PIPE FITTINGS

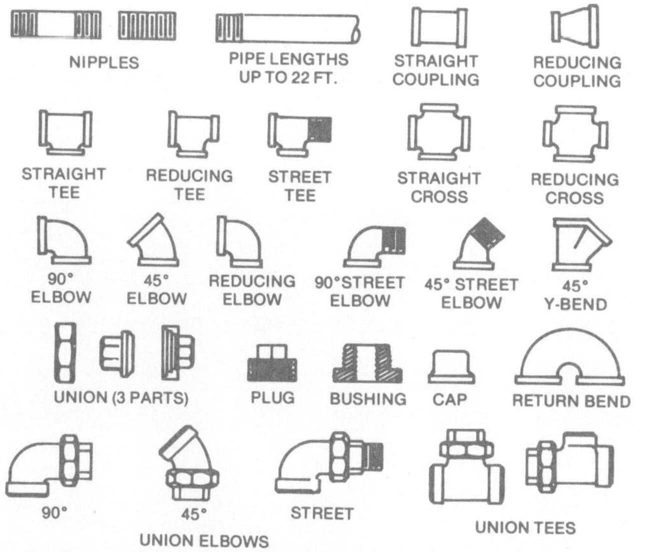

Here are the common steel pipe fittings. Nipples are simply short lengths of pipe threaded on both ends. Reducing fittings join two different sizes of pipe.

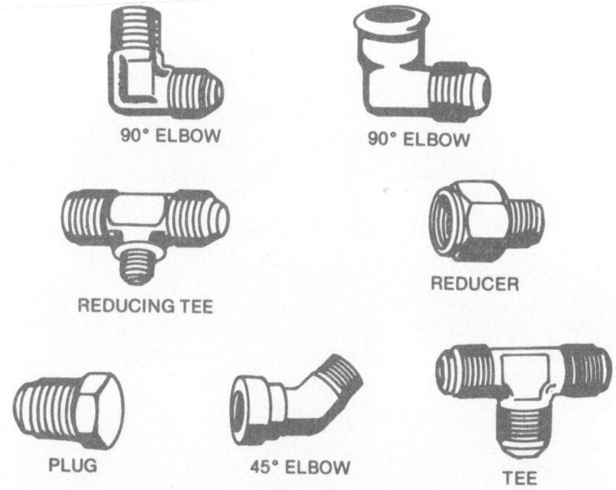

Compression fittings of the flared-tube type are the easiest for the novice to handle when working with copper tubing.

STANDARD STEEL PIPE (All Dimensions in Inches)					
Nominal Size	Outside Diameter	Inside Diameter	Nominal Size	Outside Diameter	Inside Diameter
1/8	0.405	0.269	1	1.315	1.049
1/4	0.540	0.364	1 1/4	1.660	1.380
3/8	0.675	0.493	1 1/2	1.900	1.610
1/2	0.840	0.622	2	2.375	2.067
3/4	1.050	0.824	2 1/2	2.875	2.469

SQUARE MEASURE

144 sq in = 1 sq ft
9 sq ft = 1 sq yd
272.25 sq ft = 1 sq rod
160 sq rods = 1 acre

VOLUME MEASURE

1728 cu in = 1 cu ft
27 cu ft = 1 cu yd

MEASURES OF CAPACITY

1 cup = 8 fl oz
2 cups = 1 pint
2 pints = 1 quart
4 quarts = 1 gallon
2 gallons = 1 peck
4 pecks = 1 bushel

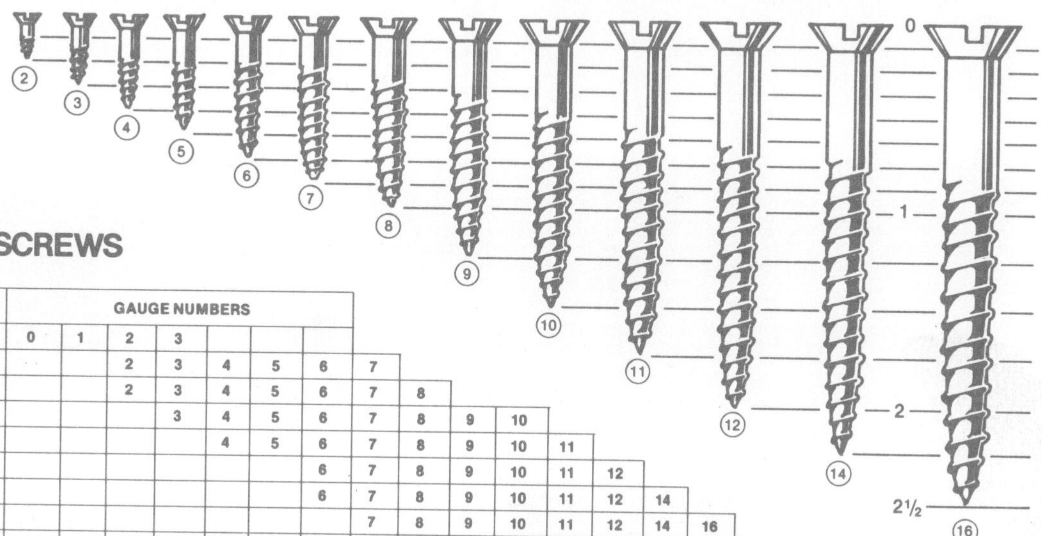

WOOD SCREWS

LENGTH	GAUGE NUMBERS																
1/4 INCH	0	1	2	3													
3/8 INCH			2	3	4	5	6	7									
1/2 INCH			2	3	4	5	6	7	8								
5/8 INCH				3	4	5	6	7	8	9	10						
3/4 INCH					4	5	6	7	8	9	10	11					
7/8 INCH							6	7	8	9	10	11	12				
1 INCH							6	7	8	9	10	11	12	14			
1 1/4 INCH								7	8	9	10	11	12	14	16		
1 1/2 INCH							6	7	8	9	10	11	12	14	16	18	
1 3/4 INCH									8	9	10	11	12	14	16	18	20	
2 INCH									8	9	10	11	12	14	16	18	20	
2 1/4 INCH										9	10	11	12	14	16	18	20	
2 1/2 INCH													12	14	16	18	20	
2 3/4 INCH														14	16	18	20	
3 INCH															16	18	20	
3 1/2 INCH																18	20	24
4 INCH																18	20	24

WHEN YOU BUY SCREWS, SPECIFY (1) LENGTH, (2) GAUGE NUMBER, (3) TYPE OF HEAD—FLAT, ROUND, OR OVAL, (4) MATERIAL—STEEL, BRASS, BRONZE, ETC., (5) FINISH—BRIGHT, STEEL BLUED, CADMIUM, NICKEL, OR CHROMIUM PLATED.

Popular Mechanics

do-it-yourself yearbook

The best illustrated home reference guide from the world's most authoritative source for today's how-to-do-it information.

1996

HEARST DIRECT BOOKS

This book is published with the consent and cooperation of POPULAR MECHANICS Magazine.

POPULAR MECHANICS Staff:
Editor-In-Chief: Joe Oldham
Managing Editor: Deborah Frank
Graphics Editor: Bryan Canniff
Home Improvement Editor: Steven Willson
Electronics/Photography Editor: Frank Vizard
Boating/Outdoors Editor: Joe Skorupa
Science/Technology Editor: Gregory T. Pope
Automotive Editor: Don Chaikin
Art Editor: John Bostonian, Jr.
Photo Editor: Nancy Coggins
Copy Editor: Kyle McGinnis

POPULAR MECHANICS
1996 YEARBOOK
Editor:
C. Edward Cavert
Managing Editor:
Beth Helfont
Book Design and Production:
The Bookmaker
Fairfax, Virginia
Editorial Assistance:
Wilma Cavert
Cover Photo:
Cy DeCosse, Inc.
Cover Design:
Beth Helfont

ISBN 0-87851-123-7
Library of Congress Catalog Card Number: 85-81760
GST Hearst Registration No. R10521891

10 9 8 7 6 5 4 3 2 1
Printed in the United States of America

CONTENTS

Arts-and-crafts chair and ottoman

The elegant ottoman and chair presented here are examples of the American Arts-and-Crafts furniture style, also sometimes called the Mission or Morris style. This type of furniture evolved from a movement in England in the late 19th century, in which craftsmen rejected the heavy ornamentation and shoddy construction of mass-produced Victorian furniture. Gustav Stickley, an American furniture designer and manufacturer, went to England in the late 1890s and returned home with great enthusiasm for the new design trends.

Characteristic of Stickley's work are heavy, unornamented rectilinear forms with through-tenon construction. Most of his pieces were built from quarter-sawn white oak and upholstered in leather. The pieces shown here are faithful to the originals, including the chair's adjustable back with five different positions. Whether reading, watching TV or taking a well-earned Sunday nap, you're sure to find a comfortable spot.

Making Chair Parts

Begin by making the legs. The best way to display the oak's unusual grain is to construct the legs so the grain is visible from all sides. The leg shown here was assembled from four beveled pieces glued to a solid square core.

Begin by ripping slightly oversize slats $^3/_4$-in.-thick stock. Set the table saw blade at 45°, and carefully rip the slat edges so that the piece has a width of $2^1/_4$ in. across its face. Do not cut the slats to finished length yet. Rip the core pieces slightly oversize, then joint their surfaces. Dry assemble each leg to check the joints.

Lay out the four facing pieces and the core piece for a leg and apply a thin film of glue to all the joint surfaces (Fig. 1). Apply the glue sparingly. Too much glue will result in a sloppy fit and make the parts hard to clamp. Assemble the leg with masking tape, and clamp the assembly until the glue sets (Fig. 2).

Next, use dado blades in the table saw to cut the tenons at the top of the front legs. Use a stopblock on the miter gauge to guarantee accuracy in the cuts. Butt the workpiece against the block. Cut the tenon slightly oversize and then pare it smooth using a sharp chisel (Fig. 3). Accuracy is important here because the tenon end is exposed, so don't remove more than the thickness of a light shaving.

The tenons on the rear legs have a shoulder that is not 90° to the tenon, so it is simpler to cut these joints by hand. Clamp a leg blank in a vise and make the

1 Each leg is an assembly of four beveled pieces glued to a core. Spread a thin film of glue on each bevel and core.

2 Tape the leg assembly together, then position closely spaced clamps around the assembly and let the glue set.

3 Using a miter gauge, cut the tenon on the leg with a dado blade in a table saw. Bevel the tenon end with a chisel.

4 Cut the leg mortises with a plunge router. To provide adequate support for the router, clamp two legs together.

5 Attach an extension fence with a stop to the miter gauge, and cut the tenon shoulders on the front and back rails.

6 Next, attach an auxilliary fence to the table saw's rip fence, and use a tenoning jig to cut the tenon cheeks.

7 Cut the slat mortises in the side rails using a plunge router. Again, clamp two rails together to suport the plunge router.

8 Cut a wedge for each arm, and glue it to the arm. After the glue has set, saw the top of the arm to produce the flat.

9 Fasten an arm to the workbench, and support it at a slope. Cut the through mortise for the leg tenon using a chisel.

10 Mark the curve on the backrest slats, and mark the biscuit location. Cut the biscuit slots using a plate joiner.

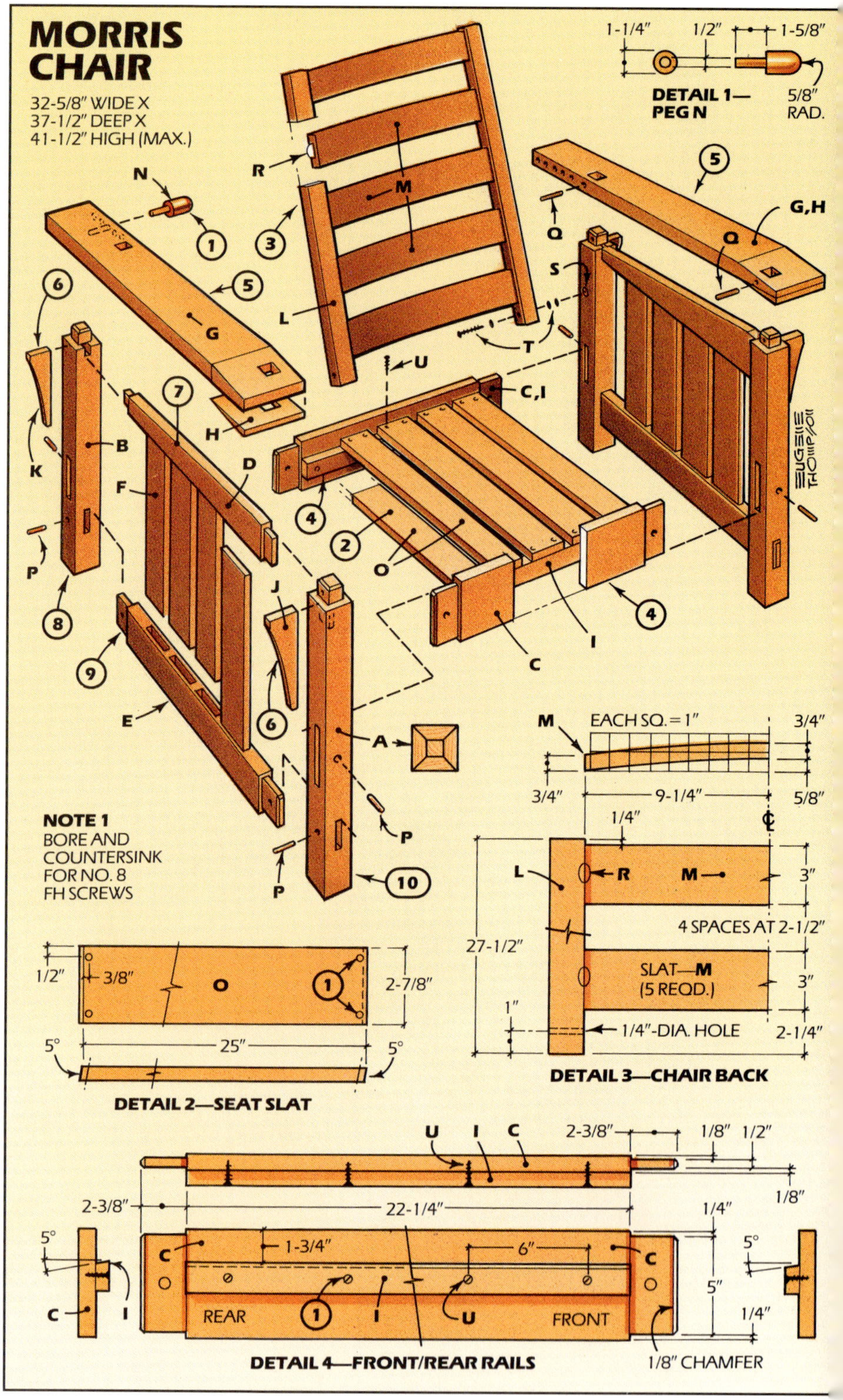

Neal Barrett wrote *Arts-and-Crafts Chair and Ottoman*. Lead photo by J.R. Rost with step-by-step photos by Neal Barrett. Technical art by Eugene Thompson. Quartersawn white oak is available from Talarico Hardwoods, RD 3, P.O. Box 3268, Mohnton, PA 19540. The threaded inserts for the chair can be obtained at most hardware stores or you can buy No. 33183 threaded inserts from The Woodworker's Store, 21801 Industrial Blvd., Rogers, MN 55374. The Solar-Lux American Walnut Stain is available from Woodworker's Supply Inc., 1108 N. Glenn Rd., Casper, WY 82601.

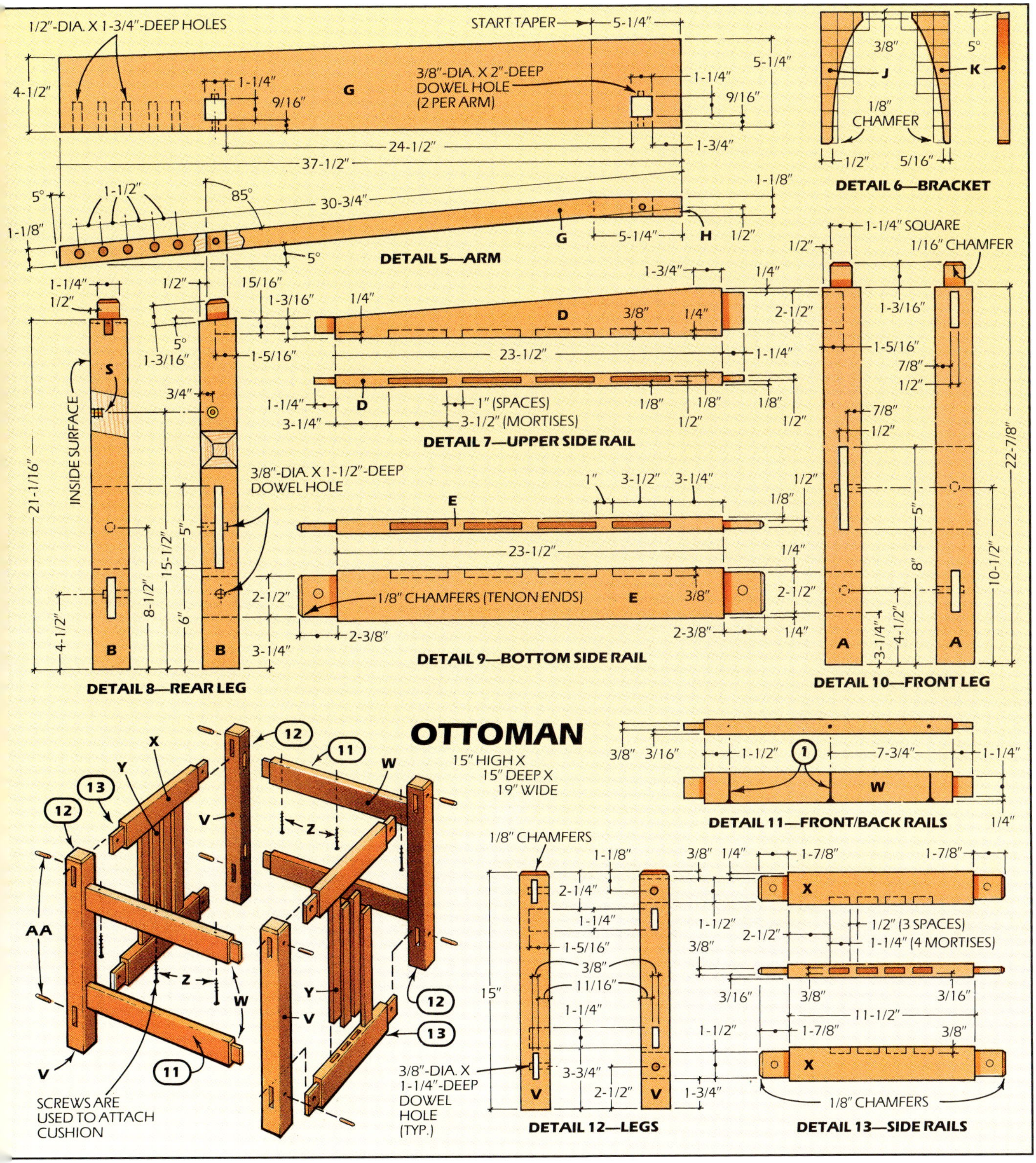

MATERIALS LIST—CHAIR AND OTTOMAN

Key	No.	Size and description (use)
A	2	2¼ x 2¼ x 24 1/16" white oak (front leg)
B	2	2¼ x 2¼ x 22¼" white oak (rear leg)
C	2	¾ x 5½ x 27" white oak (rail)
D	2	¾ x 3 x 26" white oak (rail)
E	2	¾ x 3 x 28¼" white oak (rail)
F	8	½ x 3½ x 14⅝" white oak (slat)
G	2	1⅛ x 5¼ x 38" white oak (armrest)
H	2	½ x 5¼ x 5¼" white oak (wedge)
I	2	¾ x 1½ x 22¼" white oak (ledger)
J	2	¾ x 2½ x 8" white oak (front arm bracket)
K	2	¾ x 2 5/16 x 8" white oak (rear arm bracket)
L	2	1⅛ x 1¾ x 27½" white oak (backrest side)
M	5	1⅜ x 3 x 18½" white oak (backrest slat)
N	2	1¼-dia. x 3⅜" white oak (backrest peg)
O	6	¾ x 2⅞ x 25½" white oak (seat slat)
P	8	⅜"-dia. x 1½" white oak (dowel peg)
Q	4	⅜"-dia. x 2" white oak (dowel peg)
R	10	No. 20 joining plates
S	2	¼-20 threaded insert
T	2	¼-20 x 2¼" brass rh machine screw and six brass washers
U	28	1¼" No. 8 fh screws
V	4	1¾ x 1¾ x 15" white oak (legs)
W	4	¾ x 1¾ x 18" white oak (rails)
X	4	¾ x 2 x 15¼" white oak (rails)
Y	8	⅜ x 1¼ x 10⅛" white oak (slats)
Z	6	2¼" No. 8 fh screws
AA	8	⅜"-dia. x 1¼" white oak (dowel peg)

vertical cheek cuts using a dovetail saw. Then, holding the legs flat to the benchtop, saw the tenon shoulders. Finish the tenons by shaving them smooth with a chisel.

Lay out the mortises on the chair legs. Note that the only leg mortises that are not through mortises are for the top side rails. For the through mortises, cut half the mortise depth from one side of the leg using a plunge router. Then, turn over the workpiece and complete the cut. This requires that the top and bottom limits of the mortises be accurately marked. Also, the router edge guide must be placed on the same leg face when cutting both sides of the joint.

Clamp two legs together on the workbench to provide a stable support for the plunge router. Make a series of increasingly deeper passes with the router until you have cut slightly more than half the mortise depth. Do not cut the mortise in a single pass. White oak is too tough a material to do this. Turn over the legs and complete the cut (Fig. 4). Cut the ends of the mortise square with a chisel.

Next, rip and crosscut the front, back and side rails and side slats to finished dimension. Lay out the tenons on the end of each rail. Begin cutting each joint by making the shoulder cuts using the table saw and miter gauge (Fig. 5). Attach an auxiliary fence to the miter gauge to do this, and attach a clamp on the fence to act as a stop. Butt each workpiece securely to the fence and stop to make the shoulder cut. Next, cut the tenon cheeks using a shopmade tenoning jig on the table saw (Fig. 6).

Mark the slat mortises on the side rails, and cut the mortises in a series of shallow passes until you have arrived at the depth shown in the plans. As was done with the legs, provide a stable base for the router by clamping two rails to the bench (Fig. 7). Again, use the edge-guide attachment on the plunge router, and square the cuts with a chisel when you're done.

Mark the taper on each side top rail, and cut the taper on the band saw. Cut just to the waste side of the line. Remove the saw marks from the surface and work down to the taper line using a hand plane.

Select two pieces of 5/4 stock for the arm blanks and cut them to rough size. Lay out the wedge shapes on a piece of 5/4 stock and cut out the wedges using the band saw. Feed the workpiece into to blade slowly to avoid burning it. To disguise the wedge, and make it appear that the arm is made from one piece of wood, it's important to get a good glue joint here. To ensure this, plane or sand the cut surface of the wedge so it is smooth and flat. Glue and clamp the wedge to the arm. After the glue has set, cut the flat on the top of the arm using the band saw (Fig. 8). Proceed slowly to minimize burning. Clean off the saw marks by sanding or using a hand plane.

Mark the location of the through mortises in each arm. Note that the angle of the rear leg mortises is not perpendicular to the adjacent arm surfaces. Bore a 1-in.-dia. hole in the center of each mortise to remove most of the waste. Clamp an arm to the workbench with support blocks under the workpiece to hold it at

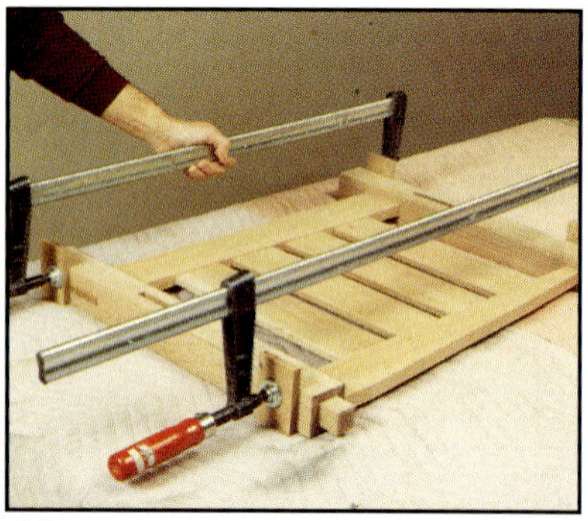
11 Glue and clamp the side slats to the side rails. Then, glue and clamp this subassembly to the front and back legs.

12 Glue and clamp armrests to the side assemblies. Use blocks to prevent marring and to spread clamp pressure.

13 After the side-arm assembly is complete, use a doweling jig to bore holes for the backrest peg in each arm.

14 Glue and clamp the side assemblies with the front and back rails. Use two clamps at the front and back.

15 Bore holes, and install the threaded inserts in the rear legs. Lubricate the inserts with wax before installing them.

16 Drive a machine screw through the backrest side and into the insert. Use three washers between the leg and side.

a slope. Cut the mortises to shape using a sharp chisel and work from both sides of the arm to prevent splintering where the mortise exists (Fig. 9).

Sand all parts before assembling the chair because it will be impossible to sand them afterward. Use 120-grit and 220-grit sandpaper, and dust off thoroughly between each grit. This should leave only minor touchup sanding after the chair is assembled. Also, ease all sharp corners with a finely set block plane or sandpaper before assembling the pieces.

Cut the backrest sides and backrest slats to dimension. Make a plywood template for the slat's curved shape, and trace the shape onto each blank.

Place the backrest sides and slat blanks flat on the worktable. Place the parts together in their appropriate positions, and mark the location of the joining plate slots on each part. Hold the plate joiner and the workpiece firmly against the table. With the plate joiner held on the mark, make the plunge cut (Fig. 10).

Cut the inside curve on each slat using the band saw, then clamp each piece between bench dogs and use a cabinet scraper to remove the saw marks. Cut the outside curve on the slats, and use either the scraper or belt sander to remove the saw marks.

Locate and bore the holes in the backrest sides for the screws that mount the backrest to the chair base. Sand the backrest parts with 120- and 220-grit sandpaper, carefully easing all sharp edges. Dust off the parts and test fit them. Glue and clamp them together using biscuits at each joint.

Assembly

Begin assembly by gluing and clamping the side slats to the top and bottom side rails. Then, glue and clamp each of these subassemblies to the front and back leg posts (Fig. 11). The bottom side rails have through tenons. To prevent glue from getting on the tenon end, apply glue sparingly on the tenon cheeks only.

Next, glue and clamp an armrest to the side assembly (Fig. 12). Again, the top tenons on the legs go through the armrests. Therefore, apply glue only on the tenon cheeks. Before you move on to the next assembly, bore holes in the armrest for the backrest pegs (Fig. 13), and bore the hole for the dowel peg that is driven through the arm into the leg tenon.

Join the side assemblies by gluing and clamping them together with the front and back rails (Fig. 14).

Now cut the seat slats and ledger strips, and bore and counterbore pilot holes in the ledger strips and slats. Install the ledgers and slats.

Using the doweling jig, bore holes in the rear legs and the backrest for the threaded inserts (in each rear leg) and the machine screw (through the sides of the backrest).

Bore the peg holes at each of the remaining joint locations that have an exposed tenon. Using just a little glue, install an overlength peg at each joint. After the glue has set, pare the peg flush with a sharp chisel.

Lubricate the threaded inserts with a little paste wax and drive an insert into each back leg (Fig. 15). Complete the assembly by installing the backrest. Separate the backrest sides from the legs with three brass washers (Fig. 16).

Ottoman

The construction of the ottoman uses the same techniques as the chair, but the legs are cut from solid 8/4 stock.

Cut the parts to dimension, then mark and cut the mortises and tenons.

Before proceeding to assembly, remember to bore and counterbore pilot holes through the top side rails (Fig. 17). The ottoman's seat is attached to the rails by screws driven through these holes.

Begin assembling the ottoman by gluing and clamping the slats to the front and back rails, then glue and clamp this subassembly to a pair of legs (Fig. 18). Bore and install pegs at the joints, then glue and clamp these subassemblies spanned by the remaining rails (Fig. 19).

You can now proceed to finish the two pieces. To achieve an authentic Arts-and-Crafts appearance, use Solar-Lux American Walnut Stain. Also use Solar-Lux retarder to prevent lap marks.

Next, apply three coats of Watco Natural Danish Oil Finish. Apply the oil generously with a rag or brush, let it sit for about an hour, then wipe it off. Allow the oil to dry overnight between coats. After the last coat is thoroughly dry, buff the finish with 4/0 steel wool and polish it with a soft cloth.

17 Bore and counterbore pilot holes for attaching the ottoman's slip seat. Use the drill press or a doweling guide to do this.

18 Begin the ottoman assembly by gluing and clamping the side rails to the slats. Then glue and clamp this to the legs.

19 Join the ottoman side assemblies by gluing and clamping them with rails. One clamp should provide sufficient pressure.

Arts-and-crafts sofa

Dominated by Victorian styles, the designers of 100 years ago drew themes from the past—Gothic, Rococo and Renaissance, to name a few—and interpreted them with new industrialized production methods. With all of this activity and the wealth of decorative information on hand, it's easy to imagine that these leading-edge designers felt that anything worth doing was probably—in some form—already done.

As is usually the case, nothing was further from the truth. In the midst of the Victorian tradition, another design philosophy took shape. Called the Arts and Crafts movement, this school of thought emphasized a return to simple, unadorned forms—designs that achieved their character through an appreciation of the materials used and the hands-on skills that shaped them.

One of the most well-known proponents of the American Arts and Crafts movement in the early 1900s was Gustav Stickley. He designed and manufactured a line known as Craftsman furniture while his younger brothers, Leopold and J. George Stickley, developed their own line of furniture. The popularity of these styles encouraged other designers to follow suit. Today, the term Mission furniture refers loosely to the work of various builders influenced by the Stickley family. This sofa project is based on one of Leopold and J. George Stickley's designs.

While you could use most any hardwood for this piece, quarter-sawn white oak is the wood generally associated with the style. After building the sofa, an upholsterer made the cushions. While leather would be the traditional choice, a vinyl material that resembled leather in both appearance and feel was chosen. The core of each cushion is Dacron-wrapped foam. To support the cushions, the upholsterer installed a rubber mat to the interior cleats shown in the drawing. Alternatively, you could modify the cleats and install slats to support the seat cushions.

Arts-and-Crafts Sofa was written by Neal Barrett. Lead photo by John Griebsch with other photos by Neal Barrett. Technical art by Eugene Thompson. One source for quarter-sawn white oak is Talarico Hardwoods, RD 3, P.O. Box 3268, Mohnton, PA 19540. A 1/2-in.-dia. carbide spiral-flute up-cutting router bit is available from Woodworker's Supply, Inc., 1180 N. Glenn Rd., Casper, WY 82601. The aniline dye used on this piece was Moser's English Brown Oak Aniline Dye No. W1230.

1 Rip the mitered leg sides on a table saw. A featherboard clamped to the fence holds stock for a more accurate cut.

2 After applying glue to core and mitered sides, clamp assembly until glue sets. Alternate clamps for even pressure.

3 Use a plunge router and edge guide to cut the leg mortises. Spare leg clamped to side of workpiece helps support router.

4 After the mortises have been routed, use a sharp chisel to square the mortise ends so the rail tenons will fit snugly.

Start with the Legs

Construct the legs by gluing up four strips of stock, with mitered edges, around a ¾-in.-square central core. First cut stock to rough size for the leg faces. Then set up the table saw to cut the 45° angles along both edges of each strip. To achieve good results, make sure your table saw is adjusted to exactly 45°, or the corner joints will not come together properly. Clamp a featherboard holddown to the table saw rip fence (Fig. 1). This will keep your fingers away from the blade and help yield a smoother surface on the mitered edges.

After ripping the mitered edges, readjust the saw and cut the four central core pieces for the legs.

Apply glue to all mitered edges and all sides of the central core strip. Loosely assemble the pieces, then apply clamps (Fig. 2). After about 30 minutes, scrape off any excess glue and let the glue thoroughly set.

Crosscut the legs to finished length on the table saw and lay out the mortises. Cut the mortises with a plunge router and edge guide. A spiral-flute up-cutting bit eases the load on the router and results in a smoother cut with no burning.

5 Use a dado blade to cut the tenon faces on the rail ends. A stopblock clamped to the table ensures consistent tenon length.

6 After cutting tenons slightly oversize, use a chisel to pare them for a snug fit. Paring also removes dado blade marks.

7 Reset the dado blade, and cut grooves for the panels and stiles. Use a featherboard to hold work against fence.

8 Bend a thin strip over the lower rail pieces to lay out a smooth curve. Clamp strip at ends and trace curve with a pencil.

9 Use a band saw or sabre saw to cut the arch on the lower rails. Stay just to the waste side of the layout line.

10 Smooth the arches to the layout line with a spokeshave. Cut down the arch from each end to avoid tearing the wood.

11 Rout a chamfer along the top front edge of the front rail. Use a 30° chamfer bit with a ball-bearing pilot for the job.

Clamp a leg between bench dogs on the workbench and make the mortise cut in several stages, with each cut taking no more than $^3/_8$ in. in depth.

To help support the router base when making the top rail mortise cuts, clamp a spare leg to the side of your workpiece, extending past its top end (Fig. 3). Square the ends of each mortise with a sharp chisel (Fig. 4).

The Frame Pieces

Choose the stock for the stiles that divide the panels, and rip and crosscut the stiles to finished dimension. Set these aside.

Select the stock for the sofa rails, and cut these pieces to finished dimension. Orient each piece as it will appear on the finished sofa, selecting for best grain figure, and mark the exposed face to indicate the top and bottom edges. Use a dado blade in the table saw to cut the broad tenon faces on the rail ends (Fig. 5). Clamp a stopblock to the saw table to aid in making the tenons the same length. Readjust the blade height to cut the top and bottom shoulders on each tenon. It's best to cut the tenons just slightly oversize and then pare to finished dimension with a sharp chisel. This practice eliminates the small ridge marks that most dado blades leave on the surface of a cut (Fig. 6).

12 After planing the panel stock to $^3/_8$ in. thick, use a crosscut table mounted on the table saw to make square panel cuts.

13 Apply warm water to raise grain, let dry and sand. Then color the panels with aniline dye according to the instructions.

14 Apply one coat of the final finish after the dye has dried. This protects the panels when the assembled sofa is dyed.

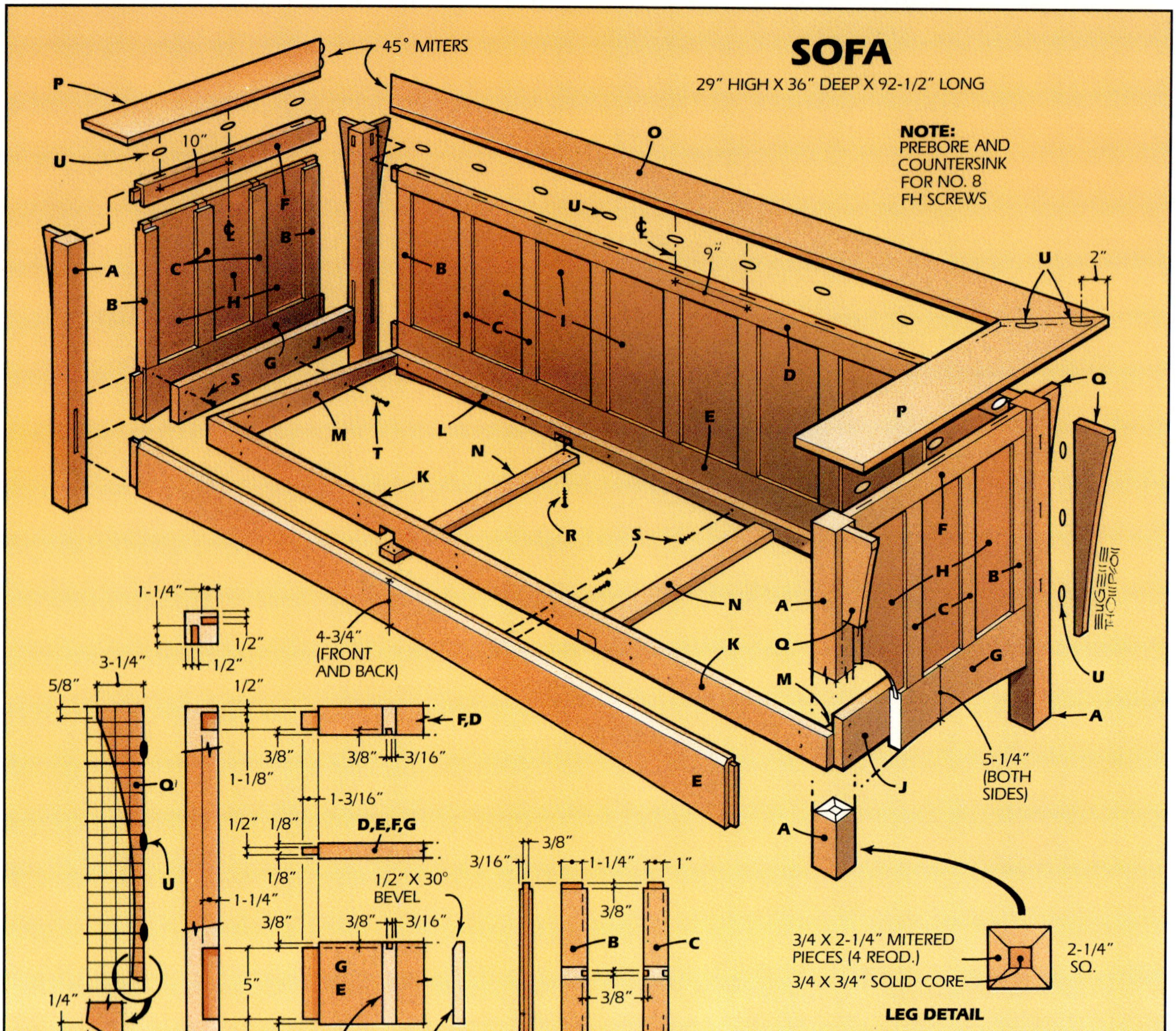

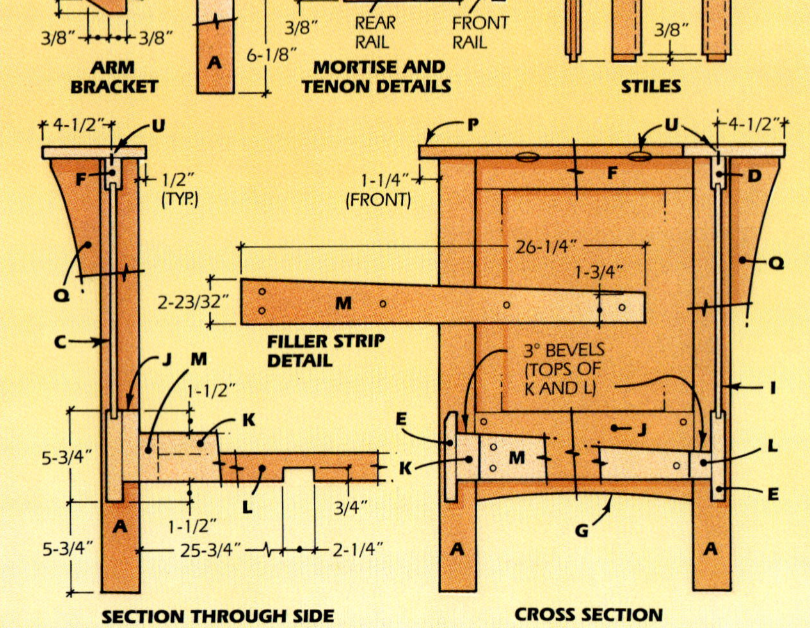

MATERIALS LIST—SOFA

Key	No.	Size and description (use)
A*	4	2¼ x 2¼ x 28¼" oak** (leg)
B	6	¾ x 1¾ x 15½" oak (end stile)
C	11	¾ x 1¾ x 15½" oak (middle stile)
D	1	¾ x 2 x 82⅞" oak (back top rail)
E	2	¾ x 5¾ x 82⅞" oak (wide rail)
F	2	¾ x 2 x 28⅞" oak (side top rail)
G	2	¾ x 5¾ x 28⅞" oak (side bottom rail)
H	6	⅜ x 7⅛ x 15½" oak (side panel)
I	8	⅜ x 8 11/16 x 15½" oak (back panel)
J	2	1⅛ x 4¼ x 26½" maple (filler)
K	1	1¼ x 2¾ x 80½" maple (front cleat)
L	1	1¼ x 1¾ x 80½" maple (back cleat)
M	2	1¼ x 2 23/32 x 26¼" maple (side cleat)
N	2	¾ x 2¼ x 28¾" maple (cross brace)
O	1	¾ x 6½ x 92½" oak (back arm)
P	2	¾ x 6½ x 36" oak (side arm)
Q	7	¾ x 3¼ x 19¼" oak (arm bracket)
R	8	1½" No. 8 fh screw
S	26	1¾" No. 8 fh screw
T	10	2" No. 8 fh screw
U***		No. 20 joining plates

Misc: Waterlox Transparent Finish; Moser's English Brown Oak Aniline Dye (No. W1230), available from Woodworker's Supply Inc., 1180 N. Glenn Rd., Casper, WY 82601.

* Overall dimension given. Build from four mitered ¾-in.-thick boards with square core as shown.

** Quarter-sawn white oak.

*** As required.

Note that the tenons are $^1/_{16}$ in. shorter than the mortise depth to allow a place for the excess glue to go.

Use a dado blade to cut the tenons on the ends of the stiles. On these tenons, however, only make the cheek cuts, as the shoulders will be automatically formed when you cut the panel grooves.

Readjust the dado blade in the saw to cut the grooves in the top edges of the bottom back and side rails, bottom edges of the top back and side rails, and the edges of the stiles. Use a featherboard clamped to the saw table to hold the pieces tight against the rip fence (Fig. 7).

Next, mark the arched profile on each bottom rail. To achieve a smooth curve, spring a $^1/_4$-in.-thick strip of pine or poplar between the clamps on each end of the rail and trace along the strip to mark the arch (Fig. 8). Use a band saw or sabre saw to cut these arches (Fig. 9), and use a spokeshave to remove the saw marks (Fig. 10).

Use a 30° chamfer bit in the router to cut the chamfer on the top front edge of the front rail. Clamp the rail to the workbench before routing (Fig. 11).

Select the stock for the back and side arms of the sofa. If you cannot cut all the arms from one board, try to match the pieces for color and grain pattern so the arm has a unified appearance. After ripping the stock to width, use the miter gauge on the table saw to cut the 45° mitered ends on each piece, then cut the square ends on the two side arms.

Make a plywood or cardboard template of the arm bracket shape, using a thin strip to create a smooth curve. Then, trace the template onto the appropriate pieces of stock. Use a band saw or sabre saw to cut out the shape, and remove the saw marks with a spokeshave.

Prefinishing the Panels

If possible, make each panel from a single board. Otherwise, glue narrower stock together to achieve the necessary width. Plane the panel stock to $^3/_8$-in. thickness. If you do not own a thickness planer, you can usually find a lumberyard or professional woodworker who will plane your stock for a modest fee. Rip and crosscut the panels to finished dimension (Fig. 12), and sand thoroughly, finishing with 220-grit sandpaper.

Prefinishing the panels ensures a neat job and eliminates the possibility of raw wood appearing if the panels shrink in a dry environment.

To color the wood, use a water-based aniline dye. Before applying the dye, wipe the wood with warm water to raise the grain. When dry, lightly sand the wood with 320-grit paper before applying the dye.

Dust off thoroughly and apply the dye according to the manufacturer's directions, and let it dry before proceeding (Fig. 13).

Next, seal the surface of the panels by applying one coat of the finish of your choice (Fig. 14). One coat of Waterlox Transparent Finish will protect the stained surface and keep any further stain from penetrating the panels when the body of the sofa is finished. Allow the sealer to dry completely before beginning the final assembly.

Assembly and Finishing

First, assemble the side frame rails, stiles and panels. Mark the stile locations on the rails to ensure proper positioning. Apply glue to the rail grooves where the stile tenons will rest, and apply glue to the tenon ends. Don't glue the panels in the grooves.

Position the stiles in the bottom rail groove, slide the panels into place, then install the top rail. Clamp the assembly, and compare opposite diagonal measurements to guarantee that the frame is square. Scrape off any glue squeeze-out before it completely hardens. After the side frames are done, assemble the back frame and clamp (Fig. 15).

When the glue dries, join the side frames to the legs. Apply glue to the mortise-and-tenon joints and to the edges of the stiles that abut the legs.

Next, join the two sides to the front and back rails. Be sure to complete the assembly on a flat surface to avoid imparting a twist to the frame.

Cut and install the filler strips on the inside of each side bottom rail. Use glue and screws to attach these strips. Cut poplar or maple stock to size for the cleats that support the sofa seat cushion. Note the beveled top edge on the front and back cleats. Use the table

15 Apply glue to the stile tenons and to the rail grooves at the stile locations. Panels are held in grooves without glue.

16 After mitering the arm pieces, use a plate joiner to cut the slots for joining the components with plates (biscuits).

17 When the arm has been assembled, flip it over and lay the inverted sofa assembly on top. Then, mark plate joints.

18 Position slots in rail using fence on joiner. Clamp a board to underside of arm, to position corresponding slots.

19 Apply glue to plate joints for connecting arm subassrmbly to frame. Then, clamp arm to frame and let the glue dry.

20 Use a plate joiner to join arm brackets to legs and arm assembly. Hold brackets in place with tape until the glue dries.

saw and dado blades, or handsaw and chisel, to cut the notches in the bottom edges of the front and back cleats. Bore and countersink pilot holes in the cleats, and attach them to the frame with screws and glue. Cut the crossbraces and install them in the notches in the front and back cleats.

Mark the positions of the two joining plates in each arm miter joint, then cut the slots with the plate joiner (Fig. 16). Apply glue and assemble the arm, clamping in two directions, to keep the miters aligned.

Lay the arm upside down on a padded surface. Position the sofa frame on the arm, also upside down, and align the two for proper overhang on all sides. Mark joining plate positions on the arm and top rail (Fig. 17). Cut the slots on the bottom face of the arm, locating the plate jointer by clamping a straightedge guide to the arm to yield the proper setback. Use the plate joiner fence to center the slots in the rail top edge (Fig. 18).

Apply glue to the rail edge, joining plate slots and plates, install the plates and assemble the arm to the sofa. Use bar clamps to pull the joints tight and let the glue dry (Fig. 19).

Mark and cut the plate slots in the arm brackets, legs and center back stile. Use the plate joiner fence to position the cuts on the legs (Fig. 20), but a straightedge guide must be clamped to the sofa back to position the slots in the center stile.

Use masking tape to hold the arm brackets in place until the glue sets. If the joints won't close, a light blow with a mallet will do the job.

Dye the sofa frame as described in the section on prefinishing the panels. When working with water-based dyes, it's important to keep a wet edge at the point of application to avoid lap marks. Start at a corner and work your way around the piece in one continuous application. If dye splashes onto the prefinished panels, simply wipe the panel dry and proceed.

When the dye is dry, use a brush, rag or sponge to apply the Waterlox, then wipe off most of the finish, leaving only a thin film. Let the finish dry overnight between coats. Three or four coats of finish, applied in this way, should be sufficient. To smooth the final finish, lightly buff the surface with 4/0 steel wool and polish with a soft cloth.

Toy chest

Begin construction using a smooth cutting blade. A simple way to handle the large crosscuts is to tack nail a strip of wood to each panel's back. The strip is sized to slide easily in the miter gauge slot (Fig. 1). To make the strip slide smoothly, rub some wax on its edges.

Next, rip and crosscut maple edge banding and glue it to the panels (Fig. 2). You can use 3-way clamps or try bar clamps or even masking tape. Note that the top edge bands of the end panels are slightly long, so they'll be sawn at an angle when the ends are cut to shape. Also, use three 19-gauge brads partially driven into each edge band to keep it from sliding. Band all the panels in this fashion—except the lid, which gets its edge bands after the chest is assembled.

After the glue dries, scrape off glue beads and plane edge bands flush to the panel surfaces.

Next, set the table saw miter gauge to 35° and make the angled cuts on the end panels (Fig. 3). Glue and clamp the edge bands onto the sawn surface.

You can cut the panel dadoes and grooves with a router and a $^{1}/_{2}$-in.-dia. straight bit. A rectangular frame is used to guide the router to make these cuts (Fig. 4). Be sure that the side rails are parallel and are spaced to fit the diameter of your router base, plus the difference between the diameter of the router bit and the width of the required dado or groove. You

Toy Chest was written and photographed by Rosario Capotosto. Lead photo by J.R. Rost. Technical art by Eugene Thompson.

TOY CHEST

15-1/2" DEEP X 24" HIGH X 28" WIDE

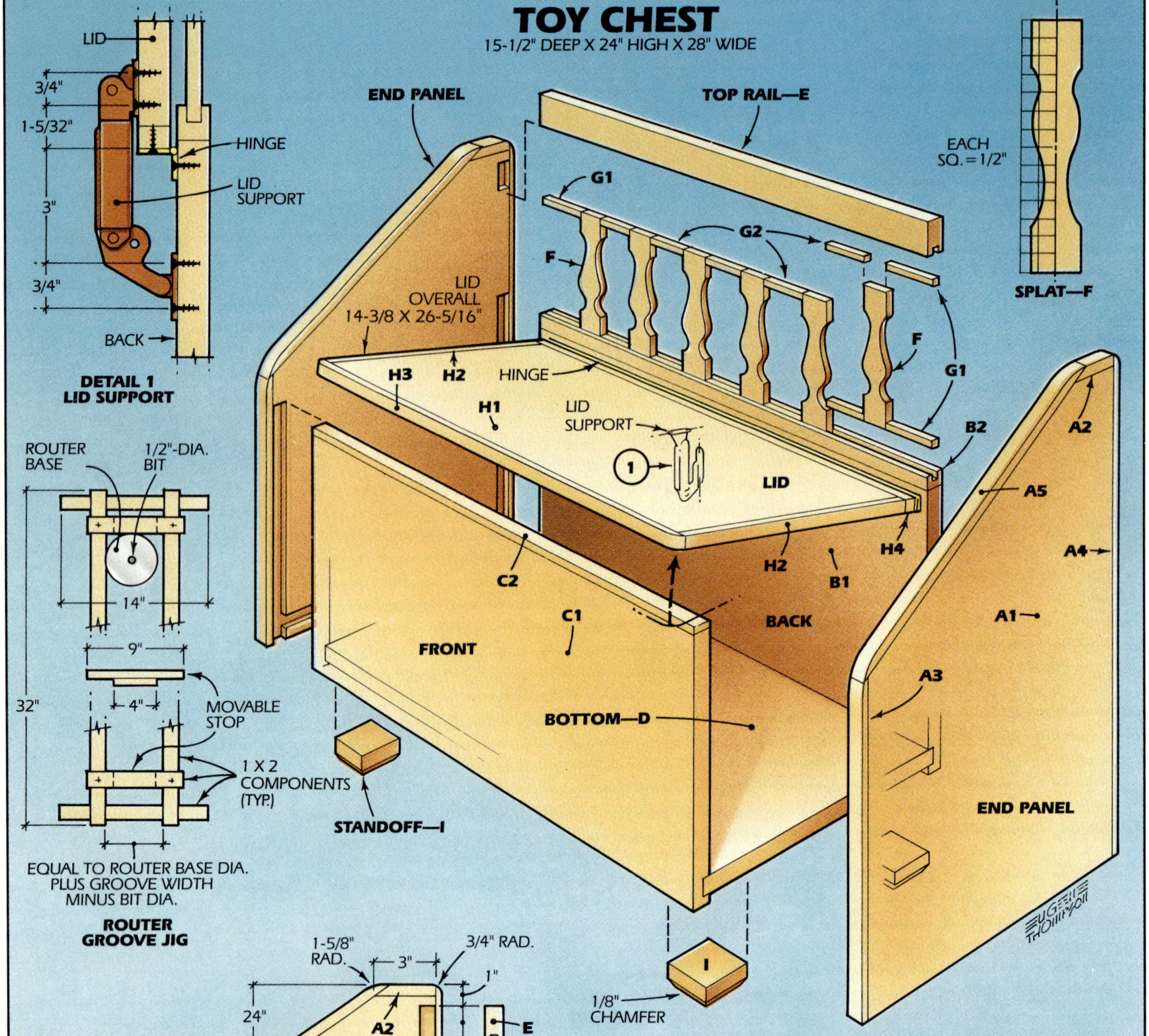

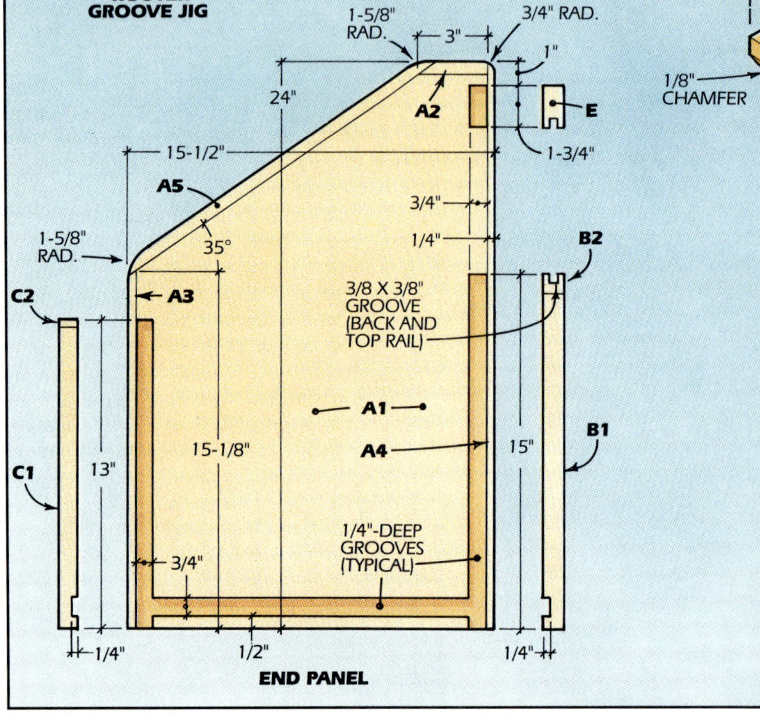

MATERIALS LIST—TOY CHEST

Key	No.	Size and description (use)
A1	2	$\frac{3}{4} \times 15 \times 23\frac{1}{2}$" maple plywood (end)
A2	2	$\frac{1}{2} \times \frac{3}{4} \times 3$" maple (band)
A3	2	$\frac{1}{4} \times \frac{3}{4} \times 15\frac{1}{8}$" maple (band)
A4	2	$\frac{1}{4} \times \frac{3}{4} \times 24$" maple (band)
A5	2	$\frac{1}{2} \times \frac{3}{4} \times 16\frac{1}{8}$" (band)
B1	1	$\frac{3}{4} \times 14\frac{1}{8} \times 27$" maple plywood (back)
B2	1	$\frac{3}{4} \times \frac{7}{8} \times 27$" maple (splat band)
C1	1	$\frac{3}{4} \times 12\frac{3}{4} \times 27$" maple plywood (front)
C2	1	$\frac{1}{4} \times \frac{3}{4} \times 27$" maple (band)
D	1	$\frac{3}{4} \times 14 \times 27$" maple plywood (bottom)
E	1	$\frac{3}{4} \times 1\frac{3}{4} \times 27$" maple (rail)
F	6	$\frac{3}{8} \times 1\frac{3}{8} \times 7$" maple (splat)
G1	4	$\frac{3}{8} \times \frac{3}{8} \times 2\frac{13}{16}$" maple (filler block)
G2	10	$\frac{3}{8} \times \frac{3}{8} \times 2\frac{5}{8}$" maple (filler block)
H1	1	$\frac{3}{4} \times 13\frac{3}{8} \times 25\frac{13}{16}$" (lid)
H2	2	$\frac{1}{4} \times \frac{3}{4} \times 13\frac{3}{8}$" maple (band)
H3	1	$\frac{1}{2} \times \frac{3}{4} \times 26\frac{5}{16}$" maple (band)
H4	1	$\frac{1}{2} \times \frac{3}{4} \times 26\frac{5}{16}$" maple (band)
I	4	$\frac{3}{4} \times 2\frac{1}{4} \times 2\frac{1}{4}$" maple (standoff)

Misc.: $1\frac{1}{2} \times 26\frac{1}{4}$" brass-plated hinge; center-mounted hinge support (No. C1088) available from Constantine, 2050 Eastchester Rd., Bronx, NY 10461; glue; polyurethane.

1 Tack nail a strip to the back of each panel. The strip should ride in the miter gauge groove as the panel is being cut.

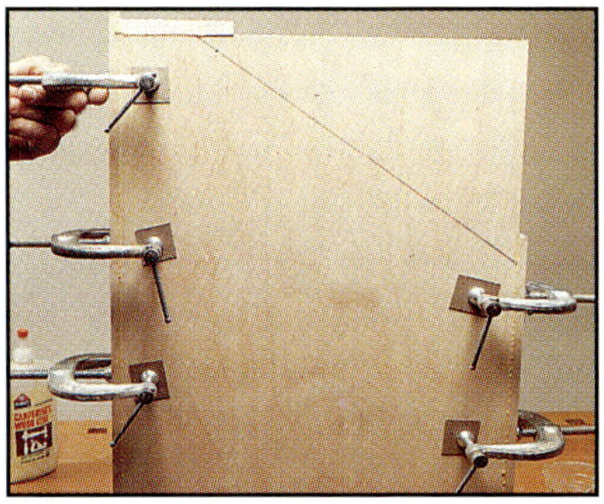

2 Glue and clamp each of the edge bands to the panels. Note that the top edge band of the end panel is just slightly long.

3 Using the miter gauge, cut the sloping edge on the end panels. Afterward, apply edge banding to the sawn surface.

4 Cut grooves and dadoes in the end panels with a router. Then tack nail a block across the rails to stop the cut.

5 Since the splats are so small, it's best to round over their edges on a router table. A ball-bearing bit usually works best.

6 Insert the splats and spacer blocks in the top rail. After the glue has dried, repeat the procedure on the back panel.

7 Begin the assembly by inserting the back into an end panel. Next, add the bottom and front, then the other end.

8 Clamp the chest using five bar or pipe clamps. Be sure to check the assembly for square before allowing the glue to set.

must precisely measure the thickness of the plywood before setting the distance between the rails. (Hardwood plywood is always slightly thinner than its stated dimension.) Tack nail a movable stop across the rails to control the length of the cut, and cut each groove or dado in two passes. Then, cut the ends of the grooves square with a chisel.

Making the Splat Rail

Cut the splats to shape, then smooth their edges. The pieces will be too small to clamp to a bench. Instead, use a $^{1}/_{16}$-in.-radius corner-rounding bit in the router table for the job (Fig. 5).

With the dado head in the table saw, cut the groove in the top rail and the edge band on the back panel. Then cut the filler blocks to length, leaving the four end blocks $^{1}/_{2}$ in. longer than the others. Remember to round off the rail edges before assembling the pieces.

Assembly

Use glue sparingly as you fit the splats and filler blocks in the top rail (Fig. 6). When they're all in place, briefly insert the subassembly into the groove in the back panel—without glue. After the glue in the top rail has set, repeat the procedure, applying glue and spacing each block to secure the splats in the back panel. During both subassembly stages, temporarily test fit the back to the side panels to ensure later realignment.

When the back assembly is dry, complete the project in the following sequence: Insert the back panel into the groove (Fig. 7). Join the bottom and front to this subassembly, then add the second end and lay the chest on its back. Next, glue and clamp the entire assembly together (Fig. 8) and check it for square.

Cut the lid panel to size, glue and clamp the side bands to it and then add the front and back bands. Install the hinge and lid support, attach the standoffs and relieve any sharp corners with fine sandpaper. Finally, apply several coats of polyurethane to finish off the project.

1 Use a dado blade in the table saw to cut the groove in the center of each half of the turning blank.

2 Push a ramrod down the center of the turning blank. This pushes out the glue that has squeezed into the hole.

3 Tap short filler blocks into the hole in the center of the blank. Trim the blocks flush after the glue has set.

Maple lamp

The graceful lines of this maple lamp will add elegance to any setting. Topped with a satin-black shade, its design harkens back to a formal, well-mannered age when even something as simple as a turned lamp had to be dignified and elegant.

The project is a good one for brushing up on your turning techniques. To make it, you need to use the basic turning tools and techniques, and a simple lathe trick to paint the black accent bands. The project, which can be finished in a couple of days, is well worth the investment of your shop time.

Making the Blank

The turning blank is made by gluing and clamping two pieces of stock after a groove is cut down the center of each piece. This creates the hole for the pipe and power cord. Start by cutting two pieces of 12/4 stock ($2^3/_4$ in. thick × 20 in. long × $4^1/_4$ in. wide). Use a dado blade to cut a $^1/_4$-in.-deep × $^1/_2$-in.-wide groove through the center of the inside face of each piece (Fig. 1).

Bore holes for alignment nails, one at each end, in the waste area of each workpiece using a $^7/_{64}$-in.-dia. drill bit. Use 3-in.-long 10d finishing nails for alignment. Drive the nails so their heads stand slightly above the surrounding surface. This will make it easier to remove them after the glue has set.

When you clamp each half of the turning blank together, glue will run into the hole in the blank's center. If left there, the glue will harden and prevent the lamp pipe from being inserted. To prevent this, make a $^1/_2 \times ^1/_2 \times$ 24-in-long ram cut from scrap wood. Also cut two 3-in.-long filler blocks for plugging the hole ends. The blocks permit the work to be mounted on the lathe centers.

Apply glue to both surfaces, then insert the alignment nails. Leave some of the nailhead exposed so it can be removed later. Next, use the ram to clean the glue out of the hole (Fig. 2). Follow this by gluing in the filler blocks (Fig. 3). When the glue has set, remove the alignment nails. Next, square the block so it is $4^1/_4$ in. wide on each side. Then use the table saw or band saw to cut 45° chamfers at each corner in preparation for turning. Also, cut the excess off the filler blocks.

The next step is to draw the full-size profile of the lamp by enlarging the grid on the drawing. Include the sizing groove marks, and number them in sequence to avoid confusion.

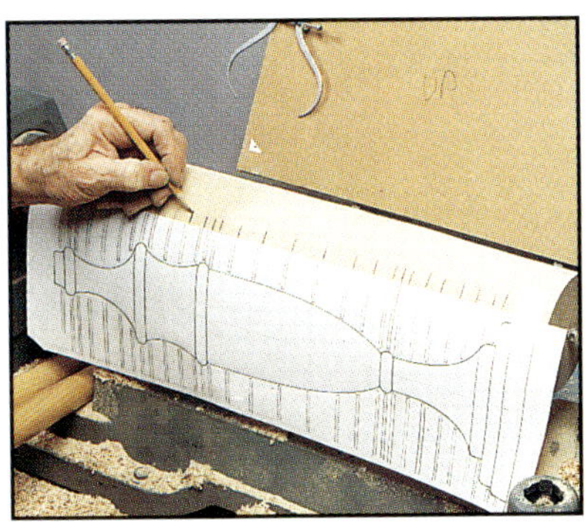

4 Rough cut the turning blank into a cylinder with a gouge, and tape the drawing to it. Mark sizing-groove locations.

5 Cut the sizing grooves and check their depth with a caliper. The drawing is positioned so it can be easily reached.

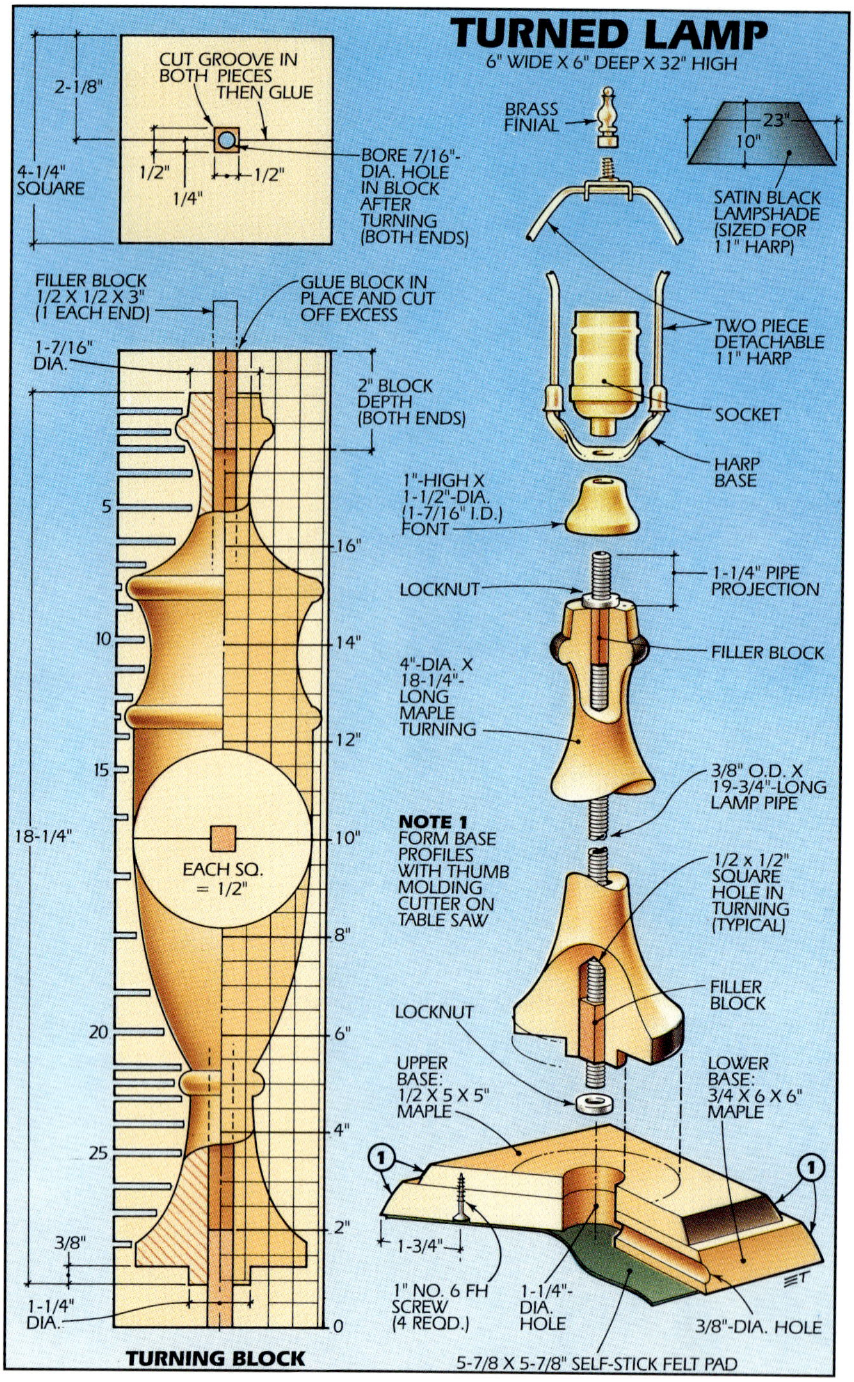

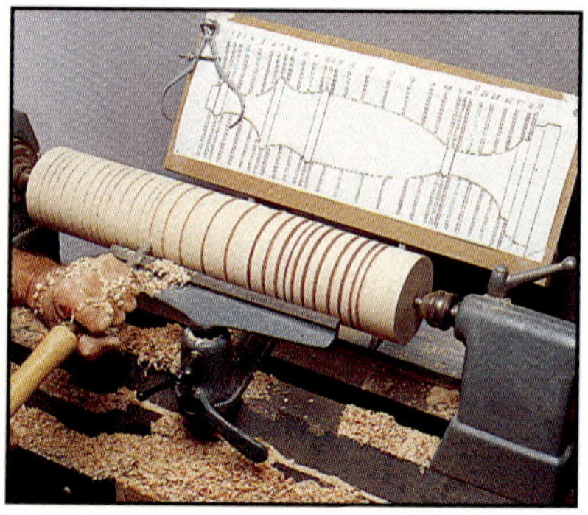

6 A parting tool can get quite hot when cutting deep sizing grooves. Widen these grooves to avoid overheating the tool.

7 The gouge quickly removes waste between sizing grooves. Once waste is removed, the turning is roughly formed.

8 Use the round-nose chisel to dress concave curves. Move the chisel in an arc by pivoting it against your thumb.

Turning the Lamp

The first turning step is to make the roughing cut to form the cylinder. Mount the blank between the lathe centers, and run the lathe at low speed. Using a gouge, start the roughing cut near one of the blank's ends, and continue the roughing cut right off its opposite end. To remove lots of material quickly, roll the gouge in the direction of the feed to produce a cutting action. For lighter cutting, hold the gouge perpendicular to the blank to produce a scraping action.

Now tape the drawing to the roughed-out cylinder, and transfer the locations for the sizing grooves by marking with a pencil (Fig. 4). Next, remove the drawing and mount it on a board positioned behind the lathe for easy visibility and reference.

Hold an outside caliper against the drawing, and adjust the caliper to the diameter. Push a parting tool into the blank to cut the sizing groove, and check the groove's depth using the caliper (Fig. 5). The diameter of the turning is kept about $^1/_8$ in. oversize at each groove. The turning will be finished to exact size later in the turning process. Widen each groove slightly when making deep cuts to prevent the tool from overheating (Fig. 6).

9 The diamond-point chisel forms small-radius beads. The convex curves can be formed with this tool or a skew chisel.

10 Sand concave areas with sandpaper backed by a flexible pad. Work the strip in a shoeshine fashion on convex areas.

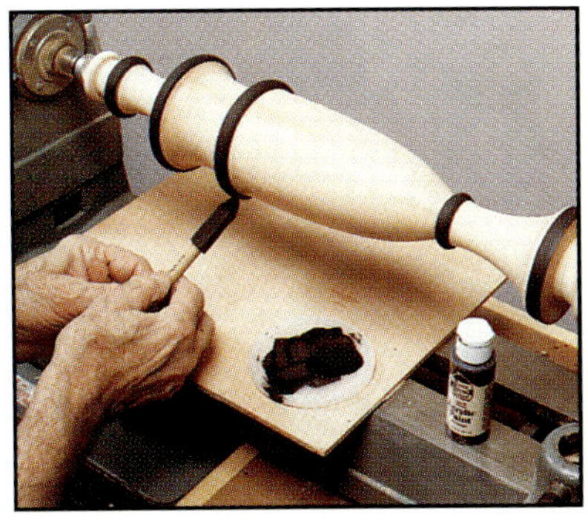

11 Run the lathe at low speed, and use a foam brush to apply acrylic paint on the beads. Steady the brush with both hands.

When all the sizing grooves have been cut, the contours of the turning are nearly formed. The basic form emerges after you remove the waste between the grooves.

Use the gouge for heavy stock removal (Fig. 7), and use the round-nose chisel to form concave contours (Fig. 8). Pivot the chisel with your thumb to swing the tool in an arc. Next, use the diamond-point tool to form the bead profiles (Fig. 9), and use the skew to cut the large convex bulb. The bulb can also be shaped by scraping with the diamond-point chisel.

Cut the 1¼-in.-dia. tenon on the turning's base using the diamond-point tool, then switch to the skew chisel to true the tenon sides parallel.

Increase the lathe speed to 2400 to 3000 rpm for sanding. Start with 120-grit abrasive paper and then work through 150-, 180- and 220-grit abrasive papers. Wrap a strip of sandpaper around a flexible pad to work concave curves (Fig. 10). Hold the strip across the turning, shoeshine fashion, to sand convex curves.

After the turning has been sanded, paint the beads, which are called accent bands after they are painted. Use black water-based acrylic paint, available at arts and crafts stores, and apply it with a 1-in.-wide foam brush for best results. Run the lathe at about 350 rpm, hold the brush steady with both hands, and lightly touch the tip to the rotating work (Fig. 11).

When the paint is completely dry, apply the clear topcoat finish. Deft Semi-Gloss lacquer is a brushing lacquer which doesn't require sanding between coats.

Making the Base

Cut both base pieces to size, then use a ⅜-in.-dia. brad point bit to bore the lamp cord hole in the edge of the lower member. Bore this hole before shaping the edge. Note that the edges do not form a quarter round but instead form an elliptical shape. They are created with a thumbnail molding cutterhead on the table saw. The workpiece is clamped to a shopmade tenon jig to make the cut (Fig. 12).

Next, bore the pilot holes, screwholes and the tenon hole in the upper and lower base pieces.

Put aside the base while you remove the turning from the lathe. Use the parting tool to cut grooves at each end of the turning. Be very careful to avoid cutting completely through the groove or cutting it to such a small diameter that the workpiece fractures. When the parting diameter is about ⅜ in., remove the turning from the lathe and use a small handsaw to finish cutting away the waste.

Finish the lamp body by boring a ⅜-in.-dia. hole through the filler plugs.

Now paint the edge of the upper base piece, glue the lamp body in place, and glue and screw the lower base to the upper base (Fig. 13). Finish the base by applying three coats of the lacquer finish.

Next, apply a square of self-stick felt to the base. This is available through woodworking catalogs and hardware stores. It shouldn't be difficult to find a lampshade locally at a lighting showroom. These don't ship well.

Maple Lamp was written and photographed by Rosario Capotosto. Lead photo by J.R. Rost. Technical art by Eugene Thompson.

12 Shape the elliptical edge on the base pieces with a molding cutter in the table saw or cut the edge on a router table.

13 Paint the edge black on upper base piece. Attach lower base to it with glue and screws, then apply finish to both.

Engineered lumber

Perhaps you've noticed, while walking through a church, theater or municipal building, a graceful arch or vaulted ceiling supported by large wooden beams or rafters. Maybe you've wondered how wood can be made to perform in situations such as these that seem to stretch the limits of the material's natural characteristics. Most of the time, especially in newer construction, these are examples of *engineered lumber.*

The idea of manufacturing structural lumber is by no means a recent one. Floor and roof trusses, for example, have long been used in both residential and commercial construction projects. These products generally incorporate lower grades of lumber in items that, by their design, maximize the structural value of the material. For truss construction, southern yellow pine—a hard, brittle and relatively inexpensive wood—is most often used. Glue-laminated beams—large beams composed of stacks of 2-in. stock laminated under pressure—have also been used to dramatic effect for at least 80 years.

In applications that are nonstructural, the engineered approach has yielded finger-jointed stock for many years. In this process, short lengths of wood are joined end to end for paint-grade work, such as baseboards, casings, doorjambs, window jams, siding and porch decking.

Today, however, the term *engineered lumber* includes a larger list of products that are fabricated from either veneers, strands of wood or lengths of solid lumber. These materials are assembled with adhesives, under great pressure, to form products that exceed the physical and structural characteristics of simple dimensional lumber.

Types of Engineered Lumber

The products that are considered engineered lumber take a number of different forms and are constructed using different techniques. Here's a quick summary of what's available and the major differences between the products.

The **gluelam**, or **glue-laminated beam**, was among the first engineered lumber products. These beams are generally used for rafters, floor support beams or stair stringers when the structural members are meant to be exposed to view. They are constructed by gluing and then applying great pressure to a stack of 2×4 or 2×6 stock to form a beam up to 30 in. deep. On special order, these beams can be fabricated to curved shapes for supporting arched roof structures.

Engineered Lumber was written by Neal Barrett with illustrations by George Retseck.

Engineered lumber maximizes wood use through modern manufacturing and design. The result is lumber that is stronger, more uniform and more stable. Products shown are (from top): open-web truss, wood I-beams, parallel-strand lumber, laminated-veneer lumber, laminated-strand lumber and glue-laminated beams.

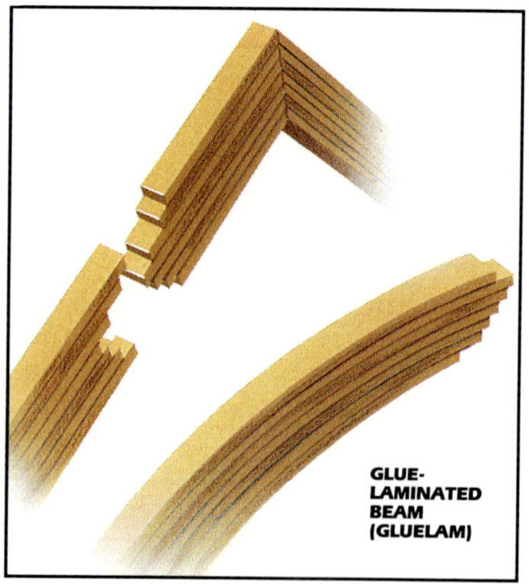

Laminated-veneer lumber, or **LVL**, at first has the appearance of a plywood beam. Instead of alternating the direction of the laminations, however, LVL is made up of $^1/_{10}$-in.-thick veneers that are all aligned in one direction and bonded under pressure. LVL is most commonly used for beams and headers when the load exceeds what can be supported by a solid wood beam of comparable size. This product is generally available in a $1^3/_4$-in. width, ranging from $9^1/_2$ in. to 18 in. deep and up to 45 ft. long. Larger sizes may be available from certain manufacturers on special order.

Parallel-strand lumber, or **PSL**, is made from 8-ft.-long strands of veneer that are soaked with adhesive and bonded under pressure to form long blocks, up to 66 ft. This material is appropriate for exposed use as posts and beams, offering an alternative to gluelam products. In addition, pressure-treated PSL beams are available for outdoor applications such as porches, decks and gazebos.

Laminated-strand lumber, or **LSL**, is a relatively new product on the market, constructed from $^1/_{32}$×1×12-in. strands of wood that are bonded with a polyurethane adhesive. LSL is available in $1^1/_4$-in. and $3^1/_2$-in. thicknesses, with varying depths up to 16 in. and lengths to 35 ft. This product is used for shorter door and window headers, rim joists for floor construction and as a core stock for flush doors with a veneer overlay. In traditional solid-wood framing techniques, a carpenter builds headers on site from nominal 2-in. stock and plywood, a slow and inefficient task. When using headers of solid LSL, the material can be ordered precut to specific length or can be cut to size on the job site. In either case, there can be a substantial savings in labor cost.

Wood I-beams look much like steel I-beams. A central web of plywood, oriented-strand board (OSB) or LVL is enclosed between top and bottom webs of solid lumber or LVL. These beams are typically used for floor and roof framing and have the notable feature of providing additional room for insulation and plumbing or electrical runs because of the recessed web. Since the top and bottom flanges are considerably wider than the conventional solid-wood joist or rafter, they provide additional surface area for securing floor or ceiling material. Some of these beams are available with a cambered construction—a feature that provides a uniform upward crown to the beams to maximize the load-bearing capacity of the floor structure, especially on long spans.

Open-web trusses use both wood and steel technology. Top and bottom chords of solid wood or LVL enclose an open web of steel tubing to form an extremely strong support for both floor and roof applications. These trusses are generally used in commercial construction projects, and are designed as an alternative to either steel trusses or gluelam beams. Open-web trusses are usually custom designed for a particular project to maximize truss performance while keeping material use to a minimum.

Benefits of Engineered Lumber

Manufactured lumber makes wood a realistic alternative in situations that might previously have called for other materials. Some of these materials, such as steel, are manufactured from resources that are not renewable, so it's valuable to set them aside for situations where they are truly needed. Also, using structural steel on a project often requires specialized tradespeople and equipment, which can add considerably to the cost of a job.

Because engineered wood uses raw materials of short length and width, trees that would normally be considered weed trees—useless for construction or trim work—can be cut up and used to make engineered lumber. These trees, aspen being the most common, are plentiful and grow quickly. Using these

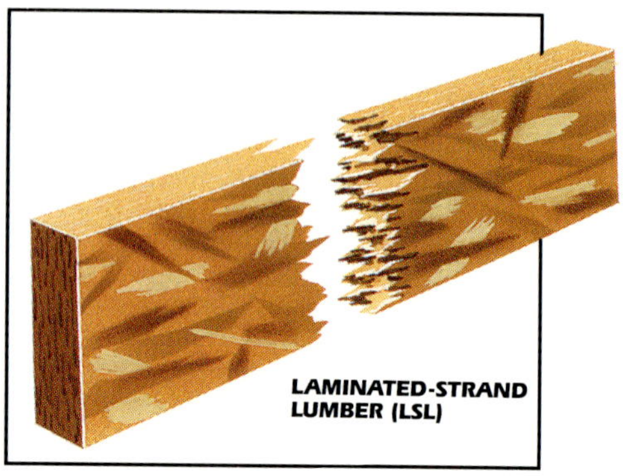

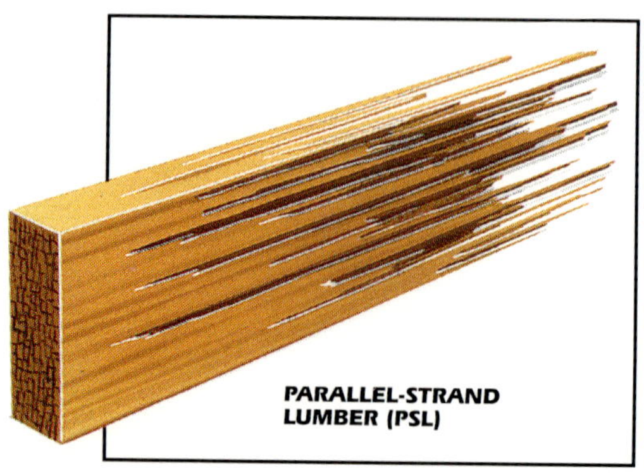

trees for structural products opens up a new, readily renewable source of raw materials.

Natural defects that occur in the wood, which would normally cause a piece of lumber to be rejected for structural use, are either cut out or spread randomly throughout the reassembled beam. This technique generates a much higher yield of usable material from any given tree. Because there is so much concern about the prudent use of our forest resources, any innovation that optimizes wood use is a positive development.

Another feature of engineered lumber is dimensional stability. In a conventionally framed house, it's common to experience squeaky floors and drywall or plaster cracks that result from shrinkage of the floor joists. Engineered joists are manufactured from kiln-dried materials that have been saturated with a resin-based adhesive. This yields a product that is extremely stable and will not change dimension either by picking up or losing moisture.

Engineered lumber can contribute in other ways to better constructed buildings. Anyone who works with wood is familiar with warped, twisted and split lumber. These solid-lumber problems not only decrease cost effectiveness, but can also compromise the integrity of a structure. Defects have become more prevalent as lumber suppliers have had to turn to faster-growing species to keep up with the demand. Since manufactured lumber is dimensionally stable, it resists these problems, providing a more uniform and predictable product.

Design, Cost and End Use

Engineered beams have opened up new possibilities for architects as well as builders. The ability of wood I-beams to carry greater loads than comparable-size solid-wood joists provides increased flexibility in placing bearing walls and support beams, while maintaining a relatively thin floor structure. The result can be a more expansive floor plan—one in which the client's lifestyle can be a greater factor in the ultimate design.

As you might expect, the benefits of these products do not come without cost. Typically, engineered wood items are priced about twice that of a comparable length of solid lumber. The manufacturers of these products are quick to point out, however, that the combined factors of less waste, greater strength, faster installation

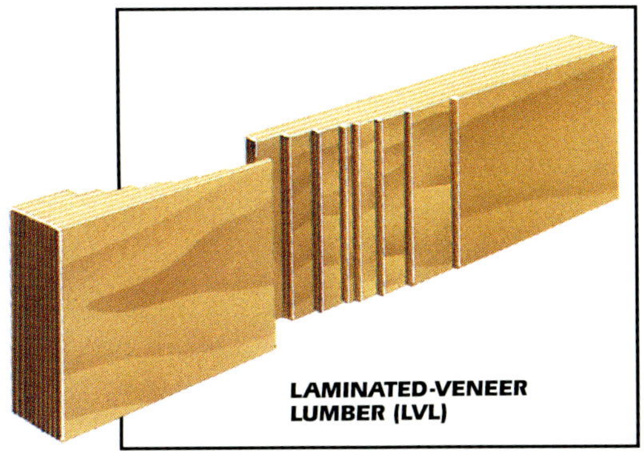

LAMINATED-VENEER LUMBER (LVL)

and lighter weight per unit length all contribute to savings that offset the higher cost of the product.

The introduction of these new products has not met with universal enthusiasm, and many builders have been slow to accept engineered lumber. The combination of increased material costs and new construction techniques has made some professionals reluctant to make the leap of faith required to use these materials. Many builders by now, however, have met with projects where engineered lumber has been specified, and they are becoming familiar with its use. In addition, the phenomenal rise in lumber prices just over the past two years, along with solid-lumber shortages throughout the country, has been a deciding factor in persuading builders to make more frequent use of these products.

If you are planning a remodeling or building project that you think might benefit from engineered lumber, consult an architect or engineer to compare product specifications with the load-bearing requirements of your project. In some cases, the structural capacity of engineered lumber allows greater spacing of supports in a floor or roof providing that the decking material is able to span the distance. These substitutions should not be made casually, and the time and money spent on a professional consultation is a good investment.

In shopping for engineered lumber products, a bit of local research will be necessary. Several companies manufacture these items, and the particular products available will vary with the distribution network, and market, in your area. In most cases, you will have the option of special ordering items that are not carried as stock material.

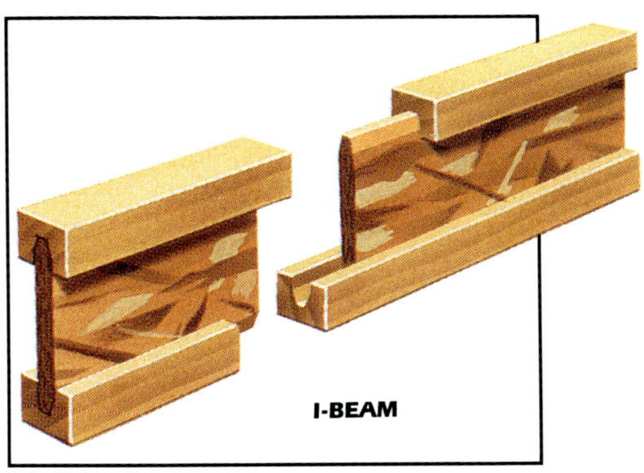

I-BEAM

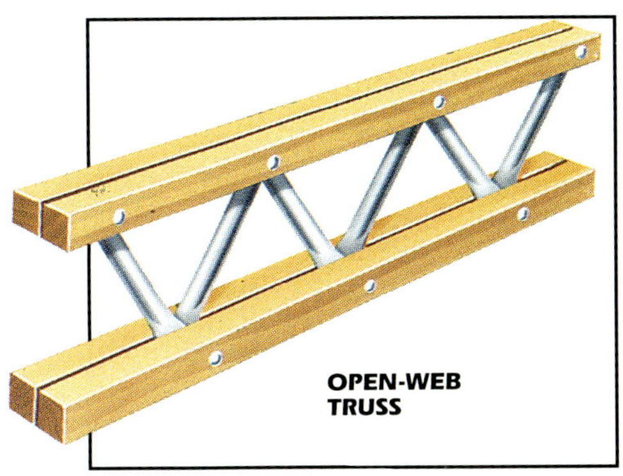

OPEN-WEB TRUSS

Reinforced joints

The simplest way to join two pieces of wood is to cut them to size, apply a little glue to the mating surfaces and put the assembly in clamps until the glue sets. Unfortunately, this method doesn't work well if there's any end grain involved. End-grain joints require reinforcing, usually with dowels or splines, so the glue joins the pieces through adequate long-grain contact.

As it turns out, dowels and splines are also handy for aligning and reinforcing ordinary edge-to-edge joints. In combination with milled joints such as tongue-and-groove joints and glue joints, you're prepared to solve a wide range of joinery problems. Best of all, you can make most of these joints quickly and accurately, using ordinary hand and power tools.

Reinforced Joints was written and photographed by Rosario Capotosto.

Basic Butt Joints

When used correctly, today's glues are stronger than the wood itself. Therefore, when laminating stock to produce wide panels, there's a good argument for leaving out any type of reinforcing. The secret to a successful edge-to-edge glue joint is perfect contact along the entire mating surface.

Begin by laying out the boards and marking them as they're to be assembled. If you have a jointer, joint each edge. Check for fit by placing the mating surfaces together and looking for any light that passes through the seam. To fine-tune a joint, or do the job entirely by hand, fold two adjacent boards together and hold them in your vise so both mating surfaces can be planed at once. Then, true the edges with the longest plane you have (Fig. 1). Because both edges are planed together, slightly out of square planing is negated when the boards are unfolded and joined.

To keep the boards aligned and flat when gluing them together, sandwich straight boards across the assembly and clamp. Then, apply bar or pipe clamps across the assembly. Alternate these clamps above and below the panel to equalize the pressure and reduce any tendency the assembly has to cup (Fig. 2).

1 Fold workfaces together and plane edges. Planing edges doesn't affect parallel alignment when boards are joined.

2 Apply glue to both mating surfaces of each joint. Use boards to keep assembly flat. Alternate clamps above and below.

Doweled Joints

Using dowels in a butt joint increases the mechanical resistance to lateral stresses and maintains alignment when gluing the boards together. In edge joints, avoid using dowels longer than about 1 1/2 in. Otherwise, the dowels may actually force the joint open if the wood dries and shrinks. Always make the dowel holes slightly deeper than necessary and either buy or make grooved dowel pins so excess glue can escape.

To add dowels to an edge-to-edge joint, first place adjacent boards together and use a square to mark centerlines on both edges (Fig. 3). Use a doweling jig to ensure that the holes will be square to the edges and at a uniform distance from the workfaces. Some doweling jigs are self centering. If you're using a noncentering type, be sure to reference one side of the jig with designated workfaces on your stock to ensure that adjacent faces will be aligned. Use a depth stop or a piece of tape wrapped around the drill bit to gauge hole depth (Fig. 4).

To do the job with a drill press, first clamp a fence to the drill-press table and place your work against it. Then, adjust the fence so the bit is centered over the stock edge. Mark an index line on the fence that corresponds to the bit center. Align hole centerlines on the work with the index mark, and bore each hole (Fig. 5). Always reference the same working face of each piece against the fence to ensure good alignment even though there may be slight variation in stock thickness.

Doweling is an excellent way to reinforce mitered-frame joints. After cutting the miters, lay each joint together and mark the hole locations on the faces. Then transfer these centerlines across the mating edges.

Align your doweling jig with the hole centers and bore the holes (Fig. 6). To assemble the frame, apply glue and join two L-shaped sections first. Then, join the assembled sections and clamp with bar clamps or a band clamp to bring the joints tight.

Use dowel centers for transferring hole locations in leg-to-rail joints or other joints with unaligned faces. (A dowel center is a small steel plug with a centered point on one face.) First, bore dowel holes in one piece and insert the centers (Fig. 7). Then, press the two mating surfaces together to transfer the centers. Use flat shims clamped to the work to gauge the appropriate face offset (Fig. 8).

3 Place adjoining boards face to face, and use a square to mark dowel hole centerlines across both edges at once.

4 Align index mark on doweling jig with centerlines on stock edge and bore holes. Self-centering jig aligns hole.

5 To bore dowel holes on a drill press, set up fence and position for centered hole. Align holes with index mark on fence.

6 Use a doweling jig to bore holes for miter joints. Use a depth stop or masking tape around bit to gauge hole depth.

7 For unaligned dowel joints, place dowel centers in dowel holes in preparation for marking adjoining hole positions.

8 Press mating pieces together to mark holes with dowel centers. Shims clamped to work sides control alignment offset.

9 To add slots to dowels for dry fitting assemblies, install dowel in scrap block. Then, cut slot on a band saw.

When dry assembling dowel-joined components to check for fit, it's a good idea to cut slots along each dowel so the project can be assembled and disassembled easily. Use a small block of wood to hold each pin and cut the slot on a band saw (Fig. 9). Use unslotted grooved dowel pins for the final glued assembly.

Milled Joints

Milled joints, such as the tongue-and-groove and shaped glue joint, make stock alignment and assembly easy while increasing the surface area for a stronger glue joint. These joints can be made on a table saw or shaper.

To make a tongue-and-groove joint on a table saw, first install a dado blade and set the width for the width of the groove—usually one third of the stock thickness. Set the fence for a centered cut, and cut the groove (Fig. 10). Making the tongue requires two cuts—one on each side of the edge of the mating piece.

You can also use a molding head with tongue-and-groove cutters. These specially shaped cutters enable you to complete the joint in two passes (Fig. 11).

The shaped glue joint is made with a single glue-joint cutter that produces both mating pieces (Fig. 12). To use the cutter, first shape the edge of the first piece (Fig. 13). Then, shape the edge of the second piece, flip the piece over and join the two. Because of the reversible profile, the faces will be aligned.

When making any of the above milled joints on a table saw, always secure a wooden board to the metal table saw fence so the fence can be adjusted up to the cutter.

10 Use a dado blade for tongue-and-groove joints. First cut makes groove. Making the tongue requires two cuts.

11 To make tongue-and-groove joints in two passes on a table saw, use a molding head with tongue-and-groove cutters.

12 Glue-joint cutter in molding head shapes both sides of joint. Shaped glue joint increases glue surface area.

13 Use a featherboard to hold workpiece against wooden auxiliary fence when using molding head. Glue-joint cutter shown.

Spline Joints

A spline is a thin strip of wood that is inserted into grooves cut in adjoining stock faces. Like dowels or milled joints, splines add mechanical strength to the joint and aid in alignment during assembly. Thin plywood, 1/8-in.-thick hardboard, and hardwood are the usual spline materials. If you use solid wood, orient the grain at a right angle to the grain direction of the work to provide greater strength. Like dowels, hardboard, plywood or crossgrain hardwood splines should not be too wide or they may force the joint open if the wood shrinks. For average work, make the spline width about the same as the stock thickness. A spline joint doesn't require a single continuous spline. For long joints, simply use short lengths placed end to end in the slot.

14 Use a router equipped with a winged slot cutter to make spline slots. Stop cut short of end for blind spline joints.

15 Referencing slot with same face of each board ensures alignment. Cut splines narrower than double slot depth.

16 Use table saw to cut kerf-width slots. Cut slots in miters with blade tilted to miter angle and slightly below center.

17 Assemble spline-miter-joint boxes in two stages. First, join adjacent L sections. Join subassembles and clamp.

18 Use a jig to support workpiece when cutting spline slots parallel to face in end of miter joint. Use two splines per joint.

19 Apply glue and fit splines in miter. Clamp across frame to tighten miters. Clamp across joints to hold splines.

To cut a spline groove with a router for an edge-to-edge joint, first install a winged slot cutter of the appropriate size. Center the cutter on the stock and make the slot (Fig. 14). This method is best for making blind spline joints that require stopped slots. Cut the splines for a slip fit that is slightly less in width than double the slot depth (Fig. 15).

You can also use a table saw to quickly cut spline slots that match the saw kerf thickness. When cutting slots in edge miters, place the slot closer to the inside miter corner to provide adequate depth for the slot (Fig. 16). When assembling a box joined with splined miters, join the two L-shaped sections first. Then, join the two sections and clamp (Fig. 17).

Splines can also be used to join mitered frames. To cut the slots on the table saw, first build a jig that supports the work vertically and at the miter angle (Fig. 18). Then adjust the fence and depth of cut and make the slot. It's best to use two slots in each joint for maximum strength. After the slots and oversize splines are cut, apply glue and assemble the frame. Clamp across the frame to bring the miters together and install clamps face to face across the spline joints to hold the splines in place until the glue sets (Fig. 19).

Plate Joints

The fastest way to reinforce a simple butt joint is with a plate joiner. In addition to being quick to make, plate joints are easy to adjust during assembly and provide good strength.

To join shelves to a side panel, first lay out the shelf positions by marking the top of each shelf on the side panel. Then, lay a shelf above its shelf position so the end is aligned on the mark and lay out slot index marks on the shelf. With the plate joiner held vertically, place the front faceplate on the side panel and butt the base of the joiner against the end of the shelf. Align the index mark on the joiner base with the slot marks on the shelf, and cut the slots down into the side panel (Fig. 20).

20 Use a plate joiner for fast assembly of shelves and side panels. First cut slots in sides, then slots in shelf ends.

21 Apply glue to plate joint slots and install plates in shelf ends. Assemble components, adjust alignment and clamp.

Rabbet and dado joints

Next to butting and gluing two boards together or driving a few nails, making rabbets and dadoes are among the simplest ways to join wood. Simple as they are, however, you'll find them in all aspects of woodworking—from finish carpentry to advanced cabinetmaking.

The *dado* is a rectangular channel cut across the grain on the face of a board. It's normally used to house the end of an adjoining board. If the cut is made parallel to the grain, it's called a *groove*. For the most part, making dadoes and making grooves involve the same techniques. Both offer increased glue surface over butt joints as well as help in alignment and provide mechanical strength.

The *rabbet* is essentially an open-sided dado on the edge of a board, either parallel to or across the grain. The resultant notch, or step, is a useful joint for cabinet or box corners, and also serves to house recessed components such as cabinet backs, panels, glass and mirrors.

Both dadoes and rabbets may be through joints, where the cut extends completely across the stock, or blind, where the cut stops short of one or both edges of the work. Dadoes that are blind, or stopped at both ends, are actually shallow mortises.

Text and photos for *Rabbet and Dado Joints* by Rosario Capotosto.

1 Cut dado shoulders with a backsaw. Use a block to keep the saw aligned. A second block acts as a depth stop.

2 After cutting the shoulders, remove waste with a chisel. Work from the ends toward the center to avoid splintering.

3 To cut a rabbet, first make the shoulder cut. Then, rest the saw horizontally on a guide block and saw away waste area.

Handcut Dado Joints

The first step in making a dado is to mark the cutting lines. Make the width of the cut equal to the thickness of the mating member and make the depth about one-third to one-half the stock thickness.

Use a backsaw to make the dado shoulder cuts with the kerf on the waste side of the layout line. To ensure square aligned cuts, clamp a square block of wood to the work so it's aligned with the center of the cutline. Then, hold your backsaw against the block to guide the cut. Ensure consistent cut depth by allowing the backsaw spine to touch the top of a second block when the appropriate depth has been reached (Fig. 1). To determine the height of the stopblock, measure the distance from the backsaw teeth to the spine and then subtract the dado depth.

After the shoulder cuts are made, use a sharp chisel to clean out the waste. Work from both edges toward the center to prevent tearout at the board edges (Fig. 2).

Because rabbets are open-sided dadoes, you can usually finish the job with two saw cuts—one starting from the face and the other from the board end (Fig. 3). When the cut is finished, fine-tune it by paring with a sharp chisel.

4 Set circular saw to depth of dado and cut dado shoulders. Strip with hinged section guides both shoulder cuts.

5 Frame-type jig guides router and constrains dado width. Initial cut through jig crosspiece helps in aligning jig.

6 To rout a stopped dado, tack a stopblock to frame jig crosspiece. After cutting dado, square blind end with a chisel.

Power-Tool Dadoes

To cut a dado with a circular saw, first clamp a straight guide strip to the work so it's parallel to the dado layout lines and offset by the distance from the edge of the blade to the side of the saw base. After making the first shoulder cut by guiding the saw against the strip, readjust the strip so the opposite side of the blade aligns with the other layout line and then make the second shoulder cut. Next, make a series of passes between the shoulder cuts and remove the waste with a chisel.

For accurate repetitive work, modify the guide strip to make both shoulder cuts without readjustment. Cut a second guide strip the same length as the first, but equal in width to the width of the dado less the blade thickness. Tape this strip to the first strip to create a hinging guide. Make the first cut with the narrow strip folded out of the way, then lay it down on the work for the second cut (Fig. 4).

While you could use a similar guide for routing dadoes with a straight bit, a frame-type jig prevents the router from drifting off course and helps eliminate

7 Rout grooves parallel to the grain with a router fence. Where a fence won't reach, clamp a guide strip to the work.

8 Install dado blade in radial-arm saw and make initial cut through new fence. Use resultant notch to align work.

9 To cut blind dadoes on a radial-arm saw, clamp a stopblock to the saw table. Motor housing contacts block to stop cut.

10 Turn radial-arm saw to rip position for cutting grooves and long-grain rabbets. Adjust anti-kickback pawls for safety.

11 When cutting dadoes on table saw with dado blade, mark exact cut position on table insert to aid in alignment.

12 For woods that are prone to splintering, use a utility knife to score the shoulder cutlines before cutting dado.

tearout (Fig. 5). Make the frame out of 1×3 stock. Space the two parallel side strips a distance apart equal to the router base plus the difference between the bit diameter and dado width. Screw two crosspieces near the ends of the parallel side pieces. Clamp the jig over the work, and nail a third crosspiece in place to back up the open edge of the work. Before routing the workpiece, remove the jig and rout a dado through the middle crosspiece. Use this cut to align the jig with the dado layout lines.

To make a blind dado, nail a stopblock to the middle crosspiece and square the finished cut with a chisel (Fig. 6).

For cutting grooves parallel to the grain and parallel to the work edge, use a router fence (Fig. 7).

To cut dadoes and grooves on a radial-arm or table saw, use a dado blade. On the radial-arm saw, first adjust the dado blade width and set the saw height for the appropriate depth of cut. Then, install a new wooden fence on the radial-arm saw table and make a cut through it. Align the dado layout lines on the workpiece with the cut in the fence (Fig. 8).

To make blind dadoes on a radial-arm saw, simply clamp a stopblock to the table to limit the forward travel of the motor housing (Fig. 9). Finish each cut by squaring the ends with a sharp chisel.

Grooves parallel to the grain and stock edge can also be cut on a radial-arm saw. First, pivot the motor housing to the ripping position. Set the dado blade at the correct width and height, tilt the blade guard back and bring the anti-kickback pawls into contact with the wood. As with ripping, always feed the stock against the rotation of the blade (Fig. 10).

To align the work with the dado blade on a table saw, mark the lines of the cutting path on the table saw insert (Fig. 11). Then, use the miter gauge to guide the workpiece. An auxiliary fence attached to the miter gauge provides extra support and helps reduce splintering. Cut long-grain grooves by guiding the work along the rip fence.

If you don't have a dado blade, you can still cut dadoes and grooves on either a table saw or a radial-arm saw. Simply make the shoulder cuts first with a standard blade, then remove the remaining waste with successive passes.

If you experience grain tearout along the edges of the dado, it may be because of a misaligned motor housing on a radial-arm saw or a misaligned arbor assembly or fence on a table saw. Some species of wood, however, are particularly prone to splintering. With these types of wood, use a straightedge and a utility knife to score along the dado cutlines before making the cut (Fig. 12).

Rabbet Joints

To cut crossgrain rabbets with a circular saw, construct an L-shaped platform jig out of two pieces of $^{3}/_{4}$-in.-thick × 4-in.-wide plywood. Make these pieces equal in length to the length of the saw base. Glue and screw the pieces together to form an L. Then, secure the jig to the saw base with bolts and wingnuts. Use slotted holes in the jig so the saw's position can be adjusted.

With the work held end up in the vise, hold the side of the jig against the face, adjust the saw position so the blade is aligned correctly and make the first cut (Fig. 13). Then, remove the jig and use a guide strip clamped across the workpiece to make the shoulder cut that removes the waste. You can use the same L-shaped platform jig for cutting rabbets with the grain. Use a rip fence instead of the guide strip, however, to make the shoulder cut (Fig. 14).

Routing small rabbets is best done with a piloted rabbet bit. Bits with an interchangeable bearing allow you to vary the width of the rabbet up to about $^{3}/_{8}$ in. Solid-pilot bits are also available. To use a piloted bit, simply hold the pilot against the edge of the work while making the cut (Fig. 15). If the cut is short, clamp scrap stock next to the workpiece to support the router base. To rout wider rabbets, use the router guide fence or guide strip and a ordinary straight bit.

To cut a rabbet on the long edge of a board using a table saw with a standard blade, first set the blade height for the depth of the rabbet and make the shoulder cut with the stock face down on the table. Next, reset the fence so the distance from the blade equals the depth of the rabbet less the stock thickness. With the workpiece on edge, make the second cut. Always arrange the cut so the waste falls on the open side of the blade. For a faster job, use a dado blade mounted in the table saw and an auxiliary wooden fence (Fig. 16).

For rabbets on narrow stock, and most cross grain rabbets, use the miter gauge to guide the work. With a standard blade, make several passes to remove the waste. Or, use a dado blade to complete the cut in one pass.

13 Build an L-shaped jig and attach it to the saw base to give extra support when making rabbet cuts from stock edge.

14 Use a rip fence accessory to guide portable circular saw when making rabbet shoulder cuts parallel to the grain.

15 For fast rabbeting along straight and contoured surfaces, use a router and a rabbeting bit with ball-bearing pilot.

16 Use a wooden auxiliary fence when cutting rabbets on a table saw with a dado blade. Featherboard holds stock down.

Combination Joint

This combination dado/rabbet joint is often used to secure drawer sides to the front panel in lieu of dovetails. In drawers, it provides additional mechanical strength and glue surface area over an ordinary rabbet joint. This is because of a short, locking tongue that extends from the inside surface of the drawer front panel into the sides (see lead photo, bottom left). As with an ordinary rabbeted front panel, the joint hides the endgrain of the drawer sides. Because this joint demands precision, it's best to do the job on a table saw.

Begin by cutting a groove in both ends of the front panel. Use a dado blade to make the cuts, and guide the workpiece with a jig that straddles the table saw fence. Secure a vertical stop to the back of the jig to hold the wood perpendicular to the table. Clamp the workpiece to the sliding jig for stability.

Adjust the dado blade cutting width so that the workpiece thickness less the cutting width is no less than twice the thickness of your standard-blade saw kerf. Set the depth of cut to be slightly greater than the thickness of the side pieces. Then, adjust the fence for a centered groove and make the cut in each end (Fig. 17).

Next, hold an end of the front panel against each side piece to mark the positions of the small dadoes. Align the inside of the front tongue with the end of the side piece, and mark the dado with a sharp pencil (Fig. 18).

Install a standard blade in the table saw and cut the small dadoes to a depth of about one-third the stock thickness (Fig. 19). Finally, cut the rear tongues on the front panel pieces to match depth of small dadoes (Fig. 20). After the joint is assembled, trim the thin exposed endgrain of the front panel flush with sides.

17 Begin combination joint by cutting grooves in end of first workpiece. Clamp work to jig that straddles saw fence.

18 Use the grooved piece to lay out narrow dado in second mating piece. Align inside of grooves with end of mating piece.

19 Cut narrow dado on second piece with standard blade. Auxiliary fence on miter gauge reduces splintering.

20 Shorten one of the tongues in the first piece so its length matches the depth of the dado in the second piece.

Inlay

Woodworkers will tell you it's all in the details that make or break a woodworking project—the little things that catch the eye and give the piece value far beyond its utility. For some, it can be as simple as a delicately tapered leg with chamfered corners, while others rely on elaborate moldings or turned spindles to give life and character. If your involvement stops there, however, you're missing out on a world of visual possibilities all based on inlay work.

Like marquetry, inlay adds a decorative element to the wood surface by incorporating patterns made up of contrasting woods. While marquetry is concerned with laminating veneer on top of the surface, however, inlay involves embedding a pattern or design into recesses cut in the wood.

A simple jewelry box was chosen to demonstrate a few inlay variations. To start, you'll be shown how to make a diamond mosaic banding. Then, you'll move to a simple triple-stripe inlay and finish with a marquetry insert. Most of the tools used are common to the typical home woodworking shop.

Diamond Mosaic Banding

The secret of a diamond mosaic motif lies in assembling the elements in the form of a board, and then slicing off thin layers.

Begin by cutting two pieces of mahogany and one piece of maple to $^{9}/_{32}$×3×20 in.; then laminate the mahogany pieces to each side of the maple piece. This blank will produce more than enough banding material for a small jewelry box.

When the glue has dried, joint the edges of the blank and tilt the blade on your table saw to 45°. Crosscut the end of the blank to produce a 45° bevel. Then, cut the board into $^{1}/_{4}$-in.-thick slices with the blade set at 45° (Fig. 1). Use an angled stopblock clamped to an auxiliary fence on the miter gauge to ensure uniform cuts.

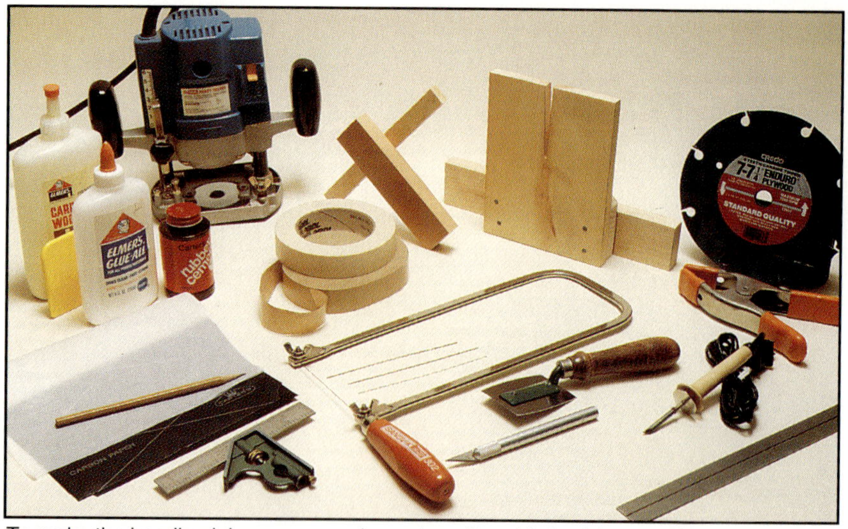

To make the banding inlays, you need a router with guide bushing, masking tape, spring clamps, shopmade T-guide, veneer saw, knife and glue. To lay out and inlay a marquetry insert, use carbon and tracing paper, a hard pencil, rule, rubber cement, gummed veneer tape, a fret saw and a shopmade birds-mouth (cutting support).

Text and photographs for *Inlay* by Rosario Capotosto. For special tools and supplies, check out mail-order outlets such as Constantines, 2050 Eastchester Rd., Bronx, NY 10461, and The Woodworker's Store, 21801 Industrial Blvd., Rogers, MN 55374.

The next step is to reassemble the strips, only offset, so a mahogany layer is adjacent to a maple layer. To hold the pieces together while the glue sets, use spring clamps and masking tape. Align a pair of sections, maple to mahogany, and apply a strip of masking tape along the mating line on one side so the two pieces hinge open. Then, apply fast-setting yellow glue to the mating surfaces and let the glue become tacky by letting it dry

1 With the saw blade tilted at 45°, cut the lamination into $^{1}/_{4}$-in.-slices. Clamp a stop-block to a miter gauge fence for uniformity.

2 Assemble the slices so each maple section abuts a mahogany piece. Use tape and spring clamps to hold pieces in place.

3 Tack strips to both edges of assembly and place between guide boards. Install a wide base on router and trim faces flat.

4 To add stripes to each side of the diamond pattern, cut maple and mahogany veneer to the size of the diamond blank.

5 Laminate a stack of maple, mahogany and maple veneer to each side of the diamond blank. Clamp until glue sets.

6 Rip $^{1}/_{16}$-in.-thick strips on outside of blade. Use a T-jig in miter gauge slot to reposition fence and work after each pass.

in the air for about a minute. Bring the faces together and apply tape to the opposite joint line. Add two spring clamps to fully close the joint (Fig. 2). Leave the spring clamps in place for at least five minutes.

Next, construct a jig to rout off the peaks on both faces of the blank. First attach a $^{3}/_{4}$×$^{3}/_{4}$-in. strip to both edges of the blank with a few 1$^{1}/_{4}$ in. finishing nails. Make sure the strips are parallel to each other and in line with the blank. Then, screw the assembly to a workboard and add a $^{3}/_{4}$-in.-thick guide board on each side of the assembly. Secure an oversize base on your router to ride on the guide boards. Install a straight bit in the router, and adjust the depth to take off the peaks of the blank while the router rides on the guide boards. A strip tacked on one side and then moved to the other keeps the router in line while you are trimming the edges (Fig. 3). When the first side is done, flip over the blank and trim the other side. When you're done, you'll have a flat board with the diamond pattern visible on the edge. You can cut off many thin strips for inlaying.

7 Rout diamond band recess with a straight bit. Use a template and guide bushing. Trim round corners with chisel.

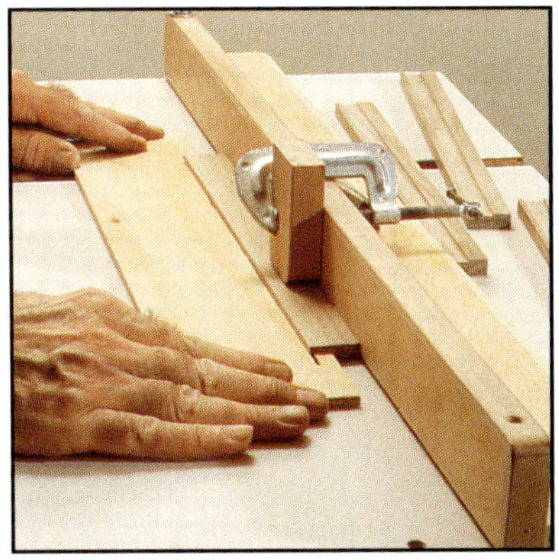

8 When inlaying banding in pieces to be assembled later, such as for a picture frame, use a router table to cut recesses.

9 To position miters, first make photocopies of the banding. Align and cut these to length and use as a pattern.

10 Test fit each piece. Apply glue and cover with wax paper and a caul before clamping. Sand flush when glue is dry.

To add triple-border stripes on either side of the diamond pattern, cut two pieces of mahogany veneer and four pieces of maple veneer slightly larger than the blank (Fig. 4). Use $^{1}/_{28}$-in.-thick veneer. The veneer and blank can be laminated in one step, but you'll have to work fast if you're using white glue. For a more relaxed pace, use slow-setting hide glue, available in a bottle.

With cauls (flat boards that distribute clamping pressure), clamps, glue and wax paper on hand, stack the assembly in correct order—each side of the blank is glued to a maple/mahogany/maple stack (Fig. 5). Then apply glue to each piece, drive a few nails through the wood at a waste area to prevent shifting and clamp the bundle with wax paper between the work and the cauls.

To slice the complete blank into banding, first install a smooth-cutting blade in your table saw and fit the saw with a close-fitting blade insert.

The $^{1}/_{16}$-in.-thick bandings must be ripped on the outside of the blade—not between the blade and the fence. To ensure uniform cuts and speed up the fence adjustment after each pass, make a T-shaped jig (or T-guide) that fits on the miter gauge slot. Trim the leg of the jig that extends toward the blade so it ends $^{1}/_{16}$ in. from the blade, and clamp the jig to the table saw a few inches in front of the blade.

With the work against the fence, adjust the fence until the work touches the jig and cut the first strip. After each cut, readjust the fence so the work touches the jig and make the next cut (Fig. 6).

To rout a recess for the banding, install a straight bit that matches the banding width, or use a smaller bit and make the cut in two passes. Set the depth of cut to slightly less than the thickness of the banding.

For a rectangular installation, such as the one shown here, make a template of the recess and use a guide bushing on the router to follow the template (Fig. 7). Be sure to size the template properly for the bit and bushing sizes you're using. Secure the template with double-sided tape or clamps. After routing the recess, square the corners with a sharp chisel.

If you're banding individual pieces that will be assembled later, such as in a mitered frame, rout the recesses on a router table (Fig. 8).

To inlay a mitered rectangular banding, first make several photocopies of the banding. Then, cut and fit the copies (Fig. 9). When you're satisfied with the placement of the miters, use the photocopies as a guide in cutting the pieces to length with a veneer saw.

Finally, test fit the bandings and trim, if necessary (Fig. 10). Then apply glue sparingly, place the bandings in the recesses and clamp. Use a flat scrap of wood as a caul to provide even pressure and place wax paper between the work and the caul.

Triple-Stripe Inlay

Like a pinstripe on a car, one of the most effective decorative elements in woodworking is a simple, single or multiple inlaid stripe.

Single-stripe inlays can be made by simply slicing solid wood. For this triple-stripe inlay, start with maple and mahogany veneer. Laminate three layers of 3×20-in. veneer, with the mahogany sandwiched between two maple pieces, to obtain a roughly $^{1}/_{10}$-in.-thick triple veneer.

To cut the assembly into strips on your table saw, tape the piece to a $^{3}/_{4}$×3×19-in. support board so that 1 in. overhangs the front end of the board. Apply the tape to the edge of the board that will ride against the fence.

Adjust the blade so it projects about $^{3}/_{16}$ in. above the table. Then, place the work against the fence and use the T-guide, described on page 39, to set the fence for a $^{1}/_{16}$-in. rip on the outside of the blade. Reference the T-guide against the 1-in. overhang of triple veneer that projects from the support board.

After the first cut, shift the fence over so the veneer abuts the T-guide and make the next cut (Fig. 11).

11 Tape triple veneer under board with 1 in. extending past end. Reference T-guide against extension to cut $^{1}/_{16}$-in. strips.

12 Cut triple-stripe recess with a fine-cutting thin-kerf blade. Then glue stripes in place, using butt joints at corners.

To install the triple-stripe inlay, make the recesses with a fine-cutting thin-kerf blade, slightly shallower than the depth of the strips. Cut the inlay strips to length, using butt joints at the corners and carefully test fit them in the recesses. Make sure that these recesses are free of all sawdust and other debris that could keep the inlay from seating properly. Then, apply a thin bead of glue to the recesses and clamp the strips in place (Fig. 12).

When the glue is dry, sand the triple stripes flush to the surface.

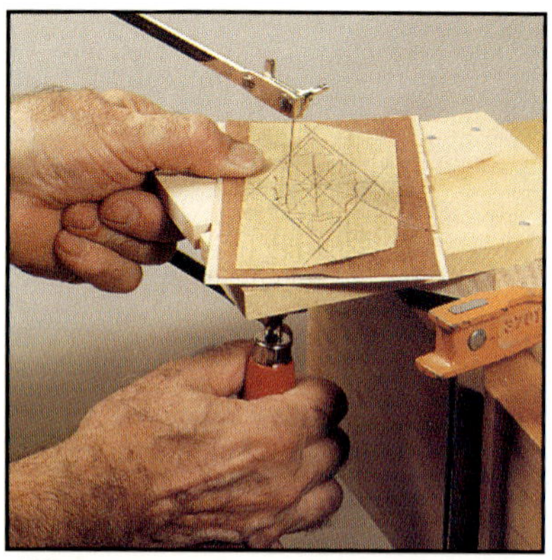

13 Support veneer on birds-mouth, and use fret saw to cut shapes. A pushpin makes holes that start each internal cut.

14 After cutting, separate the two sets of shapes. Then, assemble a contrasting set and apply veneer tape to the top face.

15 Use a template, guide bushing and straight bit to rout marquetry recess. Bushing and bit determine template size.

16 Use a sharp knife to trim round corners left by router. Apply glue and clamp marquetry assembly. Sand flush.

Inlaid Marquetry

To make an inlaid marquetry pattern similar to the central design on this jewelry box, begin by laying out the design on paper and then choose your veneer. In the project shown here, limba and mahogany $^{1}/_{28}$-in.-thick was used.

You can cut the marquetry pieces with a knife or use the fret-saw method. The advantage of the fret saw is that you can cut more intricate shapes. The sawing technique shown is called the *double-cut* because it produces two complete assemblies—one the inverse of the other in terms of light and dark.

Begin by cutting two pieces of contrasting veneer slightly larger than the complete design and stack them together with a piece of scrap veneer underneath.

Temporarily secure the veneer together with rubber cement. Trace your pattern on the stack by placing carbon paper between the drawing and the work and going over the lines with a sharp pencil.

To cut the individual veneer pieces, first install a fine blade in a fret saw—this saw is similar to a coping saw, but with an adjustable or very deep fixed throat, and capable of using blades ranging from .008 to .034 in. thick. Support the veneer stack on a $^3/_4$-in.-thick board with a narrow V notch cut into one edge. This board is called a *birds-mouth*, and the V notch provides clearance for the blade while the work is supported for cutting.

Use a pushpin to pierce starting holes at the corners of the lines of the design. Then, insert the blade in a hole with the teeth pointing down, tension the blade and begin cutting out the shapes (Fig. 13). Hold the fret saw so the blade is vertical and at 90° to the veneer stack. When all the lines have been cut, carefully pry apart the pieces with a knife and rub off the rubber cement with your fingers.

Assemble the segments of the design that are to be used, and apply gummed veneer tape over the surface (Fig. 14). Then, flip over the assembly. Because the pieces were sawn with a vertical stroke, you'll notice a slight gap between them. Fill the gap with a paste made from fret-saw dust and white glue. Just spread some very fine dust on a piece of scrap wood and squeeze some glue into the dust. Mix the two thoroughly, using a small splinter of wood, until you achieve the consistency of commercial wood fillers. With practice, you can eliminate the gaps by sawing the pieces at a slight angle. The resultant beveled edges allow the pieces to nest together snugly. The degree of bevel is related to the thickness of the fret-saw blade.

To inlay the marquetry assembly, first make a template for the overall shape that suits your router bit size and your guide bushing, and then secure it to the work (Fig. 15). It's a good idea to first test the template on a scrap board. After you've routed the actual recess, trim the rounded inside corners with a sharp knife (Fig. 16).

To glue the marquetry assembly in the recess, first apply glue sparingly to the mating surfaces and position the assembly in the recess. Lay a sheet of wax paper over the surface and then add a pad of about six sheets of newspaper to equalize the uneven pressure caused by variations in veneer thicknesses. Place a flat caul over the pad and then clamp.

When the glue has set, remove the clamps and pad, dampen the gummed veneer tape and peel it off. Allow the inlay to dry thoroughly, then sand and apply the finish of your choice.

Improving your landscape

Improving Your Landscape was written by Merle Henkenius. Photo by Spencer Jones. Technical art by Eugene Thompson. Landscape design by Bryan Poppe.

The landscaping you do outdoors can be as important in making a house a home as the decorating you do indoors. It may be even more important in terms of building equity. But while most of us know the look we're after in the family room, fewer of us can conceptualize a well-styled and self-sustaining menagerie of outdoor plants that will add real comfort and street appeal. There's design to consider, of course, but plants are living things, with specific and sometimes limiting soil and sunlight requirements. You have three options on how to proceed. You can do the job yourself. You can hire a nursery/garden center to draw up a plan and either do the plantings yourself, according to the blueprint, or contract the nursery to do it all. In this case, the planner is usually a certified landscape designer (CLD), with a background in horticulture. Finally, you can hire a design specialist—a registered landscape architect.

While these approaches can differ significantly, there is also some overlap. A do-it-yourselfer, for example, will certainly seek out the extensive free information to be found at every garden center. Moreover, while garden centers and nurseries usually employ horticulturists with design training, some also employ or contract with, registered landscape architects. While landscape architects are usually not associated with nurseries, a developing trend in the business is the "design/build" concept. In these cases, architects work with preferred subcontractors to provide turnkey services—plans, plants, plantings and all.

Designers versus Architects

What's the difference between a designer and an architect? Certified landscape designers are often horticulturists with secondary training in landscape design. Though not always the case, they tend to know more about plants and plant diseases than architects. In some areas, CLDs are tested and certified by the state, while in others, it's an industry certification. Either way, the test is no walk-through. By all accounts, it's a difficult exam. Of course, some designers are not as well trained, and in some cases, not certified either. It pays to ask.

A registered landscape architect masters most of the same things, but comes to the task from a different angle. He or she is a designer by training and temperament, but must also be versed, and state certified, in hardscape principles, including grading and drainage, property laws, irrigation and erosion control. From the consumer's point of view, there's also a significant difference in the professional relationship. A landscape designer usually works for a nursery and creates an inexpensive plan, about $50 to $200. This fee is typically credited to your account after you purchase a certain level of merchandise, say $500 to $1000. It's understood that the nursery profits from the materials you buy. The plan is a big help to the consumer, but it's also an effective sales tool, and everybody knows it. In contrast, a landscape architect—except for the design/build variety—does not profit from materials or installations. On a practical level, this means that an architect has to charge more for his plan, but may be more willing to accommodate exhaustive revisions. In addition to superior design training, his or her willingness to work your thoughts and afterthoughts into the mix is likely to yield a more striking and satisfying plan. Which is the better choice? For most of us, a garden-center design will do just fine. Simple yards, simple plans. But if you're shooting for something beyond a proportional pleasantness, or if your property is large, with multiple elevations and complicated drainage requirements, then a registered landscape architect is worth the investment.

Guidelines

Every landscape plan should be different, even when side-by-side houses are nearly identical, because the tastes and lifestyle preferences of the owners do affect the decision-making process. Still, there are a few goal-specific rules and guidelines that should be applied to each site. The first thing to consider is that the front of a home is different from the back, both physically and socially. For better or worse, the front yard is part of the larger community, while the backyard usually requires a private invitation. Metaphorically, the front door opens inward, while the back door spills outward. The front is more formal, the back less so. In addition, front yards are often lopsided, with the house, garage, driveway or entry door uncomfortably weighted to one side. Finally, the fronts of houses are usually dominated by hard lines, as viewed from the street. The line separating the yard from the foundation, the door from the walk and the vertical corners from the horizontal lawn all produce abrupt, severe edges.

A front-yard landscaping plan must complement its surroundings—its neighborhood. Any striking departure from the norm should begin modestly near the street and then develop its full effect as it nears the house. Above all, the front yard should be inviting, especially as you approach the front door. The plantings here should be chosen and placed so as to lead the visitor to the door and to focus attention there. In addition to setting an inviting tone, these plantings should also break up the hard lines near the door. In practical terms, if the door waits at the end of a long walk, or driveway, the area near the door should be softened, to diminish that end-of-the-runway feel.

How are hard edges softened? By variety—specifically, by plants that vary in height, texture and color. The plantings near the door can be placed symmetrically, as when the sidewalk is centered on the property, or asymmetrically, as when the entry is off-center, right or left. The same applies to a lopsided yard. If your house, garage or driveway hugs the left side, a prominent right-side grouping of plants can pull things back into balance. Similarly, the hard outside corners of a house can be obliterated by ornamental trees or shrubs, while the foundation line can be broken by shrubs, flowers and low-growing ground cover.

Sides and Back

Side yards are transitional, both physically and visually. They either graft together the separate sensibilities of front yard and backyard or they deliberately separate them. When a side yard is wide and spacious, shade trees and evergreens make good punctuation points and function as good dividers. When side yards are narrow, shrubs and flowers can lead the eye toward the backyard. While front-yard sidewalks are usually made of concrete, side-yard and backyard walkways can make good use of alternative materials.

Backyards are more casual. They can be cozy or structured. They can harbor Japanese gardens or sandboxes and tire swings. It all depends. If houses are like their owners, backyards are most like them. The plant selection should be less formal, with greater emphasis on variety and experimentation and plant placement can be more relaxed—less orderly. This is the place for wild clumps of tall grass, shade trees, vegetable gardens, fruited bushes, bird feeders, stepping stones, vine-covered arbors, a pool, horseshoe pits—it's your call.

Seasonal Interest

Whether you live in a semitropical climate or smack in the middle of the Rust Belt, try to include plants and trees that offer year-round interest. Though the options are limited in the northern reaches of the country, textures and colors, however muted, can make a difference. Trees and bushes that hold their fruit well into winter are good choices as are tall grasses and trees that have interesting bark patterns, such as the river birch used in this sample design. Because trees can be functional as well as ornamental, tree selection and placement is important. You'll thank yourself if you avoid the messy "self-pruning" varieties, such as cottonwoods and sycamores. Because shade trees are as good as air conditioners in summer, a few well-

ONE PLAN IN ACTION

Plans made by garden-center/nurseries are very popular these days. The reasons are apparent. Garden centers are near and familiar, and the process is low-key and manageable, allowing you to spread the work and expense over several years. To get a better handle on just how a garden-center plan works, we paid to have a design drawn up for a typical new home in a typical new development.

Every landscape plan should start with you—with your ideas, likes and dislikes. For this reason, most garden centers start with a questionnaire dealing with likes, dislikes and basic family habits. Once this is filled out, the designer has a better sense of tastes and lifestyles. He learns, for example, that we don't care to spend our weekends begging life from suicidal rose bushes. He learns that we do plan to widen our drive (though not for a year or two), and that we have a lot-width drainage swale just in front of a rear terrace, and that the drainage is slow, at best.

From a careful survey of our lot—we walked and measured it together—he learns that our rear yard is shallow, private and fenced, with a large deck, and that our front yard is large, featureless, divided by a drive and weighted heavily to the left.

We agreed that our general goal was to shade the southwest corner of the house with trees and to accent the high side of the terrace with low bushes, tall grasses and other low-maintenance plants. We also hoped to break up the front yard with bushes, ornamental trees and colorful flowers—anything to diminish the 65-ft. run of open turf.

The plan we received does exactly what we hoped it would. Starting in the front yard, our designer suggested a kidney-shaped area midway between the street and house, on the right side. This blocked-out area curls left, which serves to tie the two sides of the yard together. Within this area, we will plant three Indian summer crabapple trees that will grow roughly 15 ft. and spread about as much. Beneath these ornamental trees, we'll plant various perennials and annuals to further define the area. A second planting bed will skirt the front and right sides of the house, concealing part of the front foundation and the right-side utilities.

To balance the right-side plantings, the left of the house, extending back from the future location of the widened drive, is anchored with lentago viburnum, a bush that we'll trim into an ornamental tree. As for the backyard and left side (south) yard, our modest drainage flow dictated trees tolerant of wet conditions. We opted for two river birches, which not only thrive in wet soil but are resistant to birch blight. This area also holds moonbeam coreopsis, which are small plants with fern-like foliage and yellow flowers. These are among the longest-blooming perennials available.

At the far northern corner of the backyard, and on the high side of the terrace, we'll plant an autumn purple ash, which is a relatively fast-growing hardwood tree that turns a deep purple in the fall. We expect it to reach and spread 30 ft. Beneath this tree and against a small garden shed, we'll plant variegated porcelain ampelopsis, a vine with green leaves that have white variegation and red and purple berries. To complete the plantings along the back of the house, we opted for another viburnum, but this time we won't be shaping it into a tree. The alfredo viburnum flowers white, gets only 4 ft. tall and is noted for its brilliant red/orange fall colors.

The backyard plantings were chosen to conceal part of a not-so-handsome stockade fence, running the length of the property. Dominating the left corner will be an autumn brilliance amelanchier, an ornamental tree that will be the first to bloom in the spring. Also in this area, we'll have a mint julep juniper, another 4-ft. evergreen, a variety of viburnum bushes and several gro-low sumacs.

placed trees now can save you big bucks later. The west side of a house has seven times the heat gain of the remaining sides, so west and southwest sections of the yard are ideal shade-tree locations.

Don't Forget the Grass

Turf grasses are the foundation of every landscape plan, even when part of the plan is to reduce the percentage of grass in your yard. The only worthwhile suggestion here is to avoid traditional, short-root bluegrass varieties. These traditional turf grasses are notorious for their susceptibility to diseases and their reliance on huge quantities of water.

Today, turf-grade fescues are much less trouble, and some new bluegrass varieties have deeper root systems and improved hardiness. If you prefer the low maintenance of zoysia grass, you no longer have to live with a brown lawn most of the year. Improved varieties, such as Meyer Z-52, are less cold-sensitive, so they green-up sooner and stay green longer. If you don't care to tear up your yard, overseeding with improved varieties several years in a row will replace much of your existing grass.

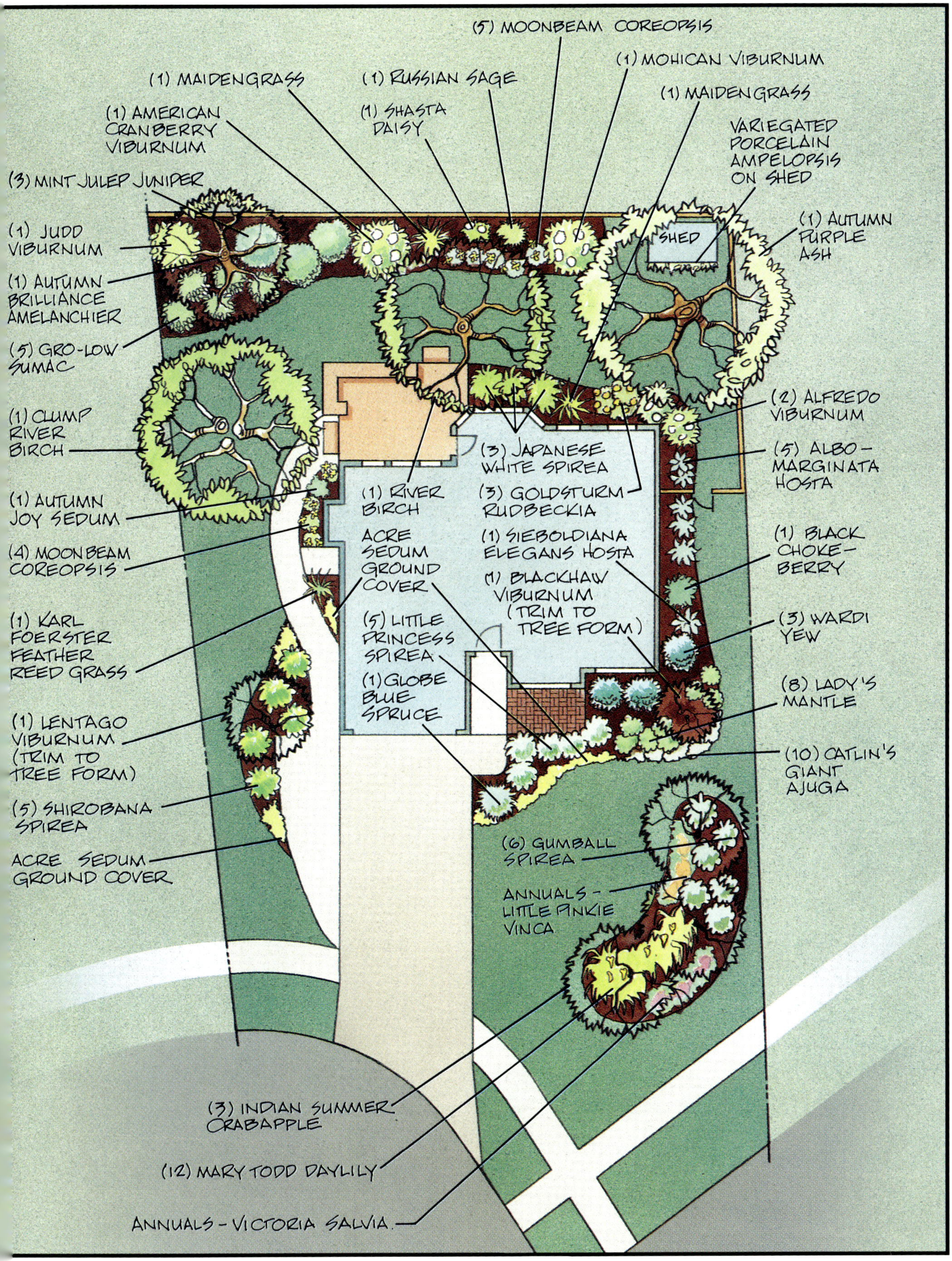
(5) MOONBEAM COREOPSIS
(1) MOHICAN VIBURNUM
(1) MAIDENGRASS
(1) RUSSIAN SAGE
(1) MAIDENGRASS
(1) AMERICAN CRANBERRY VIBURNUM
(1) SHASTA DAISY
VARIEGATED PORCELAIN AMPELOPSIS ON SHED
(3) MINT JULEP JUNIPER
(1) JUDD VIBURNUM
SHED
(1) AUTUMN PURPLE ASH
(1) AUTUMN BRILLIANCE AMELANCHIER
(5) GRO-LOW SUMAC
(2) ALFREDO VIBURNUM
(1) CLUMP RIVER BIRCH
(3) JAPANESE WHITE SPIREA
(5) ALBO-MARGINATA HOSTA
(1) AUTUMN JOY SEDUM
(1) RIVER BIRCH
(3) GOLDSTURM RUDBECKIA
(4) MOONBEAM COREOPSIS
ACRE SEDUM GROUND COVER
(1) SIEBOLDIANA ELEGANS HOSTA
(1) BLACK CHOKE-BERRY
(1) BLACKHAW VIBURNUM (TRIM TO TREE FORM)
(1) KARL FOERSTER FEATHER REED GRASS
(5) LITTLE PRINCESS SPIREA
(3) WARDI YEW
(1) GLOBE BLUE SPRUCE
(8) LADY'S MANTLE
(1) LENTAGO VIBURNUM (TRIM TO TREE FORM)
(10) CATLIN'S GIANT AJUGA
(5) SHIROBANA SPIREA
(6) GUMBALL SPIREA
ACRE SEDUM GROUND COVER
ANNUALS - LITTLE PINKIE VINCA
(3) INDIAN SUMMER CRABAPPLE
(12) MARY TODD DAYLILY
ANNUALS - VICTORIA SALVIA

Storage shed

Consider the items we now store in garden sheds. In addition to the requisite lawnmower, the selection may include a snowblower, leafblower, tiller, wheelbarrow and, of course, the usual miscellany of lawn-and-garden hand tools. The total value can easily run to several thousand dollars. With this in mind, the quality of the shed itself becomes a priority.

You do have a few options to choose from, of course. Metal shed kits have long been offered at the retail level, and site-built wood sheds are available at lumberyards and from weekend entrepreneurs.

The one shown here is a third alternative—constructing a shed from scratch, using conventional house-building materials and methods. With this plan, it's possible to accommodate the shed's size to your collection of tools and machinery. You can even tailor the trim and siding to match your house. This shed is based on a 7×9-ft. floor frame with lapped siding.

Frankly, the do-it-yourself option will cost more than purchasing a shed—for the materials alone. But in the end, you'll have an attractive, secure building that will outlast just about everything you put in it.

Because garden sheds are considered temporary structures, they're usually not constrained by building codes. Lacking code directives, you can chose a treated lumber framework for the base, set over shallow trenches filled with gravel. The gravel provides drainage away from the wood and better accommodates the pitch and heave of the seasons.

Roof trusses are also built from scratch. Trusses are easy to build, even if you've never used a framing square or haven't mastered roof geometry. The small ones seen here are a breeze to install, even when working alone.

1 Place pressure-treated floor frame on gravel-filled 4-in.-deep trenches. Then, level the frame in both directions.

2 Nail 3/4-in. tongue-and-groove plywood to the floor frame. After this is completed, coat with an enamel porch paint.

TORO

3 Nail each stud through the plates with two 16d nails per stud. Place triple studs at the ends of both long walls.

4 After sheathing, cut window opening and use 10d galvanized casing nails to secure the window to the wall.

5 Set the first wall up and nail it through the soleplate. Then, level and brace the wall with a 2×4 nailed to the floor.

6 After the end walls are set up, add a second top wall plate. Overlap the wall plates at the corners and nail in place.

Setting the Base

Build the shed base frame using three pressure-treated 4x4s and two pressure-treated 2x4s. For a 7x9-ft. shed like the one shown, cut the 4x4s to 9 ft. less 3 in. for the 2x4s at each end. Cut the 2x4s to 7 ft. long. Nail the boards to the ends of two 4x4s using 16d galvanized common nails to make a rectangular frame. To provide extra floor support, nail the third 4x4 to the 2x4s along the frame centerline, as shown in the drawing on page 50.

With the base frame assembled, level the ground at the shed site and dig a continuous 4-in.-deep trench to match the base frame perimeter and an additional trench that's aligned with the center 4x4 support. Fill the trenches with gravel, set the frame in place and level it in both directions (Fig. 1).

To make the floor, nail pieces of $\frac{3}{4}$-in. tongue-and-groove plywood onto the frame. Begin by trimming the groove from the starting sheet and nail that piece in place with 8d screw-shank galvanized nails. Using the two factory edges of the plywood, check that the framework beneath it is square, and adjust if necessary. Then, set the second piece in place, engage the tongue in the groove and nail it down (Fig. 2).

Wall Construction

Cut the four 2x4 long-wall plates to the length of the floor. Then, mark the stud positions on the plates. Position the first stud $15\frac{1}{4}$ in. from the leading end of each plate, and each subsequent stud at 16-in. centers.

To frame a utility-sash window, measure the width of the window, position a full-length stud on each side of the opening and cut a sill plate—to span between them—for the window to rest on. Leave the area above the window open. Cut the wall studs to $78\frac{1}{2}$ in. and build the corners by nailing three studs side by side. Lay each stud in position and nail to the plates with 16d nails (Fig. 3).

Build the back wall in a similar fashion, but omit the triple studs. Place the second stud $12\frac{1}{2}$ in. from the leading end of the top and bottom plates. Then, place the remaining studs on 16-in. centers.

The door opening on the front wall should be at least 36 in. wide—wider if you have a riding mower. For a 36-in.-wide opening, laminate the door header by sandwiching 39-in. 2x4s around a piece of $\frac{1}{2}$-in. plywood. To support the header, cut two jack studs $3\frac{1}{2}$ in. less than the normal stud length and nail these to full-length studs. Then frame the front wall with a centered opening, as shown. Finally, slide the header between the jack studs and the top plate and nail it from the top and sides.

Nail $\frac{1}{2}$-in. plywood or waferboard sheathing over the studs, using 8d galvanized nails. On the end walls, extend the sheathing $3\frac{1}{2}$ in. beyond the framing on both sides. This overhang will eventually cover the ends of the long walls.

At the window wall, cut out the sheathing over the opening and set the window in place. Nail through the trim with 10d galvanized casing nails (Fig. 4). Tip up a long wall and align it with the floor. Secure it with 16d nails. Then, plumb the wall and nail a diagonal brace to the floor (Fig. 5). With the side walls up, raise the end walls between then. Nail them to the

7 Build a roof truss jig on a plywood platform. Then, nail and glue $^1/_2$-in.-plywood gussets to the truss components.

8 Lay the trusses between the walls and then tip up the end trusses. Center and toenail them to the wall top plates.

9 Create a 3-in. roof overhang at the gable ends by adding double 2×4 rafters to the truss rafters already in place.

floor and to the side walls. Finally, nail second top plates to the existing plates, overlapping the side walls at the corners (Fig. 6).

Building the Roof

First, build a jig for assembling the trusses. Cut a sheet of plywood and a 2×4 to match the width of the shed and nail the 2×4 to the plywood flush with an edge.

Measure 24 in. from each end and mark the 2×4. To establish a 5-in. pitch, lay a framing square on the plywood and against the edge of the 2×4 at the 24-in. mark. Then, mark the plywood 10 in. above the 2×4. Next, lay a straight 2×4 against the corner of the jig 2×4 and angle it to intersect the 10-in. mark. Butt a second 2×4 edge to edge against the angled 2×4 and nail the second piece to the plywood. Repeat from the opposite end of the jig and mark the vertical centerline on the plywood and 2×4s.

Cut all the pieces for the first truss to fit the space on the jig. Use the first set as a pattern for the rest. Lay the members in place, and nail the joints together with gussets that are made of $^1/_2$-in. plywood (Fig. 7). Use 7d nails and construction adhesive on the gussets. Place gussets on both sides of each truss, except the two end trusses.

Mark the wall top plates every 24 in. Lay the trusses upside down on the walls, and then tip up the end trusses and align them with the top plates. Toenail these trusses in place (Fig. 8).

Run a string between the rafter ends of the two end trusses, and align the remaining trusses with this string. When all are toenailed to the walls, plumb the first truss and position the rest of the trusses to match.

To create an overhang on the ends, nail doubled 2×4 rafters to each end truss rafter (Fig. 9). Then rip $^1/_4$-in. plywood to fit underneath the rafter ends to create a closed soffit. Finally, sheath the end walls as well as the roof and add the 1×6 fascia, as shown in the drawing.

Siding and Trimwork

Install $^1/_4$-in. plywood trim spacers around the door opening and at the corners of the shed so that the $^3/_4$-in. trim will cover the ends of the lap siding. Then, install the 1×5 doorjamb (Fig. 10). Add the door face trim over the plywood, and follow with 1×4 corner trim. Use 8d casing or galvanized screw-shank nails.

Nail $^1/_4$-in. or $^1/_2$-in. plywood spacer strips to the bottom of the sheathing and install the first siding row around the shed. Leave a $^1/_{16}$-in. gap from where the siding abuts any trim and start the first row about $^1/_4$ in. below the sheathing. Measure up from the starter row and mark the trim every 6 in. (Fig. 11). Install the siding against these marks with 8d galvanized siding nails.

On the long walls, bring the siding up against the eave soffit. You'll need to finish the gable ends by trimming the final rows with angle cuts to match the roof pitch. Use a framing square or the roof truss jig to lay out the angle for the gable cuts. When you've completed the siding, caulk all joints between trim and siding and between soffit and siding (Fig. 12). When the caulk skins over, prime and paint the shed.

10 Use 1×5 pine for the door jamb. Align with $^1/_4$-in. plywood face-trim shims. Place shims under the corner trim as well.

11 To keep the siding lapped uniformly, measure up from starter row and mark the spacing on the trim in 6-in. increments.

12 Caulk all siding-to-trim joints and soffit joints. Always apply sparingly and avoid smoothing it with a finger.

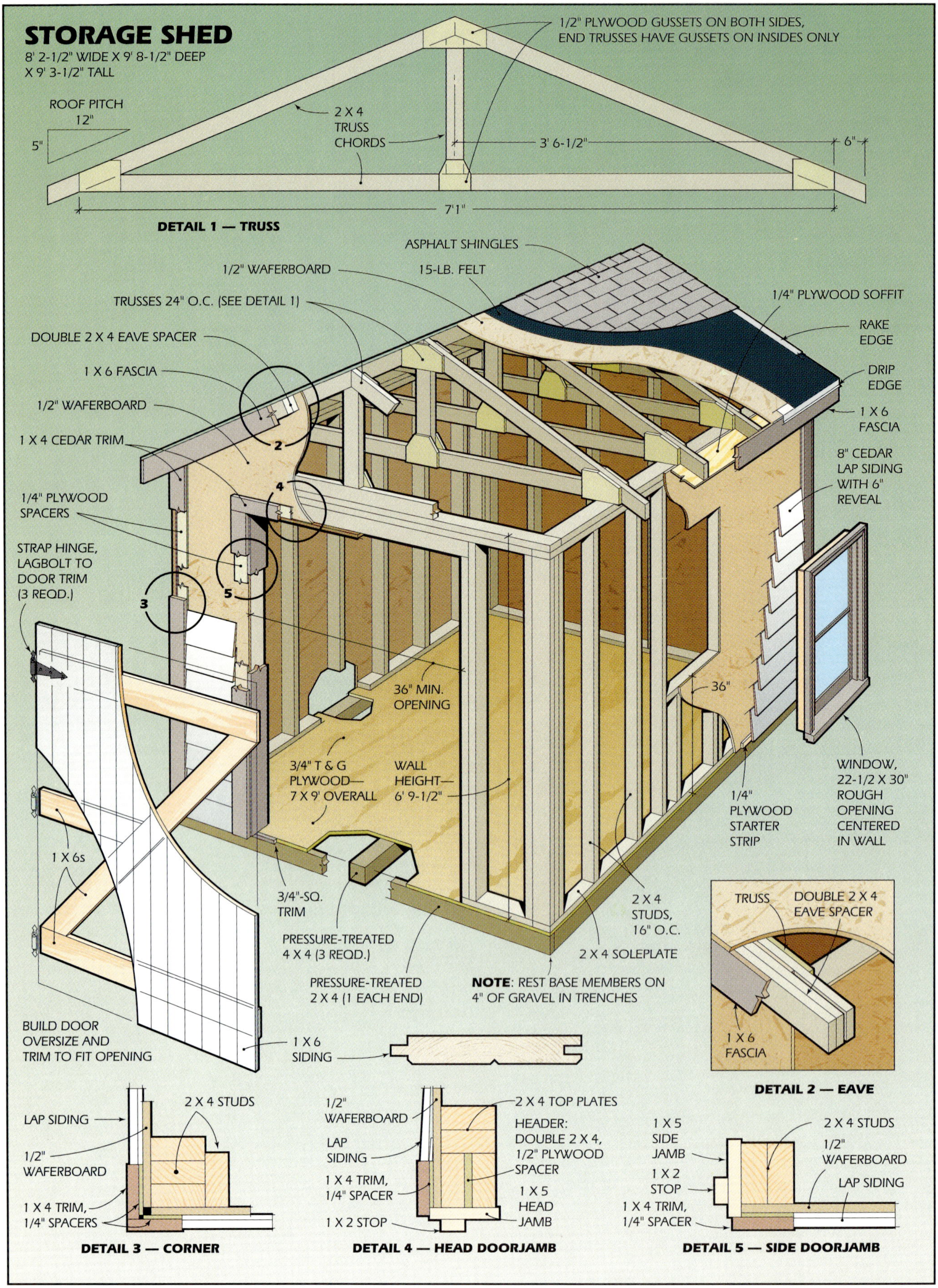
STORAGE SHED
8' 2-1/2" WIDE X 9' 8-1/2" DEEP X 9' 3-1/2" TALL
ROOF PITCH
12"
5"
2 X 4 TRUSS CHORDS
1/2" PLYWOOD GUSSETS ON BOTH SIDES, END TRUSSES HAVE GUSSETS ON INSIDES ONLY
3' 6-1/2"
6"
7'1"
DETAIL 1 — TRUSS
ASPHALT SHINGLES
1/2" WAFERBOARD
15-LB. FELT
TRUSSES 24" O.C. (SEE DETAIL 1)
1/4" PLYWOOD SOFFIT
DOUBLE 2 X 4 EAVE SPACER
RAKE EDGE
1 X 6 FASCIA
DRIP EDGE
1/2" WAFERBOARD
1 X 6 FASCIA
1 X 4 CEDAR TRIM
8" CEDAR LAP SIDING WITH 6" REVEAL
1/4" PLYWOOD SPACERS
STRAP HINGE, LAGBOLT TO DOOR TRIM (3 REQD.)
36" MIN. OPENING
36"
3/4" T & G PLYWOOD— 7 X 9' OVERALL
WALL HEIGHT— 6' 9-1/2"
1/4" PLYWOOD STARTER STRIP
WINDOW, 22-1/2 X 30" ROUGH OPENING CENTERED IN WALL
1 X 6s
3/4"-SQ. TRIM
PRESSURE-TREATED 4 X 4 (3 REQD.)
2 X 4 STUDS, 16" O.C.
2 X 4 SOLEPLATE
PRESSURE-TREATED 2 X 4 (1 EACH END)
NOTE: REST BASE MEMBERS ON 4" OF GRAVEL IN TRENCHES
TRUSS
DOUBLE 2 X 4 EAVE SPACER
1 X 6 FASCIA
DETAIL 2 — EAVE
BUILD DOOR OVERSIZE AND TRIM TO FIT OPENING
1 X 6 SIDING
LAP SIDING
2 X 4 STUDS
1/2" WAFERBOARD
1 X 4 TRIM, 1/4" SPACERS
DETAIL 3 — CORNER
1/2" WAFERBOARD
LAP SIDING
1 X 4 TRIM, 1/4" SPACER
1 X 2 STOP
2 X 4 TOP PLATES
HEADER: DOUBLE 2 X 4, 1/2" PLYWOOD SPACER
1 X 5 HEAD JAMB
DETAIL 4 — HEAD DOORJAMB
1 X 5 SIDE JAMB
1 X 2 STOP
1 X 4 TRIM, 1/4" SPACER
2 X 4 STUDS
1/2" WAFERBOARD
LAP SIDING
DETAIL 5 — SIDE DOORJAMB

13 After nailing the drip edges in place, trim the tabs from the shingles and then install a starter row along the eaves.

14 Cut the singles into three table-size pieces and use the tabs to cap the peak. Be sure to space each piece 5 in. apart.

Shingling the Roof

Cover the sheathing with roofing felt. Then, nail galvanized rake edge along the gable ends and drip edge along the eave edges of the roof. This will prevent rainwater from seeping between the shingles and the roof sheathing.

Install a starter row by trimming the tabs from a few shingles and nail what remains over the drip edge, with the grit facing up and the factory edge down. Allow the shingle edge to extend over the drip edge by about $^1/_4$ in. (Fig. 13). Offset the starter row from the first full row of shingles by trimming 3 in. from the first starter shingle you install.

After you've put the starter row down, lay the first row of full shingles over it and nail in place. On every subsequent row, cut 6 in. from the first shingle. Align shingles so that the bottom of the latest row lies across the top row of tab slots of the previous row. Nail each shingle with four $^3/_4$-in. galvanized roofing nails.

To cap the ridge, cut shingles into three pieces along the tabs. Then, nail the tabs along the peak at 5-in. intervals (Fig. 14).

Building a Door

Assemble tongue-in-groove pine to create a rectangular panel that's slightly larger in height and width than the trimmed door opening. Then, secure two horizontal 1×6 battens across the boards with $1^3/_8$-in. coated screws. Use four screws at each junction.

Next, mark and cut the door squarely to size. Finish by adding a diagonal brace between the cross battens to further stiffen the door and help prevent sagging. Add an additional short crossmember at the center of the hinge side to support a third hinge (Fig. 15).

Attach gate hinges to the door over the battens. Position the door in the opening and lagbolt the hinges to the door trim (Fig. 16). Then, install a handle, bolt and hasp. Finally, when the door swings easily and closes squarely, nail a 1×2 stop to the hasp side of the doorjamb.

Storage Shed was written and photographed by Merle Henkenius. Technical art by Eugene Thompson.

15 Build the door by using tongue-and-groove pine. Attach the crossmembers and a diagonal brace with screws.

16 Hang door with three steel gate hinges. Secure it to the trim with lagbolts, then hang the handle, bolt and hasp.

Redwood deck

Text and photos for *Redwood Deck* by Merle Henkenius. Technical art by Eugene Thompson. If you'd like to design your own deck and could use some help, you should consider the Redwood Design-A-Deck Plans Kit. It costs $19.50 ppd. from the California Redwood Assn., Dept. DDK-94, 405 Enfrente Dr., Suite 200, Novato, California 94949.

A wooden deck can be a kind of sanctuary, hosting only the invited. It can be both a party center and a quiet retreat—a place to repair, to relax or to conjure empires.

The superstructure of the deck shown is built out of pressure-treated pine because of its strength and high resistance to moisture and insects. The rich look of redwood was also wanted—to say nothing of its weather resistance—which lent itself to a box-like construction. The concealed pressure-treated lumber does most of the work, while the construction heart-grade redwood does most of the showing off.

Getting Started

The first order of business is to lay out the perimeter. Measure out from the house at each end of your future deck, 13 ft. $10^1/_2$ in. Then, drive in wooden stakes and stretch a string line between them. This line will give you the exact outer edge of the double rim joist and the posts that will support it. A redwood 2×12 trim board will eventually bring the dimension to 14 ft.

Using this line as a guide, dig posthole footings to frost level, usually 24 to 48 in., depending on the climate. Place one footing at each of the outside corners of the deck layout and equally space two more posts between these. Then, to accommodate the step and offset, dig two additional footing holes—one at the outside corner and one at the inside corner of the offset.

Pour these holes to approximately 1 in. above grade with concrete, and while the mix is still wet, insert metal 4×4 brackets into the concrete, so that the outer edge of the bracket is aligned with the string (Fig. 1). Then, level each bracket in both directions with a torpedo level (Fig. 2). Finally, allow the footings to cure a day or two before building on them.

Because this deck is built at ground level, there will be no getting under it once it's finished. For this rea-

Redwood lumber: California Redwood Assn.
Technical art: Eugene Thompson

son, it pays to strip the sod and cover the area with landscape fabric. The fabric will keep weeds from growing under the deck. Just roll out the fabric and pin it in place with galvanized nails (Fig. 3). Shovel a little sand over the fabric to hold it in place.

The next step is to mount the ledger plate on the house. In the installation shown, the first row of hardboard siding was not shimmed out at the bottom. If yours is, you'll need to either remove the shim or shim the top of the ledger plate. The point is, the ledger plate should be vertical, not canted inward.

To mount the 2×10 ledger, block under it or have a helper hold it up, then nail it to the siding-clad rim joist of the house with a few 16d galvanized nails. If your ledger will wrap around a trimmed corner, like the one shown, use a circular saw to mortise out the depth of the vertical trim on the back side of the ledger. This need not be a perfect cut, as its only purpose is to allow the ledger to fit flush against the siding. You can also continue the ledger partway around the cantilevered wall, stopping 1$^1/_2$ in. short of the adjoining 45° trimpieces.

With the ledger tacked in place, bore a series of pilot holes every 24 to 32 in. along its length and lag the ledger into the rim of the house. Galvanized lagbolts $^1/_2$×5 in. long will reach through all three layers of material. Back up each with a washer.

Installing Hangers and Posts

Start by laying out and marking all the joists along the ledger. A 14-ft. span requires joists set on 16-in. centers. With the layout complete, install a joist hanger at each marked location. To keep from getting a few of them too high or too low, use a short piece of 2×10 as a guide, aligning its top with the top of the ledger (Fig. 4). When positioned correctly, nail the hangers in place, using proper joist-hanger nails.

With the house side of the deck laid out and fitted with hangers, it's time to determine the height of the 4×4-in. posts that will support the double rim joists. Begin by cutting short lengths of 4×4 and setting them in their footing brackets. Then, set a precut joist (13 ft. 6 in.) into one of the ledger hangers opposite a footing and place a 4-ft. level atop the joist. When the joist is level, mark the post and cut it to length, then set the joist on the post and check for level again (Fig. 5). When two such posts are marked and trimmed, use their elevations to snap a string line across the remaining posts.

With all posts cut to length, nail two sets of 2×10s together with 16d galvanized nails to create the double rim joist. Alternate the nails, high and low, at 16-in. intervals. Make the outer 2×10 of the double rim 3 in. short of the overall length of the deck, to accommodate the redwood rim joist. Then, cut the inner joist 1$^1/_2$ in. short of the outer joist at each end. These stepped ends will allow you to nail the intersecting side joists from both directions.

1 After pouring each footing hole, set a 4×4 bracket into the wet concrete. Align the brackets with the string line.

2 Level the 4×4 brackets in both directions using a torpedo level, and let the concrete set a day before building on it.

3 Remove the sod, then cover the soil beneath the deck with landscape fabric. This keeps the weeds from growing.

4 Lay out the joist postions, then use a scrap of 2×10 joist to align each joist hanger. Use proper nails to install brackets.

5 Use a straight joist to level between the ledger and the support posts. Mark and cut the posts, then check the level again.

6 Anchor the footing bracket to the post with nails and the post to the double rim joist with 2×5 galvanized truss plates.

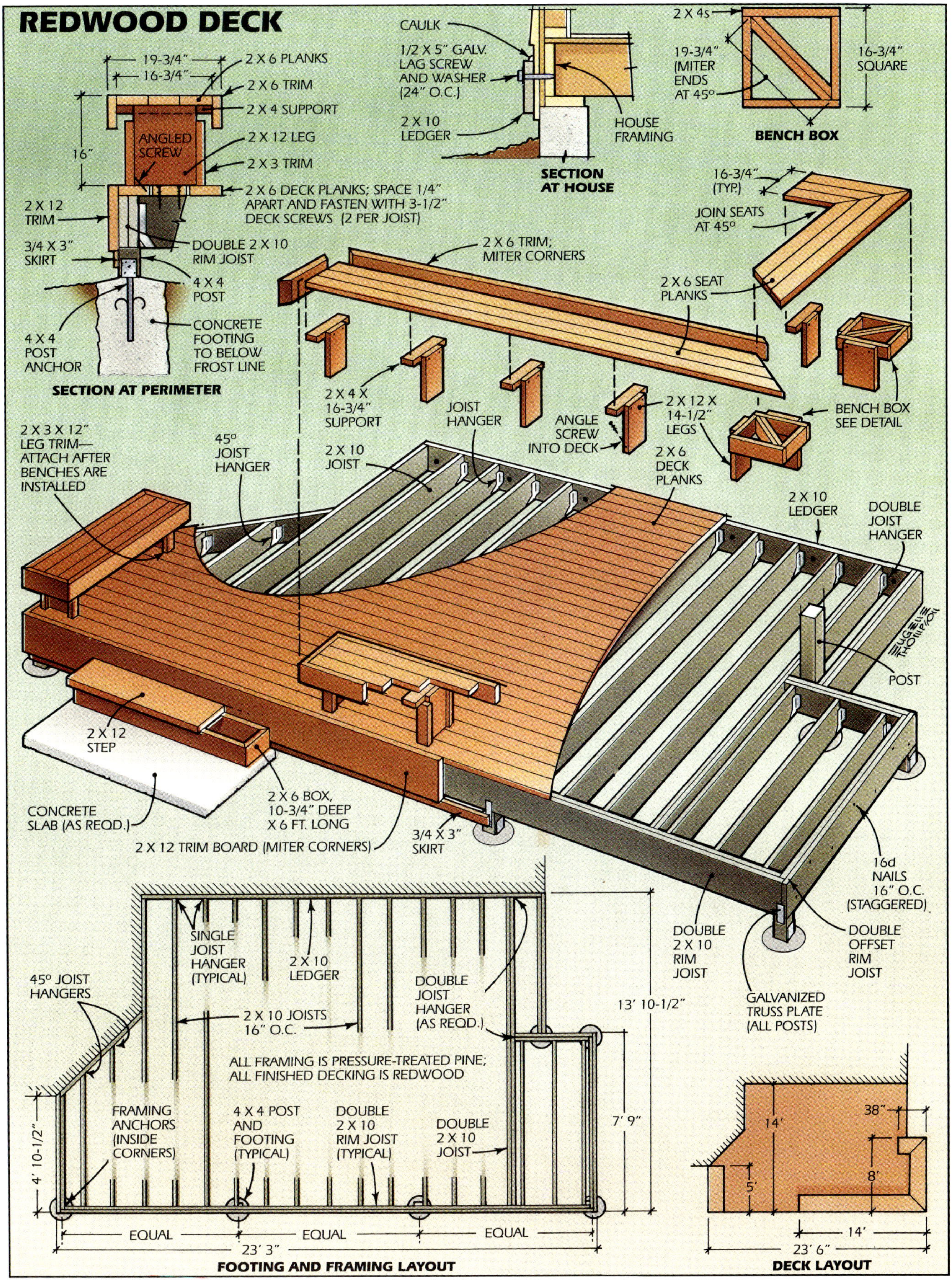
REDWOOD DECK
19-3/4"
16-3/4"
2 X 6 PLANKS
2 X 6 TRIM
2 X 4 SUPPORT
2 X 12 LEG
ANGLED SCREW
16"
2 X 3 TRIM
2 X 6 DECK PLANKS; SPACE 1/4" APART AND FASTEN WITH 3-1/2" DECK SCREWS (2 PER JOIST)
2 X 12 TRIM
3/4 X 3" SKIRT
DOUBLE 2 X 10 RIM JOIST
4 X 4 POST
4 X 4 POST ANCHOR
CONCRETE FOOTING TO BELOW FROST LINE
SECTION AT PERIMETER
CAULK
1/2 X 5" GALV. LAG SCREW AND WASHER (24" O.C.)
2 X 10 LEDGER
HOUSE FRAMING
SECTION AT HOUSE
2 X 4s
19-3/4" (MITER ENDS AT 45°
16-3/4" SQUARE
BENCH BOX
16-3/4" (TYP.)
JOIN SEATS AT 45°
2 X 6 TRIM; MITER CORNERS
2 X 6 SEAT PLANKS
2 X 4 X 16-3/4" SUPPORT
JOIST HANGER
ANGLE SCREW INTO DECK
2 X 12 X 14-1/2" LEGS
BENCH BOX SEE DETAIL
2 X 3 X 12" LEG TRIM—ATTACH AFTER BENCHES ARE INSTALLED
45° JOIST HANGER
2 X 10 JOIST
2 X 6 DECK PLANKS
2 X 10 LEDGER
DOUBLE JOIST HANGER
POST
2 X 12 STEP
CONCRETE SLAB (AS REQD.)
2 X 6 BOX, 10-3/4" DEEP X 6 FT. LONG
2 X 12 TRIM BOARD (MITER CORNERS)
3/4 X 3" SKIRT
16d NAILS 16" O.C. (STAGGERED)
DOUBLE 2 X 10 RIM JOIST
DOUBLE OFFSET RIM JOIST
GALVANIZED TRUSS PLATE (ALL POSTS)
SINGLE JOIST HANGER (TYPICAL)
2 X 10 LEDGER
45° JOIST HANGERS
2 X 10 JOISTS 16" O.C.
DOUBLE JOIST HANGER (AS REQD.)
13' 10-1/2"
ALL FRAMING IS PRESSURE-TREATED PINE; ALL FINISHED DECKING IS REDWOOD
FRAMING ANCHORS (INSIDE CORNERS)
4 X 4 POST AND FOOTING (TYPICAL)
DOUBLE 2 X 10 RIM JOIST (TYPICAL)
DOUBLE 2 X 10 JOIST
7' 9"
4' 10-1/2"
EQUAL
EQUAL
EQUAL
23' 3"
FOOTING AND FRAMING LAYOUT
14'
38"
5'
8'
14'
23' 6"
DECK LAYOUT

7 Use 45° joist hangers to attach the joists to the angled ledger. Nail the top half of the joist directly to the ledger.

8 Double joists require double-wide hangers. Install these hangers on the rim joist, then slide the two joists into place.

9 Use a 1/4-in. plywood spacer to maintain consistent gaps between planks. Drive two screws through each board into each joist.

10 Trim the perimeter of the deck with 2×12 redwood. Screw these boards into the rim joists and also into the deck planks.

11 Build the square corner boxes, then install two mitered crosspieces in each to support the mitered seat planks.

12 Set the corner boxes in position and measure for the seat planks. Prebore the ends and screw the planks to the boxes.

With the posts cut and the double rim joist nailed together, set the rim on the posts and lay out the hanger locations to match those on the ledger. Then, nail the posts through the footing brackets and join the posts to the rim joist with galvanized truss plates (Fig. 6). Nail the remaining floor joist hangers. Then check each joist to determine which side has the crown and set them into the brackets with the crown up. Nail all the joists to the joist hangers.

Building the Corners

The deck shown has two corner details that required special attention. The first was the 45° extension around a cantilevered dining room wall. To build this section, just frame-in a double rim joist to span between the ledger and outer double rim. Nail the intersecting corners, in both directions, and add a corner bracket to the inside of the double offset. Then, use 45° joist hangers to support the joists set against the angled ledger (Fig. 7).

As for the step offset, frame in a double joist on one side—in the installation shown it was alongside the porch post—using a double-width joist hanger (Fig. 8). Then, frame the outer edge of the offset conventionally, wrapping it back to the double joist. A second double-width hanger makes this an easy connection. Then, bridge between the return of the double rim joist and the ledger plate on the house with a second double rim. Finally, cut shorter joists to fill in the open spaces and hang them, 16 in. on center.

Decking the Framework

Before decking over the pressure-treated undercarriage, thoroughly caulk the joint between the ledger plate and the house siding. This will keep rainwater from entering the joint and rotting the siding. Also, keep in mind that you'll find some warped lumber in every stack you buy. These boards are still usable, but should be reserved for cutting into shorter lengths to fit tight spots. Use your straightest boards for the longest sections of exposed deck. To keep the decking running straight, measure out from the house at several points and snap chalklines to establish a straight run across the joists. Every three or four boards, re-key your decking off these lines.

Starting against the house, lay your first length of 2×6 redwood tight against the siding. Then, nail or screw it down, with two fasteners in each joist. Though nails work well enough, you can also use 3 1/2-in. deck screws. They are harder to install, but galvanized screws hold longer and are better at coaxing warped lumber back in line.

For quick gapping of all subsequent decking planks, it pays to make two 1/4-in. spacers. You can make them from 1/4-in. plywood. Slide a spacer between the preceding plank and the latest plank and nail or screw the plank in place. When screwing the end of a plank, always prebore clearance holes to avoid splitting it. When fastening a plank away from the ends, place two screws at every intersecting joist, each 3/4 in. from the edge of the plank (Fig. 9).

With all the decking in place, it's time to install the 2×12 rim-joist trim boards (Fig. 10). Miter the corners and screw them to the pressure-treated rims, so that the top of each 2×12 is flush with the top of each decking plank. To keep the top edge of this trim board from warping outward, as it surely will, screw it to the decking planks as well, about every 18 in.

Building the Benches

To construct the continuous J-shaped bench, start by building two redwood boxes, $16^3/_4$ in. square, using standard 2×4 lumber. Next, miter-cut two sets of $19^3/_8$-in. crosspieces for each box. Join them back-to-back with galvanized nails. Finally, screw them into the boxes (Fig. 11).

Set each box in its corner, just inside the 2×12 trim board, and measure for the seat planks. Miter each plank at 45°, using the positions of the boxes to establish the length of the planks. Finally, screw these planks to the tops of the boxes, preboring clearance holes in the ends (Fig. 12). To build the long runs of the bench, boxes won't be necessary. Just lay out 2×4 braces (also $16^3/_4$ in. long) about 32 in. apart, and screw three deck planks over them. With all three planks assembled, cut one end at a 45° angle.

To build the bench legs, cut $14^1/_2$-in.-long pieces of 2×12 planks and screw one to each 2×4 seat support (Fig. 13). Do the same with the boxes, placing one leg under the inside edge of each box, and one spaced between the boxes. Turn the assemblies upright and set them in position. Then, join the two mitered corners and screw the seat planks in place (Fig. 14). Assemble the short end of the J in like fashion, and build the remaining bench without corner boxes. To anchor the bench to the deck, drill the face of each leg and drive $3^1/_2$-in. screws at an angle into the deck planks (Fig. 15).

To trim out the bench, screw mitered 2×6 redwood planks to the sides of the seat, anchoring them at each crossmember location at each mitered corner. Finish the bench by nailing 3-in. uprights to the faces of each 2×12 leg (Fig. 16). These vertical trimpieces not only bring the legs into a more satisfactory scale, but also hide the anchoring screws.

Finishing Up

All that remains is to conceal the truss plates nailed to the posts with a redwood skirt and to build two box steps. To install the skirt, simply rip a redwood 1×8 into two 3-in. strips and nail them to the fronts of the posts (Fig. 17).

Because the deck shown was built so near the ground, a simple box step, set on concrete, was built. If you prefer, you can rest your steps on concrete cap blocks, set in a bed of gravel. To make the steps, build two rectangular boxes as shown on the plans. Set these boxes on their supports and drill the back of each several times with a $^1/_4$-in. bit (Fig. 18). Then, screw through these holes, into the face of the deck. The oversized screwholes will allow the step to float a bit with the seasons. Finally, screw a 2×12-in. tread to the top of each box.

13 To make the bench legs, cut $14^1/_2$-in.-long pieces from 2×12 stock ; center them on the crossmembers. Screw in place.

14 Bring the mitered bench sections together at the corners and screw them in place on top of the box supports.

15 Bore the clearance holes diagonally through the bench legs and into the decking. Then drive screws into the holes.

16 Finish the legs with 2×3 vertical trimpieces. These pieces hide the leg screws and give a more substantial feel.

17 To conceal the exposed truss plates on the posts, install a skirt of 1×3 redwood. Rip it from 1×8 stock.

18 Build a step box from 2×6 material and screw it to the deck face. Bore oversized screwholes to allow for movement.

Picket fences

Picket Fences was written by Merle Henkenius. Photos by Merle Henkenius. The sealer used on the fence posts here was Seasonite made by The Flood Co., P.O. Box 399, Hudson, Ohio 44236.

There's nothing like a fence to help define boundaries, both physical and social. In addition to its utilitarian role, a fence is part of an overall architectural plan. Like a deck or porch, a good fence complements the visual character of your home and links its design to the surrounding landscape. You can build it yourself with a few simple tools in a few good weekends.

Planning the Fence

The kind of fence you install depends on what you want it to do. If it's to corral the family dog, then it must be dog-tight, starting at ground level and rising to at least 4 ft. high. If its purpose is to keep the local kids from cutting across your lawn, then a split-rail fence will do. If it's to reduce legal liability, as when fencing off a swimming pool, then a stockade fence with a locking gate may be in order. If, however, you want to conceal the lawnmower, you're in the market for a privacy fence—a simple wooden screen that contains your outdoor life and presents an attractive façade to the community.

The most popular wooden fences are made of cedar, redwood or treated yellow pine. Redwood is the most rot resistant, but without treatment it weathers to a dull gray. Cedar is slightly more prone to rot, but can be more attractive over the long haul. Pressure-treated lumber is normally quite rot resistant, but it too can fail. The problem is that fenceposts are often made of heartwood, which is the most resistant to the treatment process.

Post deterioration is also affected by the installation method. Installing a post in concrete, for example, makes an extra-sturdy fence. But the concrete traps moisture—a situation that eventually causes rot. On the other hand, direct burial provides good rigidity along with superior drainage around the post.

The fence shown is a cedar fence made up of 4×4 posts, 2×4 rails and 1×6 rough-sawn slats with dog-eared, or chamfered, top ends. While you can buy similar fencing in 8-ft.-long sections, doing this only makes sense if your yard is level. If your yard is sloped, it's best to build the fence from scratch.

1 After digging the holes with a posthole digger, coat the ends of the 4×4 posts with a sealer made for exterior use.

2 Place each post in a hole and hold it plumb while backfilling. Tamp the soil regularly with the shovel handle.

3 Begin laying out the rail notches by partially driving nails into the posts at the lower edges of each rail location.

4 Position the uncut rails on the partially driven nails, and scribe the notch locations on the posts with a pencil.

5 Set the blade depth on your circular saw to the thickness of the rails, and make a series of cuts in the notch waste area.

6 Use a sharp chisel to remove the waste from the notch area. Then, test fit the rails and adjust notch if necessary.

Before digging any postholes, check to see what may be lurking underground. Contact your local building department and local utilities to find out what's buried on your property. Usually any interested party will be more than happy to come and locate its lines. It's then up to you to avoid digging through them. As for legality, it's your job to know where your property lines are, and to set your fence a distance inside the lines that complies with local requirements.

Laying it Out

After locating your boundaries, drive wooden stakes at the corners the appropriate distance inside the property lines. Then, stretch a string between the stakes to establish the fence line. Measure each straight run of fence and divide by the width of the slats plus the slat spacing to determine whether full-width slats will complete the run. While you can make minor adjustments to slat spacing over a long length, short fence sections require careful measuring.

Then, divide each run to produce post spacings of about 8 ft. You may have to vary the post spacing slightly from one run to the next, or modify the size of the fence. Plan gatepost positions based on multiples of your slats and slat spacing, less one-half of the slat width. This allows one-half of a slat to overlap a gatepost.

Setting the Posts

Use a posthole digger to dig the holes. To protect the grass, place the soil on a piece of plywood. Dig each hole to a depth recognized in your area as being adequate for the frost line. Plan for the bottom 4 in. of the hole to be filled with sand for drainage. After digging all holes, paint each post with a sealer formulated for new wood (Fig. 1)

After the sealer is dry, shovel 4 in. of sand into each hole and drop in the posts. With the string line in place, level and plumb each post while tamping loose soil against it (Fig. 2). Use a shovel handle to tamp 2 to 3 in. of soil at a time. Mound the soil around the post for water runoff.

Attaching the Rails

After the posts are in place, mark the rail locations and cut the rail notches. If your lawn is relatively level, you can position the rails by marking the positions on a corner post and then transferring the positions to the other posts with a line level. If your lawn is sloped, mark the rail positions on each post by measuring up from the grade. For a roughly 4-ft.-high fence, measure up 12 in. for the lower edge of the bottom rail and about 36 in. for the lower edge of the upper rail. Drive nails partway at the marks on each post (Fig. 3). Then, rest 2×4 rails on the nails and scribe the rail notches (Fig. 4).

7 After cutting the the rails to exact length, set them in the post notches and secure them with 3-in.-long deck screws.

8 At the corners, you'll have two notches. Drive screws into the post and into the end of the adjoining rail.

9 To secure a post to the house, first counterbore a $1/2 \times 1\,1/2$-in.-deep hole. Then, drive a deck screw into the siding.

10 Align the slat tops with a string stretched from post to post. Space the slats with a $3/4$-in.-thick strip, and nail.

11 After nailing a slat to the top rail, position the slat bottom with the spacer strip. Drive two nails at each location.

12 Lay out the gate slats and align the ends. Then, cut the crossmembers to length and secure them with screws.

Set your circular saw to cut $1^1/_2$ in. deep, and make several cuts through the waste area of each rail notch (Fig. 5). Then, chisel out the remaining waste (Fig. 6). With each post notched, cut the rails to length and fasten them with 3-in. deck screws (Fig. 7). At a corner post, cut notches on both sides. Screw the first rail in place and screw the second rail to both the post and the first rail (Fig. 8).

To attach a post to the house, bore a $^1/_2$-in.-dia.×$1^1/_2$-in.-deep counterbore into the post. Then drive a 3-in. deck screw through the post and into the siding (Fig. 9). Finally, cut the top of each post a uniform distance above the ground. If your grade is level, use a line level to match the post heights.

Installing the Slats

Align the slat tops $1^3/_4$ in. above the posts. First, drive a nail into the top of each post, leaving $1^3/_4$ in. showing. After stretching a string from nail to nail, use this line to sight the top of the slats. To maintain uniform spacing, place a $^3/_4$-in. piece of cedar between slats when nailing them in place (Fig. 10). After nailing each slat to its top rail, move the spacer down to the bottom rail (Fig. 11) and nail it in place. Use two 6d galvanized nails at each rail location.

Building a Gate

The gateposts are spaced so that one-half of one slat overlaps a post and serves as a stop. The crossmembers are made from slat stock.

Lay the slats out on a flat surface. Butt the slat ends against a wall, and then space them to match the fence. Then, cut two crossmembers equal to the distance between the gateposts and lay them across the slats flush with the hinge-side slat. Fasten each slat to the crossmembers using one $1^1/_4$-in. deck screw at each juncture (Fig. 12). Then, use a large square to check the assembly and add three more screws per joint. Cut a diagonal brace to fit between the crossmembers and screw it in place (Fig. 13).

You can use ornamental steel hinges and hardware to mount the gate. The hinges require $^1/_4$-in. galvanized lagbolts. Bore pilot holes for the lagbolts and then drive them in with a socket wrench (Fig. 14).

To keep the gate closed, install an adjustable gate spring mounted diagonally on the hinge side of the gate. After mounting, adjust the tension by pulling the pin from behind the large hexnut at the bottom of the assembly (Fig. 15). Tighten the hexnut with an open-end wrench, and, with the spring under tension, replace the pin. Finally, install the gate handle (Fig. 16). It's a good idea to nail a cedar strip to the inside of the gatepost to act as an additional stop. Place this so the gate's crossmembers bear the impact of the spring-loaded closing (Fig. 17).

Sealing the Fence

No matter which type of wood you've chosen, it's a good idea to seal it as soon as possible. To apply the finish, use a vacuum-pumped garden sprayer or a brush and roller (Fig. 18).

13 After the horizontal gate crossmembers are in place, check that the gate is square and secure it with a diagonal brace.

14 Use a socket wrench to drive lagbolts that secure the gate hinges. Bore pilot holes for the lagbolts.

15 After installing the gate spring, adjust the tension by removing a pin, turning a hexhead nut and reinstalling the pin.

16 Gate hardware usually comes with the necessary screws or bolts. Install the gate handle and check gate operation.

17 To withstand repeated closings, install a $1^1/_2$-in.-wide × $^3/_4$-in.-thick gate stop on the post. Use galvanized nails or screws.

18 Apply sealer to fence with a roller, brush or garden sprayer. Then, apply a UV-screen sealer to prevent weathering.

Pouring a concrete sidewalk

Text and photos for *Pouring a Concrete Sidewalk* by Merle Henkenius.

Pouring a concrete walk is a manageable do-it-yourself project. It can be hard work, and it will require careful planning and some friendly help, but concrete can be made to behave the way you want it to behave—both at the time of installation and after it's cured. The key is to understanding its properties.

Concrete is made up of sand, gravel, water, gypsum and, its key ingredient, portland cement. Portland cement is made from crushed limestone that is fired in a kiln. When water is added to cement, a chemical process called *hydration* begins. Very little water is needed to make this procedure work. The more water you add beyond what is necessary for hydration, plus some for workability, the weaker the cured concrete will be. Do not ask the delivery driver to add more water to the mix to improve its workability.

It's better to order concrete with a super plasticizing agent. This makes the concrete looser without reducing its strength. It's well worth the $4 to $8 cost it adds to each cubic yard of concrete.

1 Begin the sidewalk installation by stripping the sod from the form area. Dig a trench just deep enough for the forms.

2 Drive 1×2 pine stakes next to the form lumber. Align the stakes using a string pulled taut between two stakes.

3 Drive a double-headed nail through each stake and into the form behind it. This kind of nail is easily removed.

4 Join form lumber end to end by driving a deck screw through the edge of one piece and into the end of another.

5 The first step in installing a curved form is to drive a grade stake. Use a level to check that the stake height is correct.

6 Notch the end of the 2×4 form where the curved section will meet it. Screw the curved hardboard form to the notch.

Concrete Basics

Concrete expands and contracts with freeze and thaw cycles, and to cushion this movement, you should install expansion joints where the walk begins and ends or in any situation where concrete is placed between two other concrete slabs. A good rule of thumb is to use 1 in. of expansion material for every 30 ft. of sidewalk.

One of the unalterable truths about concrete is that it cracks. The best you can do is to encourage it to crack on your terms by cutting control joints into it. The cracks will form under the control joints.

Mixing concrete by hand is practical only for small jobs, so it can be assumed you will have the concrete delivered.

Ordering concrete is easy. Estimate the cubic feet you need and covert it to cubic yards. (Nine cubic feet equals one cubic yard.) Request a 3000-pounds-per-sq.-in. mix (referred to as a 6-bag mix, or six bags of portland cement per cubic yard of concrete). Also make sure that the concrete has entrained air, which is standard these days but still worth mentioning. Entrained air results from foaming agents being added to the mix. This disperses millions of tiny air bubbles throughout the concrete. The bubbles form air pockets that cushion the expansion caused by moisture that penetrates the surface and freezes.

Commercial concrete prices vary widely, but \$50 to \$70 a cubic yard (for 7 cu. yd. or more) is common. A substantial surcharge is applied to smaller quantities—1½ cu. yd. cost \$125 from one supplier.

Installing Forms

The sidewalk shown is 38 in. wide by 24 ft. long, including a curved section. Because of space restrictions, the job shown had to be poured right against the house foundation. Keep in mind that there are two schools of thought in placing a sidewalk next to the house. One holds that it's better to have a grass strip or flowerbed between the walk and the foundation to reduce the amount of rainwater that will splash from the sidewalk onto nearby surfaces, particularly siding. The other school says that a flower bed could cause dirt splatters to stick to the siding after a rain. Since dirt holds moisture, this could be a problem for wood or steel siding. Based on that reasoning, the sidewalk should be placed next to the house.

Use 2×4 lumber for the straight sections of the forms, and hardboard siding, ripped to 4-in.-wide lengths, to form the curve.

Begin by snapping a chalkline 1 in. below the siding along the length of the foundation. This line marks the grade of the sidewalk along the house and becomes a reference point. Position the 2×4 form 1

7 Support the curved form with stakes spaced 18 in. apart. The 2×4 form is supported every 24 in.

8 Use a pointed shovel—held at a shallow angle—to shave excess soil from the form bed. This prevents over-excavation.

9 The form bed depth should be consistent. Use a 2×4 to drag the bottom of the bed until the same depth is achieved.

10 Put the finishing touch on the form bed by filling in the low spots with sand. Don't fill these spots with soil or concrete.

11 Drive screed stakes along the length of the form. Drive a pair of angled nails into each stake to hold the pipe in place.

12 The screed pipe must be positioned above the opposite form to produce a slight slope. Check this with a level.

in. lower than the chalkline. This gives the sidewalk a slope that will shed water away from the foundation.

Begin with a shallow trench for the form itself (Fig. 1). Digging a shallow trench for the form first, then removing the soil for the form bed, reduces the tendency to over-excavate. Remember, if you dig too deeply you'll have to fill low areas with sand or gravel. You can't just shovel soil back into the space because it will settle and take the sidewalk down with it. If concrete fills the void, you'll encourage a crack where the concrete changes thickness.

Next, drive two stakes and stretch a string between them to mark the form's outside edge. Place a 2×4 against the string, and drive stakes along its edge every 36 in. (Fig. 2).

Drive stakes below the top of the form, then nail through the stakes and into the 2×4 using double-headed nails (Fig. 3). Use 3-in. deck screws to join form lumber end to end (Fig. 4).

Install the curved form last and fasten it to the straight 2×4 form. Drive a grade stake that will mark the top of the form. Check the height of the grade stake with a level (Fig. 5).

To make a seamless appearance where the straight and curved concrete meet, cut a $^1/_2$-in.-deep notch on the inside edge of the 2×4 form. Screw the hardboard to the notch using $1^1/_4$-in. deck screws (Fig. 6). Next, bend the hardboard and drive a stake there. Space stakes along the curve at 18-in. intervals (Fig. 7).

Shave off enough soil to get close to the finished depth and then drag out the finished grade with a 2×4 (Figs. 8 and 9). Finish the form bed by placing sand at low spots, then grade the bed again with a 2×4 (Fig. 10).

The final step is to install a screed. This is only necessary if you are pouring concrete against a surface other than a form, such as a foundation. Use $^3/_4$ - in. black pipe as a screed and install it on top of stakes spaced 3 ft. apart. Drive 6d nails into each stake to hold the pipe (Fig. 11).

Set the pipe on the stakes so it's level with the chalkline, and check it with a level (Fig. 12).

Pouring and Finishing

A concrete truck is heavy enough to crack a driveway, so have the truck park on the street, and haul the concrete with heavy-duty wheelbarrows (Fig. 13). With several loads of concrete in the form, use a straight 2×4 as a screed board to strike off excess concrete (Fig. 14).

After there is about 6 ft. of concrete in the form, pull the screed pipe back and sprinkle new concrete into the gap left by the pipe (Figs. 15 and 16). Repeat this until all concrete is poured.

Next, work over the surface with a hand float (Fig. 17) to bring water and cement paste to the surface. Follow this by running an edger around the walk's perimeter (Fig. 18).

Next, cut control joints with a groover at about 40-in. intervals using a 1×4 as a guide. Every few inches cut through the slab along the control joint, using a

13 Use a heavy-duty wheelbarrow to haul concrete to the forms. While one person hauls, another spreads the concrete.

14 Once all the concrete is in the form, saw a screed board across the form. This strikes off excess concrete.

15 Every 5 to 6 ft., withdraw the screed pipe from the concrete. Leave the screed stakes buried in the slab.

16 Use a shovel to sprinkle new concrete into the gap left by the screed pipe. Work rough concrete smooth with a float.

17 After all the concrete is poured, use a wooden or magnesium float to bring water and cement paste to the surface.

18 Use an edger to round the concrete perimeter. This looks nicer and is less likely to chip than a square edge.

19 To make a control joint, lay a 1×4 down as a guide, then run a groover along it. Place a control joint every 40 in.

20 Cut into the control joint every few inches with a pointed trowel. This ensures that cracks will be under the joint.

21 Hold the trowel flat and apply more pressure to its trailing edge to prevent it from chattering. Sweep it in wide circles.

22 Use a broom to rough the surface for better traction. Cover the concrete with plastic for six days to keep it moist.

pointed trowel (Figs. 19 and 20). Finally, smooth the top edge of the cut with the groover.

Knowing when to trowel is critical. If the trowel leaves gray water and bubbles in its wake, wait 20 minutes and try again. This moisture is called *bleed water* because it is the excess that bleeds from the concrete. Allow it to evaporate before troweling or you will produce a weak surface. Work with the trowel held flat, and place slightly more pressure on the trowel's trailing edge than on the front edge (Fig. 21). This technique ensures that the trowel will move smoothly over the surface without catching on pieces of gravel. Most surfaces require two separate trowel passes.

After the troweled finish begins to set, draw a soft-bristle broom over the surface to produce a slip-resistant finish (Fig. 22). Cover the concrete with a plastic sheet for about six days to help it cure slowly. This greatly increases its strength. Finally, gently pry the form away from the concrete using a claw hammer.

1 Stretch a mason's string tightly between the layout stakes. The line should fall just above the outside edge of the walk.

2 Using a pick and shovel, remove all the sod, stones and other obstructions to a depth of about 4 in. Rake the bottom flat.

3 Tamp the soil in the work area and then cover the excavation with landscape fabric. The fabric inhibits weed growth.

Traditional stone walkway

When landscape designers are faced with the task of creating an interesting environment, some of the most powerful tools they can use are the varied paving materials available today. The choice of material for a walkway, for instance, can dramatically alter the feeling of an outdoor area—whether it is a short passage from a driveway to the front door, or a meandering footpath through a large country garden.

The most commonly seen materials are poured or precast concrete, and while these walkways are quite serviceable, they're also rather uninteresting. A brick or cut-slate walk, for example, suggests a formal elegance and makes reference to Colonial American design. A walk fashioned of wooden decking or blocks or rounds cut from a log has a casual feeling, and may be most appropriate for a retreat or summer home. A walk of randomly shaped flagstones falls somewhere between the previous alternatives in the feeling it conveys. The variety of sizes and shapes of the stones creates an interesting texture, while maintaining a feeling of solidity and permanence. Flagstone is an excellent option in many situations, and is the material chosen to construct the garden walk shown.

A stone walk can be installed three different ways. The first method involves setting the stones directly on the soil and letting grass or a ground cover grow

Traditional Stone Walkway was written by Neal Barrett. Lead photo by John Griebsch; step-by-step photos by Neal Barrett.

4 Spread crushed stone over the fabric to a depth of about 4 in. Make sure all the corners are filled, then rake the surface flat.

5 Use a 2×4 screed to even out the crushed stone. A uniform base at this point provides a useful reference for later work.

6 Once the bed is basically flat, use a hand tamper to compact the crushed stone. Compact the area uniformly.

7 Begin laying stone in a corner. First spread a thin layer of crushed stone onto the bed. Then lower a flagstone into place.

8 Level each ensuing stone in place. Because the surfaces are rough, the level is bound to rock. Shoot for approximate level.

9 Use a rubber mallet to make small adjustments. The stones are heavy and the less you move them the better.

around each stone—a series of stepping stones. Another system is to set the stones in concrete. The third procedure, and the one which is used here, is to set the flagstones on a base of crushed stone, and to fill the joints with the same crushed stone. This method yields a permanent and stable walk that still has a rustic feel and fits well in a garden location.

Flagstone is generally available as either slate or sandstone. In some areas, most of the irregularly shaped stones are sandstone, while slate is sold in square-edged rectangular sizes.

When flagstone is taken from the quarry, it is split from the bedrock rather than cut. This technique results in stones of varying thicknesses. The stone used here varied from $1^1/_4$ in. to 2 in. thick. This irregularity presents a special challenge to the installer, but one that is easily accommodated by the installation technique.

Flagstone is generally sold by the square foot. There can be some waste, particularly if you want a look that's primarily large stones. To be sure that you have enough material to complete your project, measure the area to be paved and add about 15% to allow for breakage and fitting.

To form the base for your walk, you will need a quantity of crushed stone. This material is sold under several names, but is most widely known to stone suppliers as dolomite dust or "1-Bs." This is a combination of very small stone chips and dust. It forms a stable base and provides good drainage. In addition, when used as a filler between the stones, it compacts well to lock the stones in place and provides a poor medium for weed growth.

In areas of the country where severe winters are a factor, a base of 4 in. of crushed stone is recommended. To determine how much stone to buy, take the square footage of your path and divide by three to give the amount of crushed stone in cubic feet. Divide that figure by 27—there are 27 cubic feet per cubic yard—to give the amount in cubic yards. Most stone suppliers sell either by the cubic yard or by the ton. For crushed stone, you can figure $1^1/_2$ tons per cubic yard. Again, add an additional 10% to 15% for filling joints and building up thinner stones.

Most homeowners will already have many of the tools required for this type of installation. A good shovel, pickax, steel rake, wheelbarrow and level are all necessary. In addition, a mason's brick chisel and hammer, layout string and hand tamper are also required. You will need some stakes for layout of the walk and a short length of 2×4 to act as a screed for the crushed stone.

10 To cut a stone, position it on a flat piece of ground and score the cutline with a mason's chisel. Score the bottom too.

11 Once scored, place the stone over a 2×4 block, with the waste area unsupported. Then, strike it with a hammer.

12 Lay all the large stones in place first, then fill in the gaps with smaller stones. Gaps should be 1 in. wide or less.

13 When you're finished laying the flagstone, spread crushed stone over the surface and into the cracks with a broom.

14 To keep the large stones from shifting, use a wide-blade mason's chisel to pack the joints as tightly as possible.

15 Finish up by giving the walk a thorough rinsing. This will remove the stone dust and further compact the joints.

Since this type of walk is intended to have a rustic feel, you do not need to install any type of edging at the borders. It may be much more appropriate to have the stones abut the grass and garden directly, providing a natural transition between the two.

Layout

Begin your walk by staking out the perimeter. Drive 2×2 stakes at the outside of each corner for a rectangular walk, and every 1 to 4 ft. along the edge of a curved side, depending on the severity of the curve. Tie a nylon mason's sting between the stakes, stretching the string tightly, to outline the walk (Fig. 1). Study the size and shape of the outline. It's a simple matter to make changes at this point, and much more involved once the installation has begun.

Before beginning to excavate the site, examine the flagstones you have purchased. Measure the thicknesses of the stones to determine the required depth of your excavation. The simplest method is to find the thickest stone that you plan to use and add 4 in. to that dimension. When setting the thinner stones, you simply place additional fill underneath to yield an even top surface.

Excavation

Start digging at the perimeter of the walk. Use a sharp shovel to dig down just inside the line created by the mason's string. The sides of the hole should be as vertical as possible to provide a stable base for the walk along its edges.

Once the entire outline of the walk has been excavated to the required depth, you can dig out the body of the walk. You will need a pickax to remove any sod, stones and roots that you encounter (Fig. 2). It is important that the base for the walk be firm and free of obstructions. Stones and roots must be removed, even if they require additional digging. To check the depth of your hole, use a 2×4 to span the width of the walk and measure to the board's bottom edge from the bottom of the hole.

Check the bottom of your excavation when the digging is complete. The base should be reasonably flat and well packed. Use a hand tamper to compact the soil. This will prevent uneven settling of the stones after installation. Next, cover the bottom with landscape cloth (Fig. 3). This material will discourage any weed or plant growth under the walk.

Spread the base of crushed stone approximately 4 in. deep over the landscape cloth. Use the back edge of a steel rake to distribute the stone around the hole (Fig. 4). Then use a piece of 2×4 that is about 4 in. shorter than the width of the walk to even the surface of the stone (Fig. 5). This 2×4 screed eliminates any high and low spots in the stone base, providing a smooth, flat surface. Use the hand tamper to compact the stone base (Fig. 6). To further promote settling of the base, thoroughly soak the stone with water.

Laying the Stone

At this point, you are ready to begin laying the flagstone. You will notice that not only do the stones vary in thickness from one to another, but also within an individual stone. This variation must be accommodated by adjusting the base layer—either building it up or carving it away—to provide a stable foundation for each stone.

Begin by laying the first stone at one corner of the walk. Spread some loose crushed stone over the base, then position the first stone over it. Wiggle the stone into position, then check that it is at the proper height—that is, even with the surrounding sod or garden. Add or remove crushed stone to adjust the level of the flagstone and to provide a base that keeps the flagstone from rocking (Fig. 7).

Select the next stone for a reasonably close fit along one side of the first stone. Since flagstones are irregular in shape, you will have to sort through your stones to find appropriate shapes. Keep in mind, however, that this material is not meant to fit together too tightly. Variation in joint size is natural and even desirable in this type of installation. Aim for joints of $^3/_8$ in. to 1 in. in width.

Again, adjust the thickness of the base for the stone, providing an even transition between stones. You can use a 2-ft. level to check the surface of adjacent stones, but the uneven surface of the stones makes this an imprecise job (Fig. 8). It is best to rely on a combination of factors in positioning each stone: the reading from your level, the height of both the adjacent stone edges and the surrounding lawn or garden and, most important, your eye. Use a rubber mallet to make minor adjustments in the position of a stone (Fig. 9). You may be surprised at how quickly you can develop a sense of what is a proper placement of a stone. A slight pitch is desirable to promote drainage, but should not exceed $^{1}/_{4}$-in. in 4 ft. This pitch can be created in one direction, or by crowning the walk in the center.

Cutting the Stone

Given a limited number of flagstones to work with, it is inevitable that you will run into situations where you need a stone of a particular size or shape that you don't have. When this occurs, it is a simple matter to cut a stone to shape. Begin by tracing the desired contour onto the stone. It is sometimes helpful to place the stone into approximate position to better envision the shape. Mark both the top and the bottom of the stone.

With the stone resting firmly on the ground, use a mason's brick chisel and small sledgehammer to score the stone along the line. Turn the stone over to score the bottom side as well (Fig. 10). Next, rest the stone on a 2×4 block, with the scored line directly over the edge of the block and the waste portion hanging freely. Use the hammer to tap the waste portion of the stone to break it along the line (Fig. 11). Cutting these stones is generally not too difficult, but there are times when the grain of a stone or a pre-existing crack will yield an unpredictable result. It's generally possible to make use of these stones somewhere in the walk, so try to keep your frustration in check. It is also important to keep track of the waste pieces when cutting stones. These small pieces are used to fill shapes that cannot be accommodated with large stones. Used either singly or in combination, these small stones add interesting texture and contrast to the mass of the larger stones (Fig. 12).

It is important to note that the large flagstones can be very heavy. Plan to have a helper available to assist in moving these pieces to minimize the risk of serious back injury.

When the flagstones have been placed, all that remains is to fill the joints between the stones. Place one or two shovels full of crushed stone on the walk. Then use a broom to sweep the material into the joints (Fig. 13). It is important that the joints are packed full of crushed stone to keep the flagstones from shifting. Use a mason's chisel to tamp down the stone in the joints, encouraging the material to settle (Fig. 14). Apply more crushed stone as required to fill the joints, then spray thoroughly with water to encourage further settling (Fig. 15).

Finally, sweep the walk one more time to clean up the joints and remove any excess crushed stone.

Backyard swimming pools

Swimming pools can be both fun and healthful for people of all ages. Many of us would consider installing a backyard pool if it could be made affordable and easy to maintain.

The first option is an in-ground pool, usually made of concrete and tiled at the water line. Given a choice, most would-be pool owners would rather have an in-ground pool. They appear—and are—more substantial, but they are also more expensive. A base price of about $20,000 is common for a medium-size pool.

At the opposite end of the spectrum are the small, aboveground models sold by discount stores. These shallow, steel-walled pools (usually round and measuring about 3×15 ft.) can be purchased for less than $200. Naturally, at these prices, quality is an issue. Thousands of soaking-wet first graders, however, might beg to differ. Still, these are, at best, starter pools, meant mostly for splashing and wading. The broad middle ground of the pool market is claimed by larger, more elaborate aboveground pools. These pools can offer the best of two worlds. They can be large enough to accommodate real swimming, while remaining quite affordable, especially when installed by the homeowner. It is possible to buy an oval or rectangular steel-walled pool, in the 15×30-ft. range, for about $2,000—pump, ladder, and filter included. If you'd rather have a professional do the installation, add $500 to $1000.

Most medium-size, aboveground pools center in the $1200 to $2500 range, though some pool packages with installation and specialty equipment can reach $8000 to $14,000. On the other hand, if a quality smaller pool will work for you, the material costs can dip as low as $600 to $800. Keep in mind, however, that the lower figures are for the pool and basic equipment costs. City codes and insurance companies may

K-D's portable pool is easy to assemble and has adjustable sides. In its shallow form, it's only 24 in. deep, which is safer for young children. When sides are raised, it measures 45 in. deep.

well require fencing, and possibly some additional safety equipment. You may also wish to upgrade the water-treatment system to one that requires less maintenance. Because aboveground pools can appear a bit stark, many homeowners build decks around them, which naturally adds to the total cost.

The Aboveground Advantage

In addition to modest initial costs, aboveground pools may offer some less obvious long-term savings. Because they are considered portable, or at least removable, they do not usually raise property taxes. In contrast, an in-ground pool is considered a permanent capital improvement, and its contribution to the value of the property will be taxed accordingly. Site limitations may also come to bear. Narrow side yards, mature landscaping, rocky soils and climates that leave the ground frozen for much of the year all favor aboveground pools. Finally, because aboveground pools are portable, they can be removed when you move, or when the kids are grown and leave home.

This Doughboy pool showcases the traditional design with support posts and metal sides. These pools come in a wide range of styles and sizes from small, round pools to oblong designs.

On the downside, aboveground pools are not diving pools. While some are available with one deep end, abovegrounds are primarily swimming and wading pools. Moreover, every pool can be dangerous, no matter how diligent you are. For that reason, it's a good idea to raise the liability limit on your homeowner's insurance. While the premium increase is usually modest, it is an increase. No matter which cleaning system you choose, you'll need to budget some money for upkeep. This should include the electricity needed to run the filtering-system pump 8 to 12 hours a day, plus chemical costs ranging between $20 and $50 per month.

Three Sample Pools

There are a great many pool manufacturers in business these days, and most offer quality products. Here are three that represent the wide variety of pools that are available. The abovegrounds made by Hoffinger Industries and marketed under the Doughboy label are fairly typical. These steel-walled pools come in a variety of sizes, including round models ranging from 12 to 28 ft. and ovals as large as 21×41 ft. Water depths are in the $3^1/_2$-ft. range, but the heavier liners are flexible enough to accommodate some center excavation. One end of the pool can be as deep as 7 ft.

Inflatable Zodiac pools require no support structure. Just roll out the pool on your lawn, inflate the sides and fill it with water. The sides are wide enough, and firm enough, to function as a seating deck.

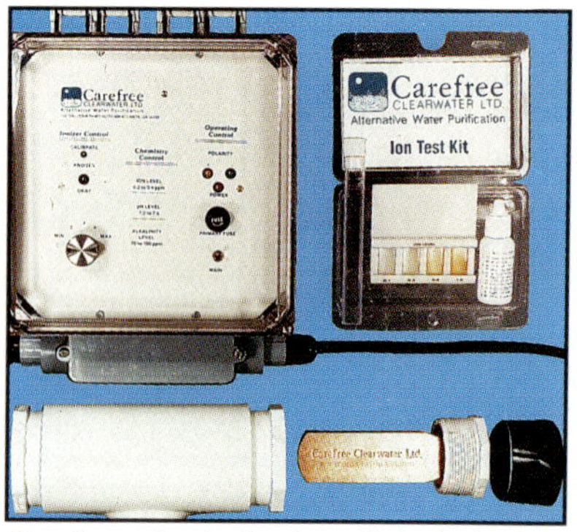

One form of water treatment is by ionization. This unit introduces a low concentration of ions into pool water that neutralizes any disease-causing microorganisms.

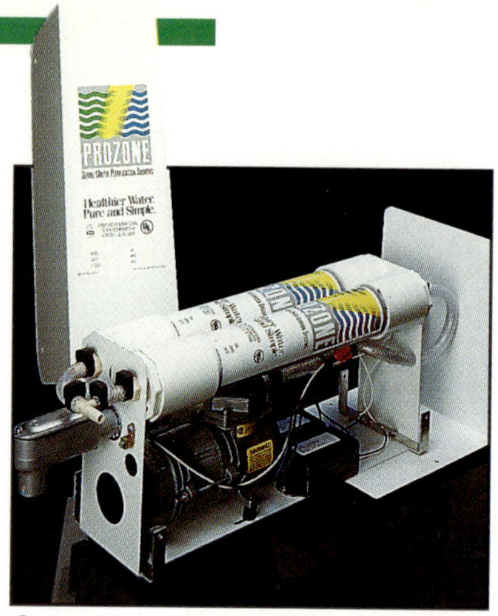

Ozone treatment can clean water, revert to oxygen, and in the process reduce the amount of chlorine needed by nearly 90%.

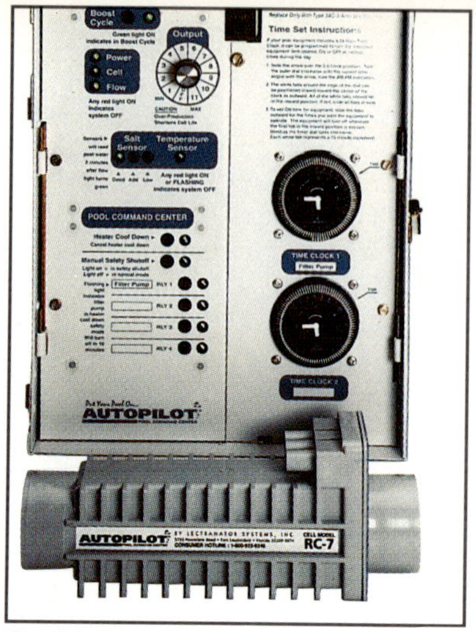

Traditional water treatment requires adding lots of chlorine. Newer alternatives, like this chlorine generator, convert common sodium chloride into chlorine.

Round pools are the simplest to design and build because the water pushes against the sidewalls in all directions equally. All that is needed is a secure band of steel and modest vertical supports. Oval pools require a bit more strength in the elongated sections of the walls, but the ends are nearly identical to round pools.

While steel-walled pools can be taken down and set up elsewhere, it's not something you'd want to do very often. Moreover, each installation would require a new liner. These pools are portable in only the most limited sense—only when compared to in-ground pools. With this fact firmly in mind, several manufacturers have designed pools that are truly portable and that take only an hour to set up.

One version is made by Zodiac Pools. These are a little like the tiny, inflatable wading pools we've all seen. The difference, of course, is that they're larger and stronger. They gain their strength from a fiber mesh that is heat-bonded between layers of tough, rubberized plastic. Projected problem-free use is about 10 years, and each pool comes with a patch kit that works underwater, which extends its life.

Pool shapes include rounds, ovals and rectangles. Round pools range in size from 16 to 24 ft., and rectangular pools can be as large as 37×24 ft. Prices go from $800 to $6500, and include sand-type filters and pump.

The height of an aboveground pool can be visually unappealing. Good site selection and beautiful landscaping, as shown here, can completely hide the sides.

One of the Zodiac advantages is that the inflated sides make a built-in deck. To inflate one of these pools, you can use a foot pump (included), or a shop vac with the motor reversed. When the sides are inflated, you add about 18 in. of water to the pool and remove the discs. Water from the pool then rushes into the inflated walls and compresses the air, creating a sturdy deck. Then fill the pool, connect the pump and filter and you're set.

Taking the concept of portability one step further, K-D products has come up with a design that focuses on child safety. The unique aspect of this pool is that it converts easily from a shallow, 24-in.-deep pool for small children, to a deeper, 45-in.-deep pool for older children and adults. As your kids grow, you simply add another vertical section to the framework and lift up the pool liner to full height. The skimmer/filter works at both levels. Come winter, the entire pool can be folded and stored.

A K-D Konvertible pool can be assembled by two people in about an hour, and entirely without tools. It consists of an anodized aluminum-tubing frame and a heavy-vinyl liner, sleeved to accept the framework. The pool can rest on any kind of surface. These round pools are available in 12-, 16- and 20-ft. sizes, with suggested retail prices between $1200 and $2900.

Support Equipment

Every pool must have a pump and filter system. The pump piping is attached to a skimmer box, usually located in the side of the pool and partially submerged. The box is equipped with a vacuum fitting and a basket. Floating debris, such as leaves and twigs, are caught in the basket, while smaller impurities, such as dirt and oils, are drawn through the skimmer and pump into the filter.

Three types of filter media are commonly used. One of the most popular is the sand filter. In these, water is drawn across layers of sand, which trap impurities. Next are cartridge filters that contain a fibrous fabric that screen impurities. Finally, some filters contain a white, powdery substance known as diatomaceous earth.

Backyard Swimming Pools was written by Merle Henkenius. Pool photos by: Zodiac Pools, K-D Pools, Doughboy Pools, Olympic Pools, National Spa & Pool Institute, Olectranator Systems, Carefree Clearwater and Prozone International. Portable pools are available from Hoffinger Industries, 10959 Jersey Blvd., Rancho Cucamonga, CA 91730; from Zodiac Pools, 401 E. Thomas St., Wilkes-Barre, PA 18705; and from K-D Products, 1015 Calle Amanecer, San Clemente, CA 92673. The National Spa & Pool Institute is located at 2111 Eisenhower Ave, Alexandria, VA 22314. The Electro-Tester is made by World Industries International at 17955 Arenth Ave, City of Industry, CA 91748. The ozone treatment shown was made by Prozone International, 1019-A Old Monrovia Rd., No. 233, Huntsville, AL 35806. The electrolytic ionizer shown was made by Carefree Clearwater, 2307-A Browns Bridge Rd., Suite 148, Gainesville, GA 30501. The chlorine generator shown here is called the AutoPilot, and it's made by Olectranator Systems, 5755 Powerline Rd, Fort Lauderdale, FL 33309.

Maintenance

If you suspect that water-quality maintenance is a perpetual nuisance, you're at least partly right. If you start with water that may be high in dissolved minerals and metals, or that is too acidic or basic, and then add airborne and swimmer-borne bacteria, suntan lotion, body oils and virtually any substance that could fall from the sky, you have a mix that can grow algae, damage equipment and make swimmers sick. Though there are a broad range of chemical treatments available, chlorine compounds are the most common.

While you don't have to be a chemist to treat your pool water, some people would rather not bother. These homeowners turn the job over to professionals, who test and treat on a weekly basis. This adds to the cost of operation, of course, and may not be right for you.

Another approach is to have the dealer test the first water in the pool—or of the season—treat it for minerals, metals and pH balance, and then set up a purification regimen for you to follow. The National Spa & Pool Institute also offers easy-to-follow information on pool care and chemical safety.

pH Balance

The key to effective chemical use is the relative pH balance of the water. On the pH scale, which ranges between 0 and 14, the ideal balance is 7.4 to 7.6. If the balance is tipped too far toward the alkaline side, the bacteria-killing capacity of the chlorine is reduced, water may appear cloudy and scale will begin to form on pool walls and filtration equipment. If the water is too acidic, equipment will begin to corrode, chlorine residual (chlorine left after the initial killing shock) will drop and the water will irritate eyes and skin. Manufacturers package products formulated to raise pH (soda ash, sodium carbonate) or lower pH (muriatic acid, sodium bisulfate).

How can you know what the pH balance of your water is at any given time? The usual choice is a chemical reagent test. In this case, you'd take a sample of water in a test tube, add a few drops of reagent, shake it up and compare the color change to a graduated color chart. Chlorine content can be tested in a similar manner.

While this method is still the most popular, electronic probes are now on the market that do all the work for you, without the mess. One such product is the Electro-Tester, which retails for about $40 and is made by World Industries International. You do, however, have some alternatives to chlorine treatment. Here are three.

Alternate Treatments

Ozone has long been used in purifying drinking water, so it stands to reason that it might work well in swimming pools as well. Because ozone has little residual—it reverts to oxygen—some chlorine is still needed, but the reduction in chlorine is said to approach 90%, which is quite a savings. Ozone does require a balanced pH, however. The equipment, a small electrified cartridge spliced into the piping, is easily installed on new pools and just as easily retrofitted to existing pools, and prices start around $350.

Another reduced-chemical approach uses electrolytic ion exchanges to strip microorganisms of their sustaining atomic structures. Keep in mind that ionization, like the ozone treatment method, does require management of the water's pH balance, plus enough chlorine to sustain a 0.4-parts-per-million residual. Electrolytic ionizers for pools start at about $900.

A final category of purification equipment is able to convert common table salt (sodium chloride) into chlorine and do so in a way that allows the chlorine to revert back to salt when its work is done. Chlorine production is a simple process—usually consisting of passing electricity through an inline chamber containing sodium and water. The electrical charge causes the chemical components to separate and realign. One of the resulting byproducts is chlorine, which is the basis of most pool chemistry products. Unlike regular chlorine additives, however, this treatment is said to be strong enough to eliminate the need for heavy, chlorine shock treatments. Because the spent chlorine reverts to salt, and does not linger as chloramine leftovers ready to assault eyes, skin and hair, this process should be welcomed by many. A chlorine generator for a backyard pool should start at about $350.

Another way to hide the pool sides is with an elaborate deck. This one provides easy access to the pool from all sides and still yields plenty of space for entertaining.

1 The first row of polystyrene blocks is set into a wet concrete footing or on top of dry concrete. The forms are set level and plumb. Subsequent forms snap onto the top of the first row.

2 When the blocks are built up to a sufficient height, they are braced with framing lumber. Next, concrete is pumped into the forms, and when the concrete hardens, the braces are removed.

Concrete forming methods

Fill a plastic foam coffee cup with concrete and you have demonstrated what many builders see as the next great wave in construction technology: using polystyrene as a lightweight, insulating concrete form.

That's right, polystyrene, the same lightweight plastic that has made millions of coffee cups, can just as easily be molded into interlocking blocks, planks and panels into which you pour concrete. The best part is, when the concrete cures, you leave the polystyrene forms in place. This results in a wall with an R-20 to R-25 insulating rating that is ready to accept both interior drywall and exterior finish. A typical 8-in.-thick concrete wall has an R-value of approximately 1.3, and even a well-insulated wood-frame wall is usually no more than R-15 to R-18.

There are many people in the construction industry who say this method of forming concrete will usher in a new era in building, the scope of which has not been seen since sawed lumber replaced hewn timbers in the 19th century. Furthermore, because of the high R-value that these systems deliver, some builders advocate them as a method to build anything from a foundation to an entire house.

Are these methods accessible to people building their own house? The answer is a limited "yes." Several manufacturers say their dealers have sold their products to do-it-yourselfers who have built a foundation, a house or a structure such as a garage.

It's tough to nail down a specific price for these systems, but they appear to be competitive with standard concrete. Using these methods, an 8-in.-thick concrete wall ready to receive interior drywall costs about $5.50 to $7 per square foot of foundation wall. Research indicates a standard 8-in.-thick concrete wall that has been insulated to an R-5 to R-15 rating and is ready to receive drywall costs about $8 to $9 per square foot. Keep in mind, however, that in some markets there may be little or no price difference.

The more things change . . .

The same influence that compelled builders to switch from hewn to sawed lumber more than a century ago is still in force today. Builders make their living by making a high-quality house as quickly as possible.

When you consider increasing land costs, complex environmental regulations, stringent building and zoning regulations and a manufacturing environment that propels the cost of building materials skyward, it seems that one of the few things that you or your builder can control directly is the speed of construction. That's where polystyrene enters the picture.

The Polystyrene Connection

Polystyrene is an odd material, part plastic and part air. Chemical manufacturers mix its components and blow gas or air through it, causing it to foam. Once cured, the plastic is lightweight, easily cut and a good insulator. You can extrude the foam into sheets, or expand it into molds to make blocks, panels and planks.

If you mold polystyrene components so they interlock, they form a quickly assembled and surprisingly sturdy structure.

Here are the specifics on how this method works. Bear in mind that there are several variations to the basic method described.

The concrete footing is poured, and the first row of polystyrene forms is either placed in the wet concrete, or it is positioned after the footing is set. Polysteel forms can be used for footings. The Polysteel forms are leveled and plumbed (Fig. 1). Each block is snapped to

3 Polystyrene forms don't necessarily have to be blocks. They can be planks or panels. These planks can be fitted with any one of three different length plastic connectors.

4 Manufacturers are refining lightweight forming methods to make them still more convenient and faster to install. Prefrabricated corners are available as are folding forms.

the one next to it. Some builders glue the blocks together, though manufacturers don't recommend it. Reinforcing steel bars are inserted in the forms, and the rest of the forms are slipped over the bars and snapped together. The polystyrene forms are braced with construction lumber, and the builder forms the openings for doors and windows by making lumber boxes. Polystyrene forms are installed around these boxes.

Pumpable concrete is flowed into the forms (Fig. 2). Rather than strip the forms after the concrete cures, they are left in place and no further insulation is needed. An added benefit to this system, say the manufacturers, is that since the forms are left in place, the concrete is kept moist longer and thus cures more slowly. This increases the concrete's strength. With this in mind, many polystyrene forms shape the concrete into posts and beams, rather than a thick, rectangular slab. That way, less concrete is used.

Inside the house, plumbing and electrical services are run in channels cut into the polystyrene foam. Outside the house (or foundation), stucco is applied over the insulation or siding is attached to furring strips that are fastened directly to the concrete. Another method is to attach the siding or its furring to the plastic or metal webs that are part of the forms.

Variations on the Theme

Polystyrene doesn't have to be confined to making blocks. It can be shaped into planks that are snapped together with plastic tie bars, such as with American ConForm's product (Fig. 3). Lite-Form Inc. makes forms that fold open on plastic hinges to form blocks (Fig. 4). To further speed construction, Lite-Form prefabricates corners and wall jogs (inset, Fig. 4).

Polystyrene is a form and an insulator that surrounds concrete, but it can work in reverse, too. For instance, the Insteel 3-D building system consists of an expanded polystyrene sheet with reinforcing wire mesh around it (Fig. 5). It comes in 4-ft.-wide sheets in lengths up to 26 ft. After it has been stood on its footing and braced, a sprayable concrete is applied to both sides of it. Insteel says it delivers an exterior wall that costs about the same as brick siding ($5 to $8 per square foot) with an R-value in the R-11 to R-18 range, depending on the thickness of polystyrene you choose.

Concrete Forming Methods was written by Roy Berendsohn. Photos by Merle Henkenius and Rosario Capotosto. Additional photos by American ConForm Industries, Insteel Construction Systems, Hebel USA and ThermaLock Products, Inc. Technical art by Eugene Thompson.

5 These polystyrene panels have built-in reinforcing mesh. A sprayable concrete is applied to both sides of the forms.

6 These blocks have a core of polystyrene insulation. Note that the insulation is grooved to accept reinforcing mesh.

7 These lightweight, aerated concrete blocks are bonded with thin-set mortar, as opposed to $^3/_8$-in.-thick mortar joints.

8 The blocks can be sawed to length with a crosscut saw from the manufacturer. They're finished with stucco or thin-set tile.

Insul Block from ThermaLock Products also centers the polystyrene between concrete (Fig. 6). Here the polystyrene is limited to an insulator and does not form the wall—the block is mortared together like conventional block.

An 8-in.-wide Insul Block costs in the \$1.85 to \$2.15 range, while a standard 8-in.-wide concrete block costs from 60 to 96 cents. The Insul Block, however, delivers an R-15 rating whereas the concrete block is in the R-1 to R-2 range.

It has several interesting features. Note that it maintains a thermal break by completely separating the concrete block faces from each other. Also, the insulation is raised $^3/_8$ in. above the block face. That way, horizontal and vertical mortar joints are insulated.

Grooves in the insulation allow for reinforcing mesh to be installed in the mortar joints, much like how standard concrete block is reinforced. Finally, the block is available with pre-applied exterior finishes.

Self-Insulating Thin-Set Concrete Block

The previous systems use polystyrene as an easily installed concrete form, an insulator or both.

Hebel, a German concrete-block manufacturer, takes a different approach. It makes lightweight concrete blocks, panels and lintels that are self-insulating because each component has thousands of tiny air pockets. It accomplishes this by adding aluminum paste to the concrete mix. The paste sets off a chemical reaction in the mix that forms hydrogen gas bubbles. The still-wet concrete is formed into large blocks that are cut into smaller blocks. The cut blocks are cured in a pressurized steam vessel called an *autoclave*.

The blocks are installed on thin-set mortar beds, as opposed to the $^3/_8$-in.-thick mortar joints (Fig. 7). Further, the blocks can be cut and drilled with hand tools. The manufacturer even supplies a large crosscut saw for cutting the block to length (Fig. 8).

In the southeastern United States, an 8-in.-thick Hebel wall costs in the \$3.85 to \$4.10 per square foot range while delivering an R-11 rating.

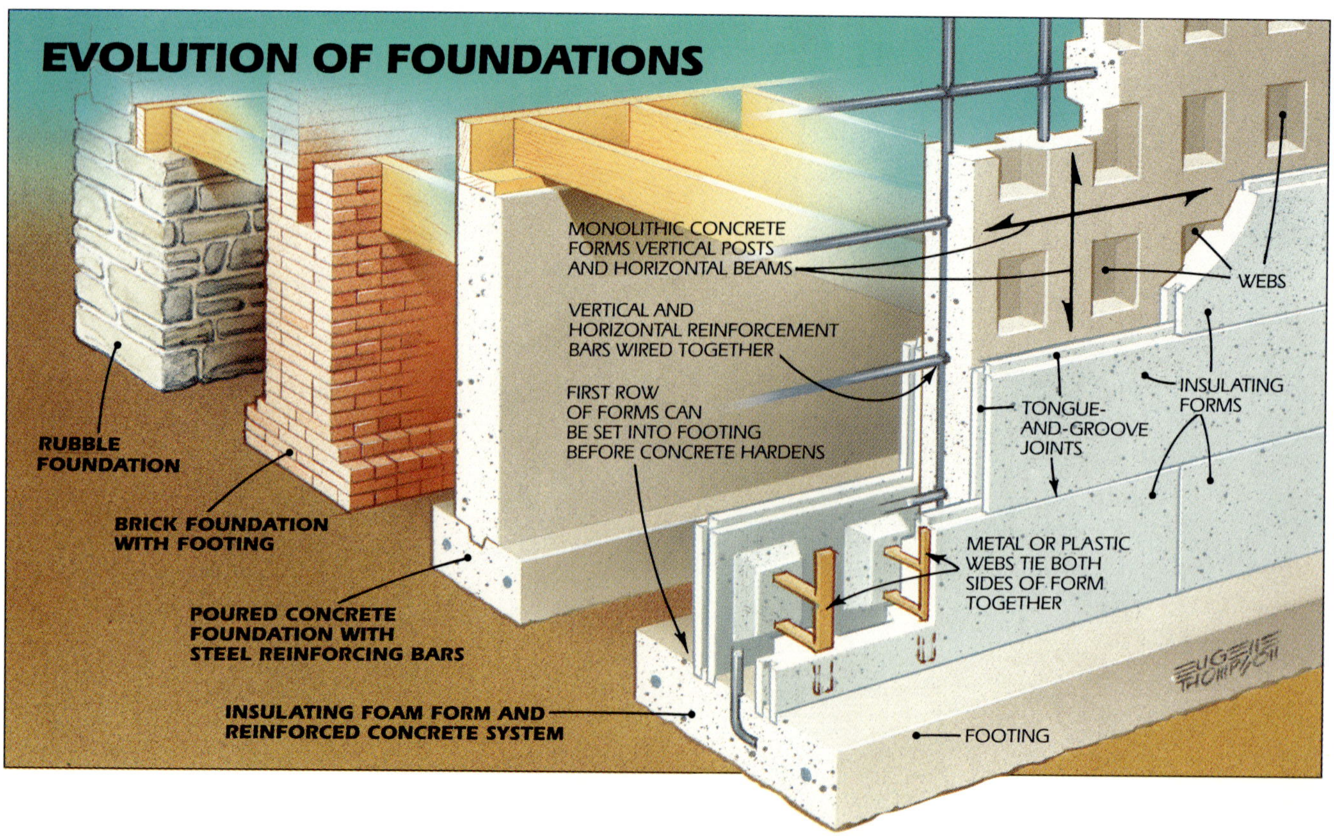

Installing an entry door

Whether your home is new or old, you've probably learned to live with its minor shortcomings. If, however, a more convenient entryway is high on your list, the solution is simpler than you may think. The home shown lacked a separate exterior door on the attached garage. To enter the garage, you had to go through the house or open the large overhead door.

To solve the problem, a new 9-light insulated steel door was installed. The door comes prehung in a wooden jamb, complete with molding and an aluminum threshold. In addition to the door, you'll need a few pieces of framing lumber, nails and basic power tools.

When ordering a door, you'll need to specify a left- or righthand swing. A good way to determine which version you need is to imagine yourself standing in the doorway with your back to the hinges. In that position, a lefthand door would swing to the left and a righthand door would swing to the right.

Bear in mind that these instructions are based on a garage-entry-door installation. Unless your situation is similar, you may have to modify the procedure. Installing a new entry door in a finished home requires locating studs, electrical wiring and plumbing runs and cutting through drywall or plaster. In this garage, all the framing is exposed. Additionally, cutting through load-bearing walls requires temporary supports appropriate to the structure. Be sure to check with your local building inspector to obtain the necessary permit for structural work.

Installing an Entry Door was written and photographed by Merle Henkenius.

Framing the Door

Structurally, a doorframe consists of two king studs—vertical framing members that extend the full height between the horizontal soleplate and the top plate of the wall. Nailed against the inner edges of the king studs are two jack studs, which reach only slightly higher than the doorjamb. A laminated header rests on top of these jack studs and bridges the door opening. Any supports located above the header are then framed conventionally.

To determine the rough opening width—the space between the jack studs—add 1/2 in. to the jamb width of the door. The extra 1/2 in. allows you to shim the door and accommodate any out-of-square framing. The height of the rough opening—the distance from the floor to the laminated header—equals the jamb height plus 1/2 in. This dimension, less the thickness of the soleplate (1 1/2 in.), equals the length of the jack stud.

Locate an existing stud that will serve as the king stud for one side of the door. Measure the rough opening width from this stud, add 3 in. to allow for the two jack studs, and mark the second king stud position on the soleplate. Then cut two jack studs and the second king stud.

Nail the first jack stud to the existing king stud (Fig. 1), and toenail it to the soleplate. Then nail the second jack stud to the new king stud and secure the assembly by toenailing it to the soleplate and the top plate.

Before cutting the studs between the new jack studs, add the temporary framing to support the structure until the new door framing is complete. If your site is similar to the one shown (a one-story home), nail an 8-ft.-long 2×6 across the edge of each stud, centered over the door opening and near the ceiling (Fig. 2). This supports the roof above the wall long enough to frame in a permanent header. For added strength, use 16d common nails with duplex heads. A 2-story home may require post supports to temporarily handle the load.

To build the header, cut two 2×8s to fit between the king studs. Sandwich the 2×8s around a piece of 1/2-in. CDX plywood cut to the same size. Apply a liberal bead of construction adhesive between the plywood and the 2×8s, and nail the three parts together (Fig. 3).

1 Use an existing stud as the first king stud. Nail a jack stud to this stud and then toenail it to the soleplate.

2 After the second king and jack studs are in place, support the wall by nailing an 8-ft. 2×6 across the studs near the ceiling.

3 Sandwich the piece of plywood between the 2×8s and nail through from both sides. Use eight 16d nails on each side.

4 Cut studs at header location. Use a circular saw to start the cuts, then finish the job with a reciprocating saw or handsaw.

5 Use a reciprocating saw with a metal cutting blade to cut the nails that hold the sheathing and siding to the studs.

6 Lift the header into place and secure it to the king studs by nailing with 16d nails. Use four nails per header end.

7 In a garage installation like the one shown, use an L-bracket to secure soleplate to floor at opening. Otherwise nail to floor.

To install the header, measure $7^1/_4$ in. up from the tops of the jack studs and mark cutting lines across the center studs at this height. After cutting most of the way through with a circular saw, finish the cuts with a reciprocating saw (Fig. 4).

Then use a reciprocating saw with a metal-cutting blade to slice through the nails holding the sheathing and siding to the studs (Fig. 5). With the studs removed, lift the laminated header in place and secure it with 16d nails driven through the king studs (Fig. 6). Finally, toenail the studs above the opening to the header. Once the header is in place, you can remove the 2×6 temporary support beam.

Because the garage floor is concrete on the installation shown, the soleplate was anchored with an L-bracket on each side of the opening (Fig. 7). If the floor is wood framed, nail the soleplate to the floor and into the framing below.

Cutting the Opening

When it comes to cutting siding and sheathing, you'll need to make two cuts. The first is a rough cut through both layers that follows the inside perimeter of the rough framing. The second cut is through the siding only and will follow the line of the door's casing, which is usually made of standard molding, sometimes called brick molding.

Begin by drilling a $^1/_4$-in. hole in each corner of the framed opening, from the inside (Fig. 8). Then, move to the outside and use a straightedge to draw lines connecting each hole on the siding. Using a circular saw, set deep, cut along these lines until the siding and sheathing fall away (Fig. 9).

With all but the bottom portion of siding and sheathing removed, use a reciprocating saw from the inside to finish the cut, slicing through the soleplate and siding at the same time (Fig. 10).

8 To locate opening on the outside of the house, bore $^1/_4$-in. holes through the wall from the inside at the opening corners.

9 Using the holes as a guide, mark the opening and cut through the siding and sheathing with a circular saw.

10 Where the circular saw can't reach, use a reciprocating saw from the inside. Cut through the soleplate, as well.

11 Set the door in place with the molding against the siding. Then, trace the molding perimeter on the siding.

12 Use a circular saw to trim the siding. Set the saw for a $1^1/_4$-in.-deep cut, or just enough to go through the siding.

13 To protect the header and door casing from rot, install a sheetmetal rain cap under the top section of the siding.

Set the door in the opening so that the molding rests against the siding. After checking to make sure that the door is square, mark the siding around the molding (Fig. 11). Set the circular saw depth to match the thickness of the siding, and cut the remaining strip of siding from the perimeter of the opening (Fig. 12).

Mount a length of galvanized rain cap under the siding at the top of the opening. Cut this formed sheetmetal to match the opening width, and slide it under the top length of siding (Fig. 13). Tack it through the siding with 4d galvanized nails.

Setting the Door

Press the doorjamb through the opening and center it between the siding cuts. Then nail the molding on each side using four 12d galvanized casing nails (Fig. 14). Don't drive in the nails all the way just yet, however, in case you need to adjust the door.

Then, go inside and check the door position. With the threshold resting firmly on the floor, make sure that the gap between the door and the jamb (about $^3/_8$ in.) is equal all the way around. If it isn't, pull the two bottom nail from the molding and move the bottom of the door, side to side, until you've corrected the problem.

To permanently secure the door, first shim the spaces between the jamb and jack studs. Do not shim the header. Each side of the door should get three sets of shims, one near each hinge on the hinge side, and three corresponding shims on the lock side.

When shimming the jamb, use two pieces of cedar shingle. The goal is to provide support without altering the critical gap between the jamb and jack studs. This takes a little experimenting, but it's not difficult. Feed one shim into the gap thick-end first, and back it up with a second shim, thin-end first. When the gap is filled, nail through the jamb and shims into the jack studs with 8d casing nails (Fig. 15).

Manufacturers typically leave one screw out of each lower hinge and two out of the top hinge. This allows you to drive longer screws through the jamb and into the jack stud behind it. To avoid splitting the jamb, bore pilot holes first (Fig. 16).

At this point, all that remains are the finishing touches. Drive a few more nails through the casing and countersink them about $^1/_{32}$ in. Then caulk the gap between casing and siding (Fig. 17), paying particular attention to the rain cap at the top. Finally, caulk the inner and outer edges of the threshold, paint the door and jamb and install a lockset.

14 Temporarily secure the door by driving 12d galvanized casing nails through the molding. Leave $^1/_2$ in. of nail showing.

15 After checking door alignment and operation, shim casing and drive 8d casing nails through casing, shims and jack studs.

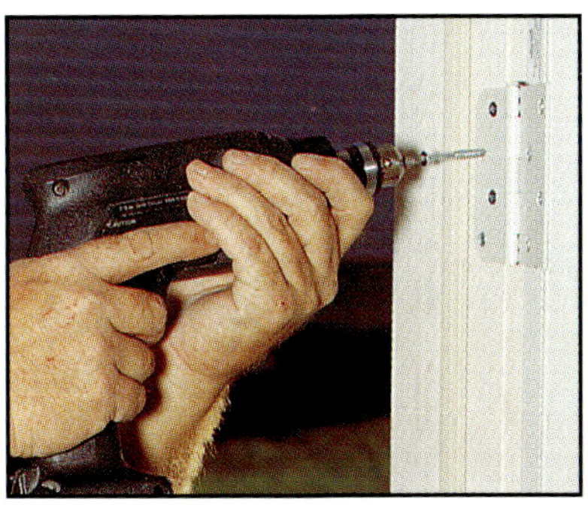

16 Fill open holes in hinges with long screws. Drive these screws through the casing and into the jack stud.

17 Seal the door against the weather with a bead of high-quality flexible caulk applied around the casing perimeter.

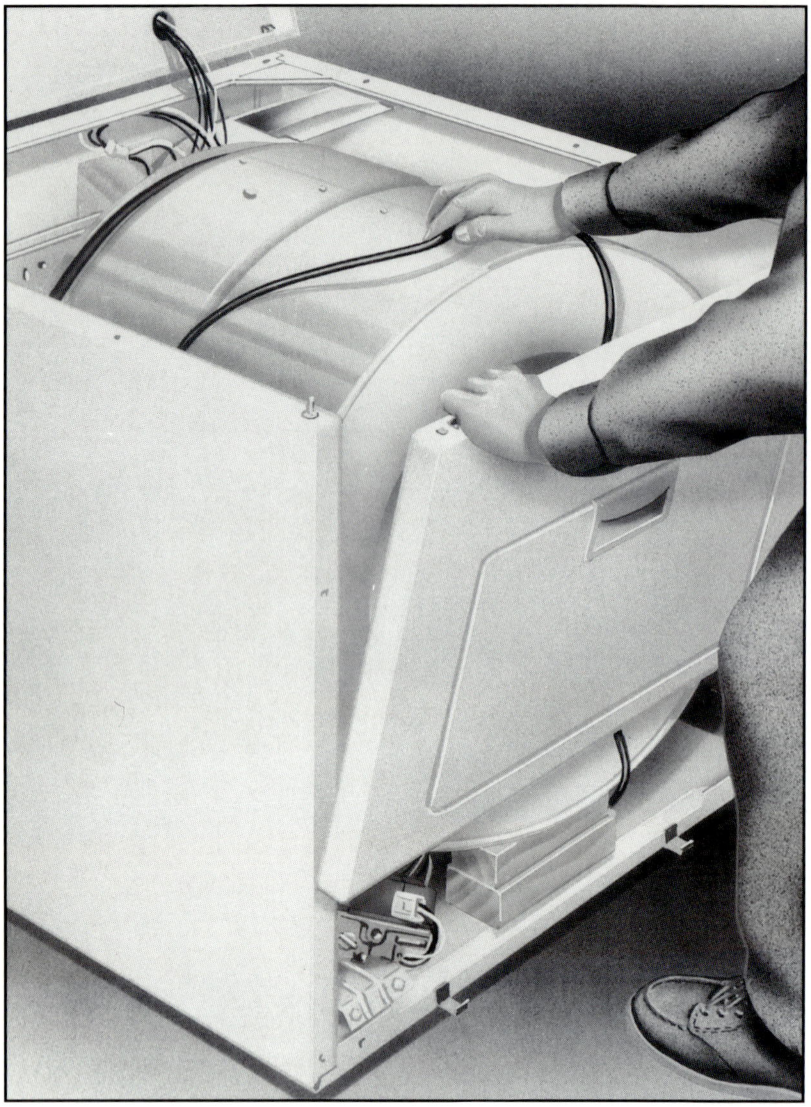

Replacing a dryer belt

Replacing the belt is a fairly straightforward operation that can be handled with a few simple tools. A Whirlpool (or Sears Kenmore) electric dryer was used to show how this job is done. The procedure is much the same on a gas dryer.

Opening up the Dryer

First, unplug the dryer. Lift the lint-screen cover and pull out the lint screen (Fig. 1). Then remove the two screws that are under the cover (Fig. 2). To unlatch the dryer top, insert a thin-blade putty knife between the top and front panel, about $2^1/_2$ in. from one corner (Fig. 3). Push in on the knife to release the locking clip, lift the corner, then release the clip on the other side. Swing the top up and lean it against the wall.

Move to the lower toe panel. Slip the putty knife between the lower panel at one side and twist the knife to release the clip (Fig. 4). Then release the opposite clip and lift the panel off the hinge springs. To support the dryer drum while the belt is being replaced, place scrap wood under the front of the drum (Fig. 5).

Loosen the two screws at each side of the bottom of the front panel about $1^1/_2$ turns (Fig. 6). Move to the top of the panel and remove the screws from the inside of the cabinet that hold the front panel to the sides (Fig. 7). Slide the old belt off the drum.

Replacing a Dryer Belt was written by Steve Toth with illustrations by George Retseck.

1 Prepare for replacing the dryer belt by lifing the lint-screen cover on the top of the dryer. Then remove the lint screen.

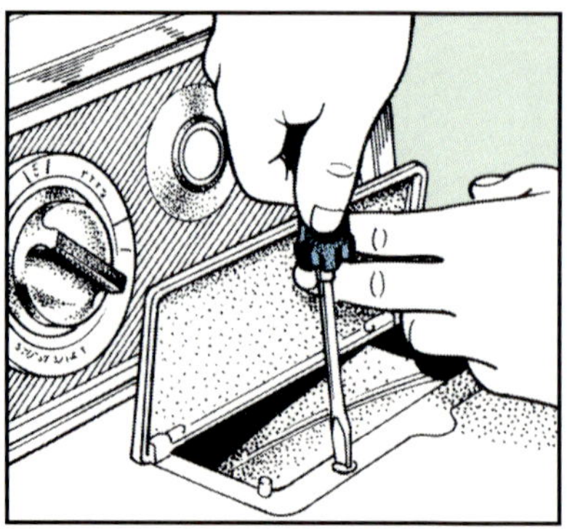

2 After removing the lint screen, lift the cover and remove the screws that hold the lint-screen housing to the dryer top.

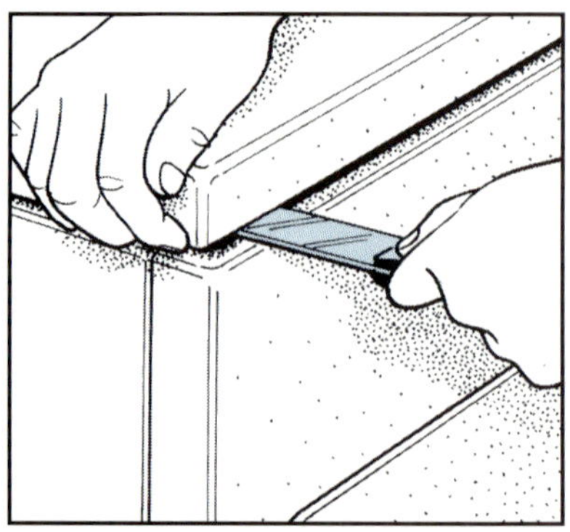

3 Slide a putty knife between the front panel and the top near a corner. Lift the corner and repeat on the other side.

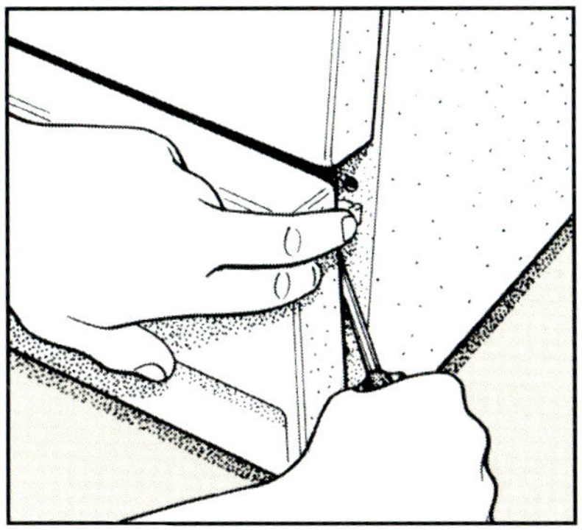

4 To remove the lower panel, insert the putty knife between the panel and each side. Then twist to release clip.

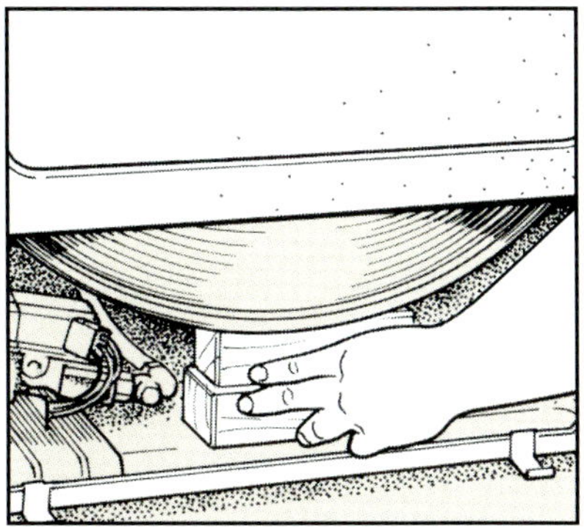

5 Place a few wood blocks under the drum. These support the drum when the front panel is moved away from the sides.

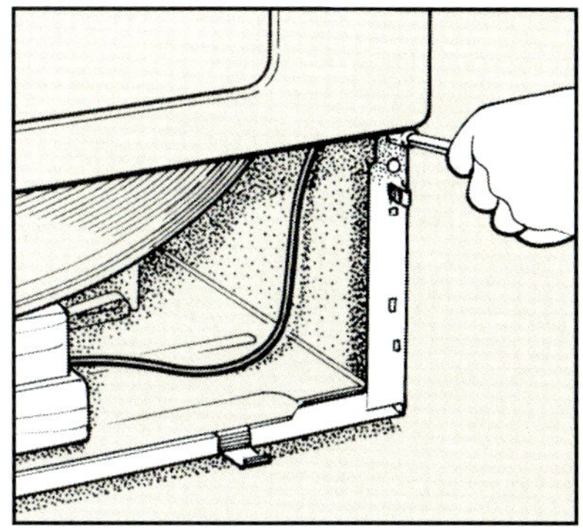

6 Loosen the screws that secure the bottom of the front panel to the dryer sides. Do not completely remove the screws.

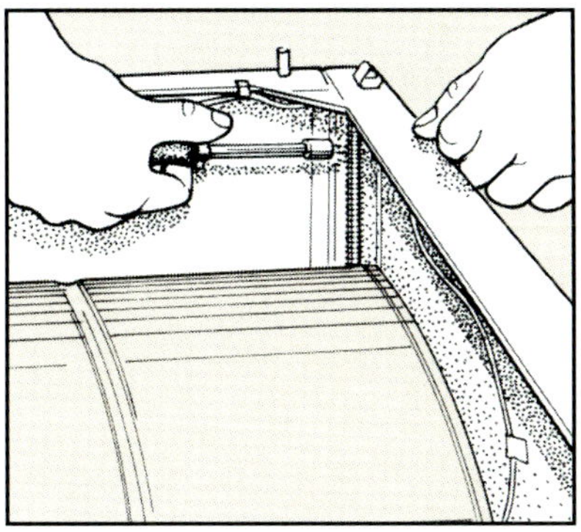

7 Remove the screws that secure the front panel to the dryer sides at the top. These are accessed inside of the cabinet.

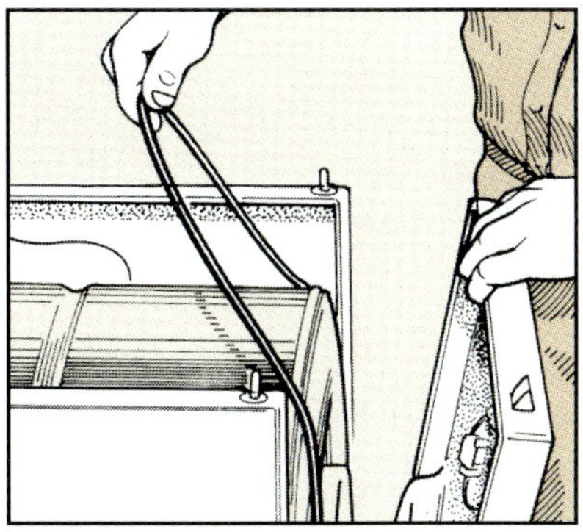

8 Lean the front panel away from the sides and slip the new dryer belt over the drum. Then secure the front panel.

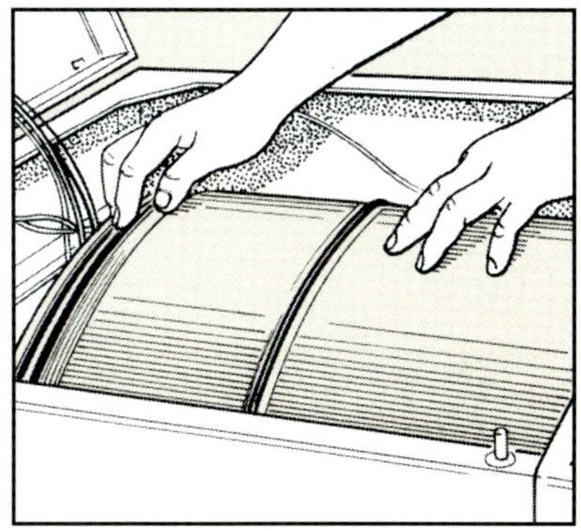

9 Check that the lip on the back of the dryer drum fits properly against the seal on the rear bulkhead of the dryer.

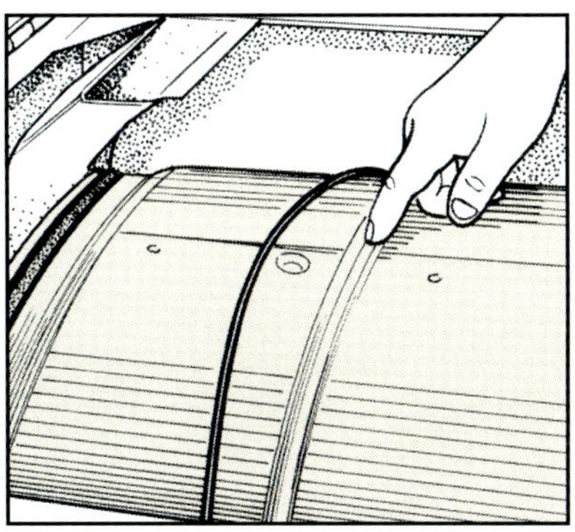

10 Locate the original position of the old belt and slip the new belt in place. Keep the grooved side of the belt down.

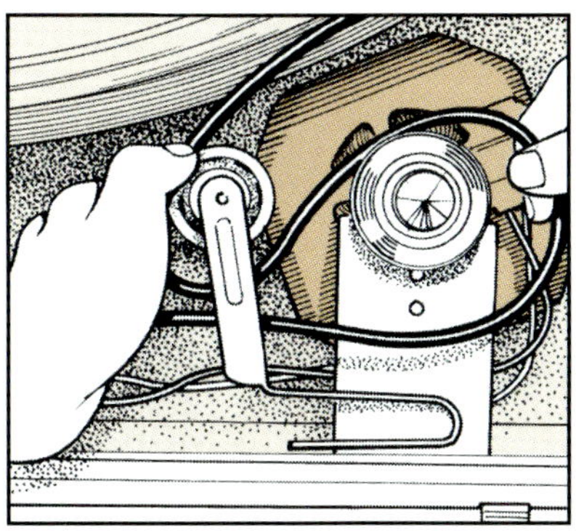

11 Push the idler pulley toward the motor and loop the doubled-up belt around the idler pulley. Slip belt around pulley.

12 Rotate drum counterclockwise a few turns to check belt tracking. Then replace remaining components and test run.

Installing the Belt

Lean the front panel out slightly and allow the drum to rest on the scrap wood support. Drop the new dryer belt between the front panel and the drum, and loop it over the drum (Fig. 8). Then, lift the drum slightly while pushing the front panel back into position.

Replace the screws at the top inside of the front panel, tighten the lower panel screws and remove the scrap wood from under the drum. Check to make sure that the rear drum seal fits properly over the lip on the rear bulkhead (Fig. 9). Position the new belt where the old belt was, with the grooved side of the belt facing down (Fig. 10)

To route the new belt around the idler and drive pulley, first pass the entire belt, doubled up, under the idler pulley. Then, push the idler belt toward the motor, slip the belt around the motor pulley and release the tension on the idler pulley (Fig. 11).

Open the dryer door and rotate the drum counterclockwise a few times to make sure the belt is tracking properly (Fig. 12). Lower the top and press down at each corner to engage the clips. Lift the lint-screen cover, replace the two screws and reinstall the lint screen. Finally, secure the lower front panel and turn on the dryer for a test run.

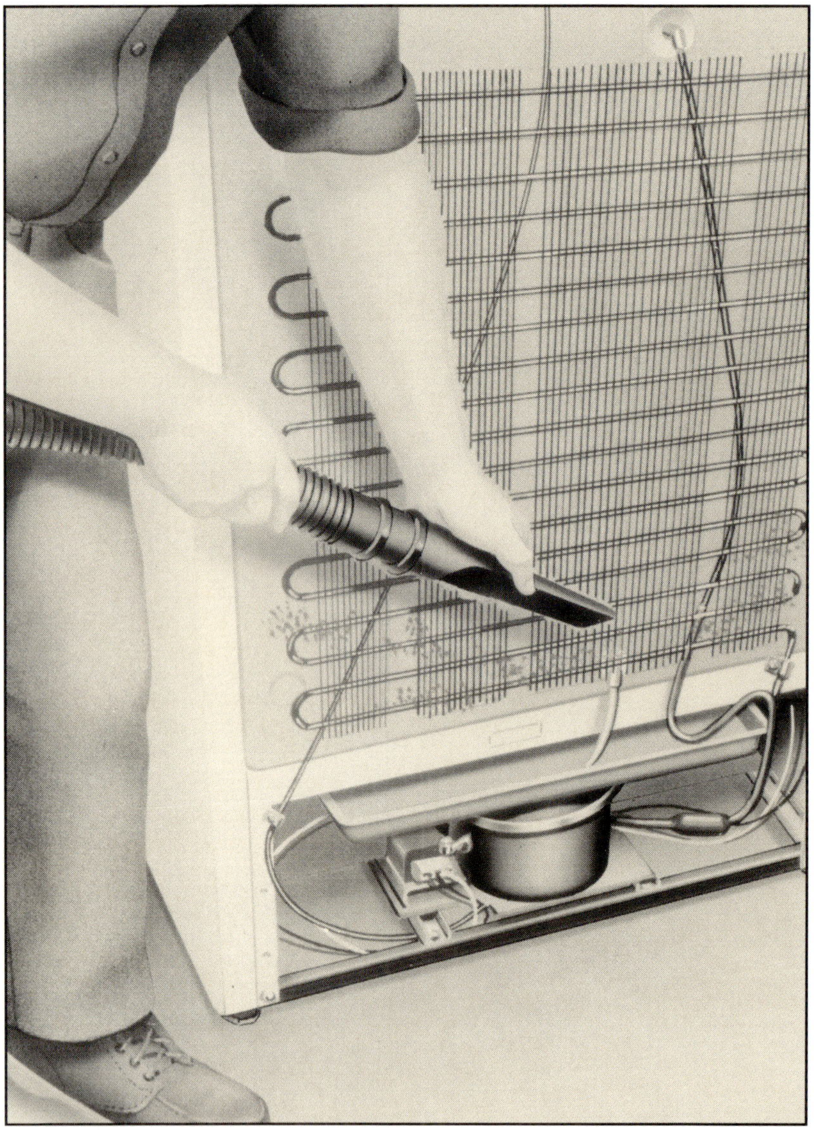

1 To remove a refrigerator's lower grille cover, grasp the cover on both ends and pivot it down and forward.

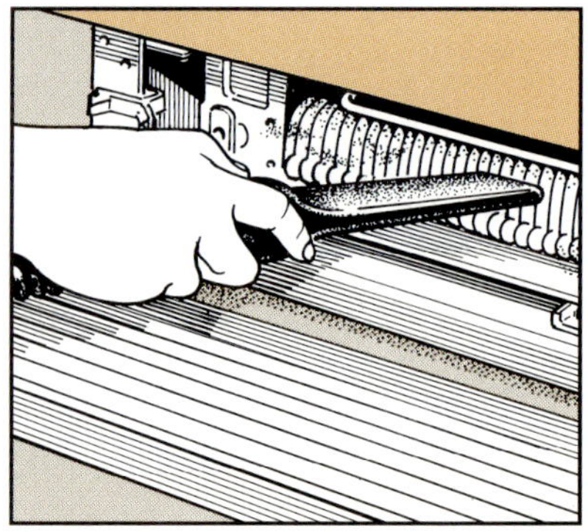

2 Vacuum off dust from the condenser coils and condenser coil fins. A crevice tool attachment on a vacuum works best.

Refrigerator Maintenance was written by Steve Toth with illustrations by George Retseck.

Refrigerator maintenance

The condenser is an important part of your refrigerator's sealed refrigerant system, and it is the only part that needs maintenance. Fortunately, all that's required is to clean the condenser's coils by vacuuming off the dust that accumulates on them. You should do this every three months or so.

Here's why it's important to keep the condenser coils clean: The condenser cools hot refrigerant vapors inside its tubes. If the condenser coils are dust covered, they cannot expel this heat efficiently. The dust acts as an insulation and prevents the heat from escaping. In turn, the temperature inside the refrigerator compartment is higher than it would be if the condenser coils were clean.

This increase in temperature also causes the compressor to cycle refrigerant through the cooling system more frequently than it otherwise would. Not only does this increase the amount of energy the compressor uses, but the additional waste heat given off by the compressor further reduces the refrigerator's efficiency.

Efficient cooling, therefore, is the ability to pump heat out of the refrigerator using as little energy as possible and creating minimal waste heat.

Looked at another way, a little dust on your refrigerator can cost you a lot of money on your utility bill.

Condenser Coil Location

The first step is to determine what kind of condenser your refrigerator has. It either has a static condenser mounted on its back, or it has a fan-cooled condenser mounted underneath in the compressor compartment. The fan blows air across the condenser to cool it.

Cleaning a Fan-Cooled Condenser

In the case of a fan-cooled condenser, first unplug the refrigerator and then remove the front lower grille cover (on most models this is held in place with spring clips). Grip the cover on both sides, pull it down from the top, then lift it off (Fig. 1).

There is often a small tag on the cover's top edge that states how often the condenser should be cleaned or inspected (usually every three months).

Clean the condenser using the crevice tool attachment on your vacuum (Fig. 2). After vacuuming, check that the condenser is clean by shining a flashlight through its coils (Fig. 3). Incidentally, the flashlight should have fresh batteries in it so it throws a nice sharp beam. Shining a dim flashlight under the refrigerator won't do you any good. If the flashlight is dim, and you don't have spare batteries, you can also use a drop light to check inside the appliance, though it is less convenient than a flashlight.

Next, go to the refrigerator's back and remove the rear access panel by backing out the hexhead sheetmetal screws that hold the panel to the refrigerator body (Fig. 4). Use a nut driver to do this or a small socket on a cordless drill. Vacuum the coils clean from the back. If need be, use a paintbrush to dislodge dust that the crevice tool did not pull out or that was pushed toward the back of the appliance (Fig. 5). Check with a flashlight to make sure they're clean (Fig. 6).

Cleaning a Static Condenser

The process is nearly the same in cleaning a static condenser. You vacuum it and brush it clean. You should, however, check that there aren't any papers or pens stuck between the condenser coils and the refrigerator cabinet. Often these slide off the top of the refrigerator and fall behind it.

Next, pull out the condenser drain pan and wash it with mild soap and water. Dry it thoroughly and slide it back in place (Fig. 7).

Finally, plug the refrigerator back in, and clean the floor behind it before pushing it back into place. Leave enough space behind the refrigerator to allow air circulation (this is especially important with static condenser models). If you're not sure how much space to leave, look in the owner's manual, or contact a servicing appliance dealer or manufacturer.

3 Shine a flashlight through the condenser coils and fins to find remaining dust. Continue vacuuming until parts are clean.

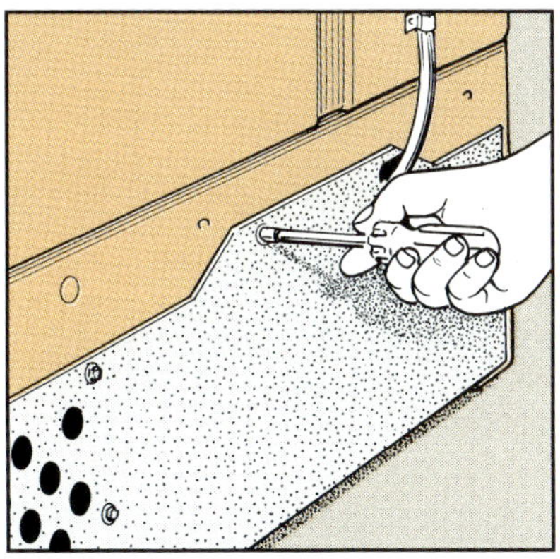

4 Using a nut driver, remove the hexhead sheetmetal screws that fasten the rear access panel to the refrigerator cabinet.

5 Use a paintbrush to dislodge dust in hard-to-reach areas. Follow this by vacuuming with the crevice tool.

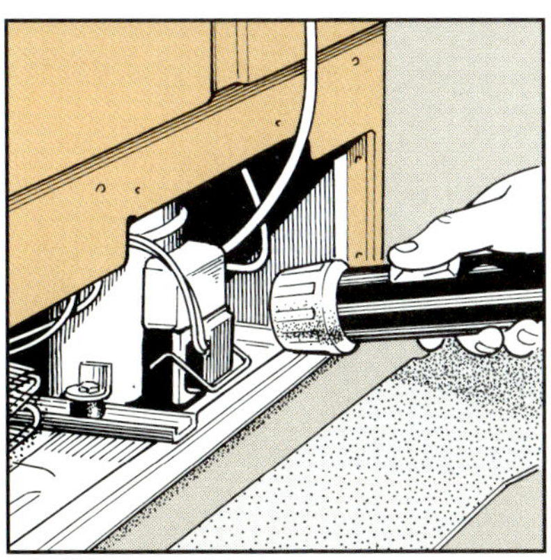

6 Shine a flashlight through to the front of the refrigerator. All of the interior surfaces should be clean and dust free.

7 Slide out the condenser drain pan. Clean it with mild soapy water, dry it and then slide it back under the refrigerator.

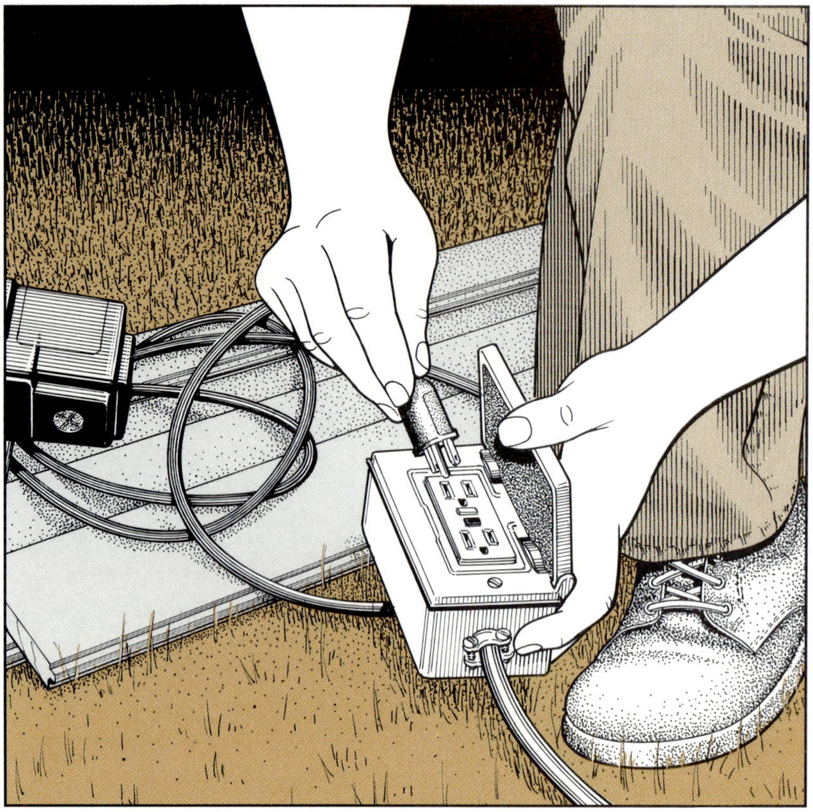

Making a ground fault extension cord

Making a Ground Fault Extension Cord was written by Gene and Katie Hamilton. Illustrations by George Retseck.

Your best guarantee of safety while using electrical tools outside or in damp areas is to be sure that everything you use is plugged into a GFCI or ground fault circuit interrupter. This electrical device instantly detects a hazardous situation and cuts the flow of power before a fatal shock is delivered.

Electrical codes require outside outlets and those in the bathroom and kitchen or in damp areas to be protected by a GFCI. New homes must have these protective devices, but homes built prior to 1974 have only grounded circuits with a circuit breaker or fuse protector. Neither is as safe as a GFCI protection with a fuse or circuit breaker.

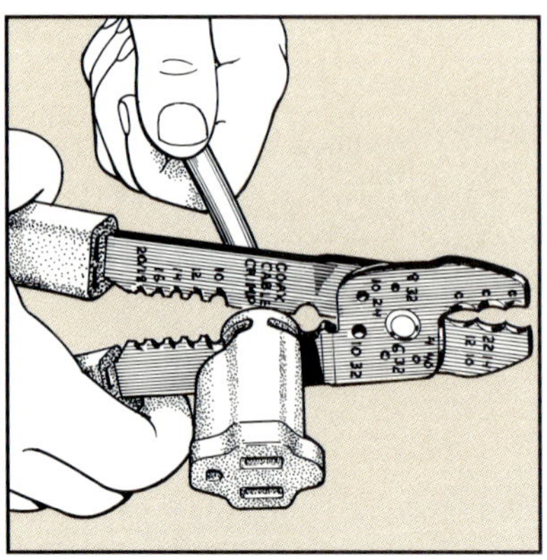

1 Begin by cutting off the receptacle end of a heavy-duty 3-wire grounded extension cord with wire cutters.

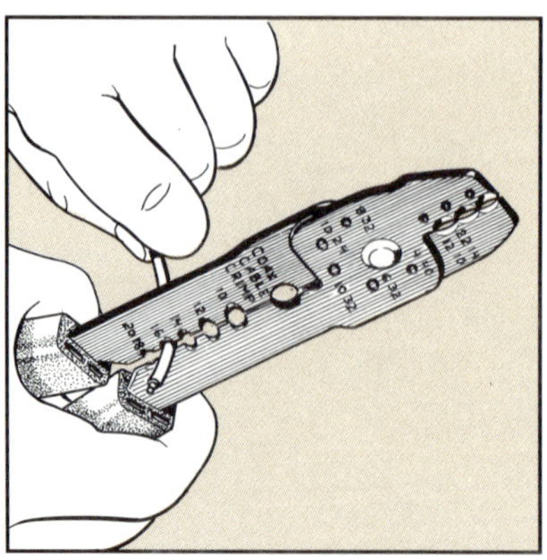

2 Strip 1/2 in. of insulation from the end of the cord's black, white and green wires. Twist the strands together.

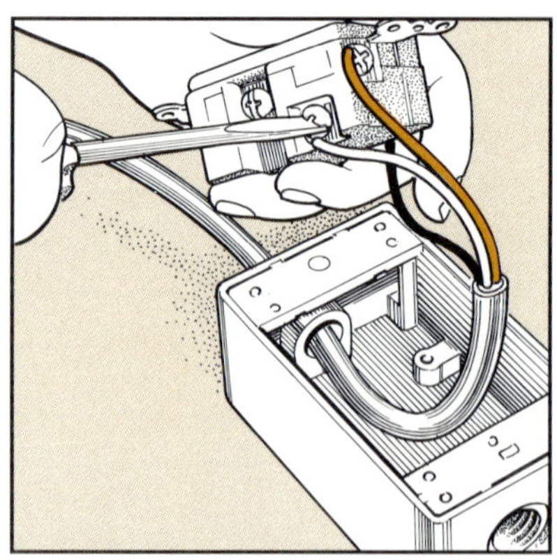

3 Attach wires to the receptacle. On a metal box, connect a ground wire from the receptacle to the wall box.

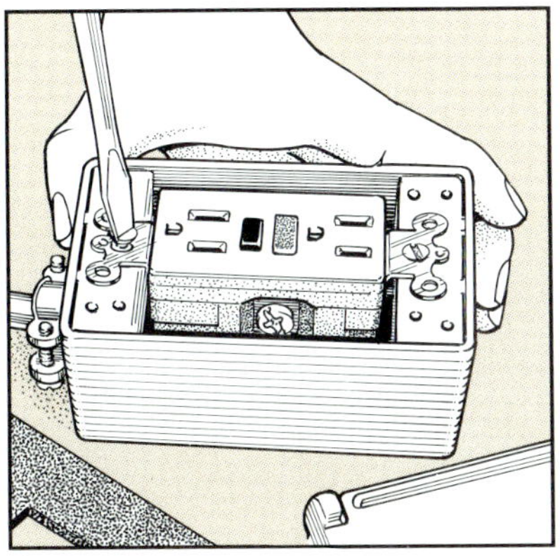

4 Center the GFCI receptacle in the box and screw it down. The cover must align properly with the receptacle's slots.

5 Then, tighten the box-connector clamp screws to secure the cord to the box. Don't overtighten the clamp.

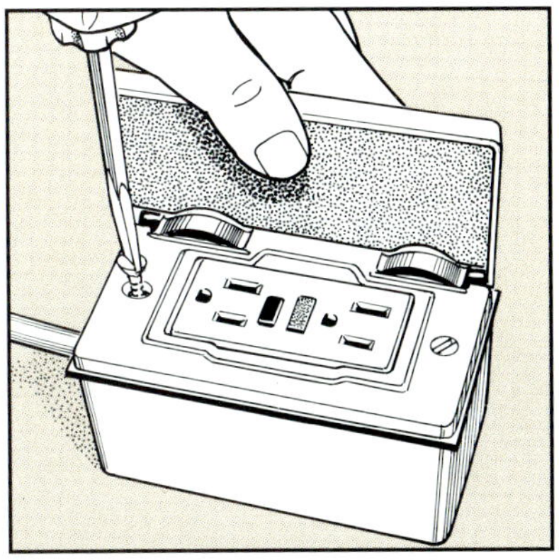

6 Place the rubber gasket on the box, and place the cover over the gasket. Fasten the cover with two screws.

Also, double-insulated tools and tools with a heavy-duty 3-wire grounded cord offer good protection against shock, but their safety features can be interrupted by accident or improper use.

GFCI devices are inexpensive and easy to install. It's a simple job to add a GFCI to a 3-wire cord. To do this, you replace the receptacle end of the cord with a GFCI receptacle housed in a weatherproof box.

How a GFCI Works

A GFCI device senses current (amps) flowing to and from electrical tools and equipment. Under normal operating conditions, the current flowing to the tool is the same as that returning to the electrical panel. When a ground fault occurs, some of the current is diverted to the ground by a short somewhere in the circuit. If the short is through you to the ground, you are in for a shocking experience.

A GFCI device senses current-flow imbalance. It can detect a current imbalance as little as 5 milliamps (which can't hurt most people) and shuts off current flow in a fraction of a second.

Adding GFCI Protection

A GFCI can be added to a metal or plastic box. Metal exterior boxes come threaded for box connectors. Plastic boxes may be threaded, but many brands require an adapter. If you plan to use a plastic box, get the necessary plastic parts so the box can accept a standard clamp-type box connector.

Besides the GFCI receptacle, you also need the following materials and tools: a 25-ft. 14/2 extension cord (14-gauge wire, 2 wires with ground), a weatherproof rectangular outdoor box that accepts dual receptacles, clamp-type box connectors, a combination wire cutter and stripper, locking pliers and a screwdriver.

Making the Cord

Begin by cutting off the cord's receptacle (Fig. 1). Strip about 6 in. of the outer cover from the cord's end, being careful not to cut the insulation on the inner conductors. Remove the insulation to expose black, white and green wires. Strip off about $^1/_2$ in. of insulation from the ends of each wire (Fig. 2).

Next, screw the box connector into the end of the box and tighten it with locking pliers. Loosen the clamp on the box connector and pass the end of the extension cord through the connector into the box. Pull a foot or so of the cord into the box.

The GFCI receptacle has either terminal screws (like a standard receptacle) or it has wire pigtails. In either case, you must connect the extension-cord wires to the terminals or the lead-out wires marked "Line." If the device is like the one pictured with screw terminals, wrap the black wire clockwise around the copper-color terminal screw. Tighten the screw and check that there are no frayed strands to short out against the box.

Wrap the white wire around the silver screw in the same way (Fig. 3). Then connect the green ground wire to the green screw at the top of the device. If you use a metal box, you have to connect a ground wire to the box. To do this, run a short section of wire from the green screw on the GFCI receptacle to the ground screw inside the box. Use wire connectors to join the conductors to the GFCI receptacle if the receptacle is equipped with wire leads instead of terminal screws.

Now, pull the excess cord out of the box to make room for the GFCI receptacle. Secure the GFCI with the mounting screws provided (Fig. 4). Check that the protective outer cover of the cord is inside the box, and tighten the screws on the box connector to clamp the cord in place (Fig. 5). Put the gasket in place and install the cover with the two screws provided (Fig. 6).

These stacking blocks are relatively small, measuring only $5x7^1/_2x12$ in., and are designed to be laid up dry. The finished wall functions as a whole because each block has a retaining lip on the bottom edge that prevents it from moving.

1 Begin by locating the best position for the wall, then drive a stake at each end to firmly support some mason's string.

2 Tie mason's string around one stake and then stretch it out and loop it over the other stake. Pull the string tight and knot it.

Building a Retaining Wall was written By Steven Willson. Illustrations by George Retseck. Blocks for the installation shown were selected from the Aztech Wall System designed by Block Systems, Inc., St. Paul, Minnesota.

Building a retaining wall

Retaining walls are a real staple of the landscape business. Not only can they solve a wealth of erosion problems but they can also lend a lot of character to otherwise uninspired grounds. A decent, serviceable wall can be made out of a wide range of different materials to suit just about anyone's personal taste. There are concrete, concrete block, brick, stone, log and even railroad-tie walls. Many of these still look wonderful after years of great service. Unfortunately, many of them don't look so wonderful. In fact, it can seem that for every wall you see in good condition, there are at least two that are falling. Some are cracked, some are crumbling and some are leaning so far they seem to defy gravity.

One of the biggest troubles with traditional retaining walls is that they are difficult to build well, especially for the inexperienced worker. It's relatively easy to erect a wall that looks good when you're done, but it's quite another to have the same wall look good in three months and still another for it to look good after a cold, hard winter.

3 If the retaining wall is to be perpendicular to the foundation wall, check the string for square using a framing square.

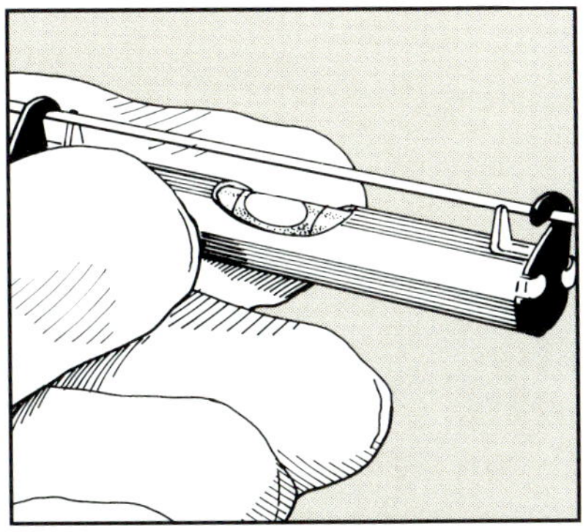

4 Hook a line level onto the string at the middle of the line and check it for level. Make any adjustments before proceeding.

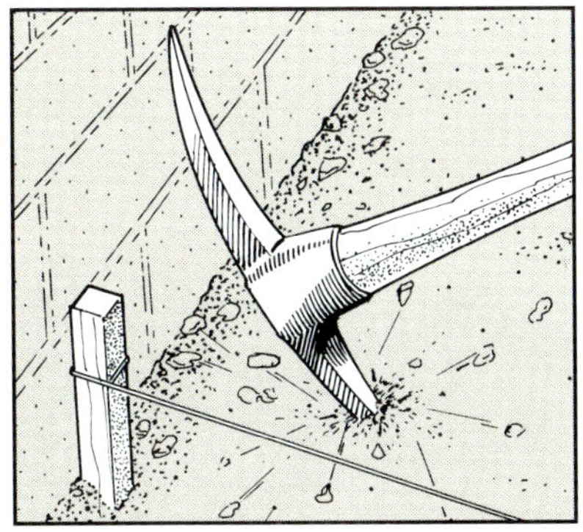

5 Begin by breaking the soil with a pick. Stand on the same side of the string as the pick to avoid hitting the string.

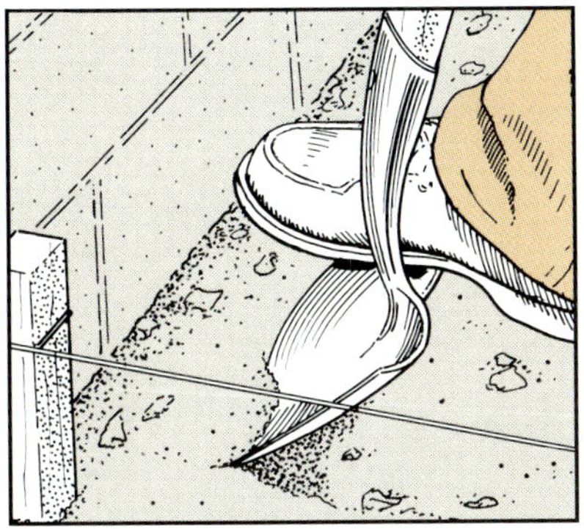

6 Once the soil is loose, remove it with a shovel. Throw the soil on the uphill side of the trench to reduce backfilling work later.

7 Periodically check the progress of your excavation by holding a tape on the bottom of the trench and against the string.

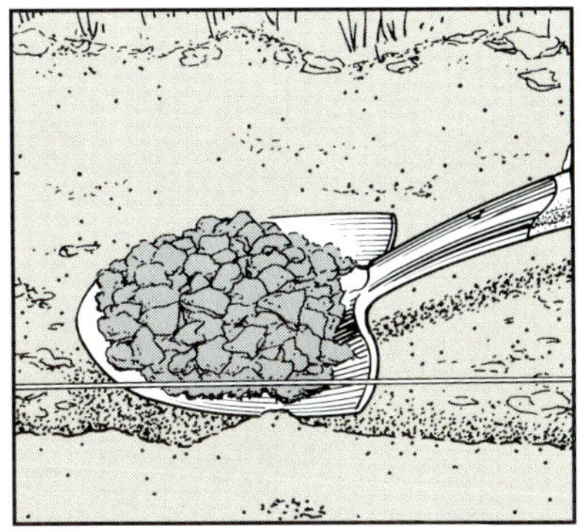

8 Remove soil to a depth of 14 in. Rake the bottom of the trench reasonably flat and add a 4-in. layer of crushed stone.

A Better Idea

The construction difficulties normally associated with retaining walls have all but disappeared with the invention of today's simple interlocking block systems. Several are on the market and each has a slightly different method of interlocking and a somewhat different palette of colors. All are made of cast concrete with a single block weighing about 20 to 30 pounds. All are designed to be laid up dry, so no mortar and no mortaring skills are necessary. Finally, because the blocks aren't joined together with mortar or by other means, hydrostatic pressure cannot build up behind the wall because the water simply seeps through the cracks between the blocks.

All these advantages wouldn't be worth much if the blocks were ugly. They aren't. The exposed sides of the blocks are heavily textured, which is the result of the block being cast and then broken at the factory. The irregularity this causes lends an authentic stone-like appearance to the wall when it is finished. Is it authentic enough for everyone? Who knows. One way to find out if you like it is to visit a masonry supply yard where various blocks are on display. Don't be satisfied with just looking at an individual block. It's much better to see a whole wall. If the supply house doesn't have the blocks on display, ask for some locations where they know the blocks have been installed and take a ride by to see if you like the results.

The manufacturers aren't giving these blocks away. Prices vary, but you can pay about $1.75 per block, and that includes a good discount for buying in volume. If you want to build a small wall of only 100 blocks or less, expect to pay at least $2 a block, delivered.

Getting Started

Once you've determined exactly where you want your wall, lay out the location with a mason's string. This string will not only serve to keep your excavation straight but it will also supply you with a reference point to check each block and each course to make sure it is level.

Drive a stake at each end of the wall location (Fig. 1) and hang a line between both stakes (Fig. 2). This line should be about 4 to 6 in. away from the finished face of the wall. These extra inches provide room for digging without disturbing your reference line.

If your new retaining wall is to be perpendicular to a foundation wall, like the one shown, then you should check the line for square before proceeding. One of the best ways to do this is by simply placing a framing square against the wall and the string (Fig. 3). Adjust the string as necessary to achieve a square location.

9 Firmly tamp the crushed stone along the bottom of the trench. Use a tamper or a simple piece of plywood nailed to a 2×4.

10 Begin the first course by placing a full block in the trench. Rock the block back and forth until it's seated firmly.

11 Using a torpedo level, check the block for level in both directions. Add or remove stone from under the block until it's level.

12 Once the first block is properly installed, use a framing square to establish how far it rests below the reference line.

13 Lower the second block alongside the first and make sure the two align precisely. Then level the second in place.

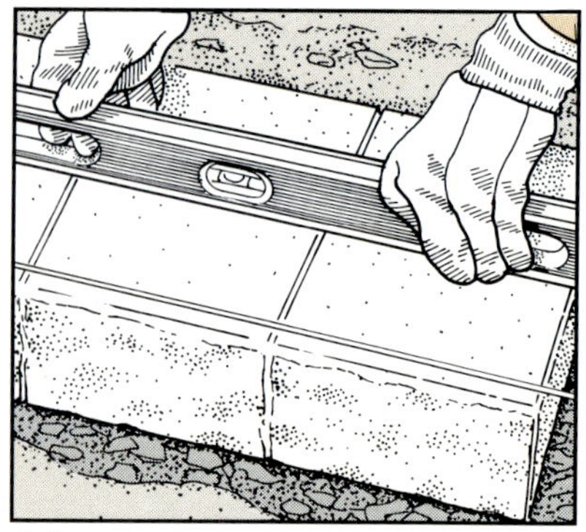

14 Repeat the same installation process for the third block, and check your progress across all three using a 4-ft. level.

You also have to check the line for level. Hang a lightweight line level on the string near the middle of the span and check the reading (Fig. 4). Remember, for the line level to be as accurate as possible, you should have the line pulled very tight.

Once you're satisfied that the line is square and level, proceed with the excavation. If your wall is going to be relatively short (no more than 24 in. high), then you have to install only one course of block below the finished grade to prevent the wall from moving out over its lifetime. But if you want to go higher, like the installation shown, then plan on burying two courses below grade for increased stability. Because the blocks are 5 in. thick and you need 4 in. of gravel in the trench before you install any blocks, you have to make the trench 14 in. deep. Using this method, a lower wall would require a 9-in.-deep excavation.

Keep in mind that most of these block systems stipulate a height limit between 36 and 48 in. You can use these blocks for higher walls, but such walls must be designed by an engineer and require extensive reinforcement, which defeats much of the purpose of using them in the first place.

Excavation

Digging a trench—especially a long one—with a pick and shovel is just about no one's idea of a good time. They say it builds character, but the people saying that aren't usually the ones who are doing the digging. Still, it must be done and if it's done with some care, everything that comes later will work out easier.

Begin with a pick (Fig. 5), making sure to avoid hitting the reference line while you work. Continue loosening the soil for several feet and then remove the soil with a shovel (Fig. 6). Throw the excess soil on the uphill side of the string to make the backfilling process easier later.

Continue removing soil and check your progress regularly with a tape measure held at the bottom of the trench and against the reference line (Fig. 7). When you are satisfied with the depth of the entire trench, smooth out the surface so it's fairly uniform and then cover the bottom with gravel or crushed stone (Fig. 8). Add about 4 in. of stone and tamp it firmly in place (Fig. 9) to give a nice firm base that is still very porous. This allows any water to drain away easily.

You can also use sand for the base, which many people prefer because it makes leveling the first course of blocks easier. In areas where water drainage isn't an issue, a sand base is actually a better idea.

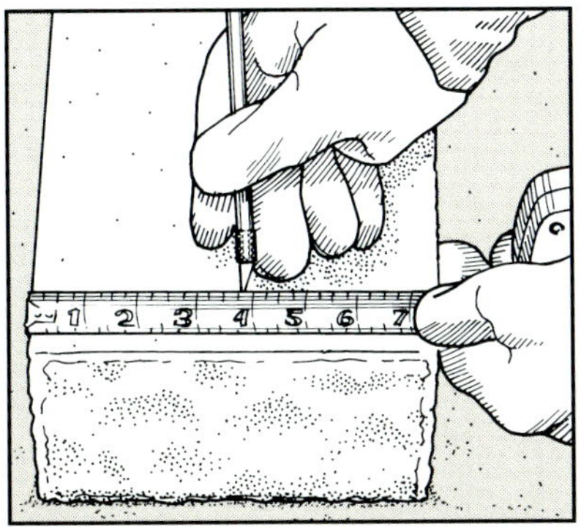

15 Begin the second course with a half block. Start by marking the centerline on all four sides using a soft-lead pencil.

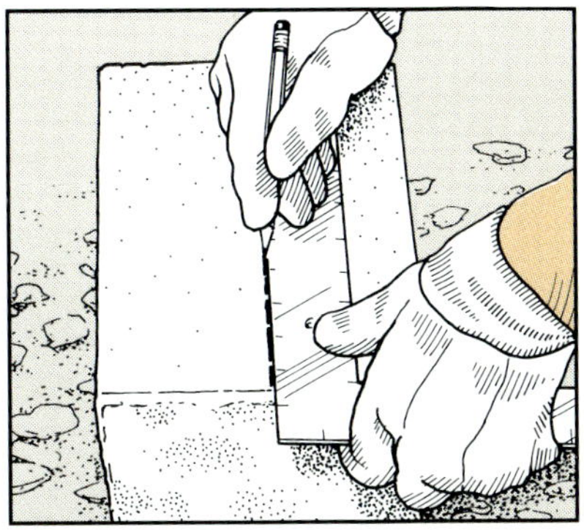

16 Draw the centerline around the block using a pencil and framinjg square. For the best results, accuracy is important.

17 Using a mechanics hammer and mason's chisel, score all the cutlines. Then break the block in half with a single blow.

18 Slide the half block in place, making sure its lip bears fully against the beveled edge of the block below.

19 Once blocks are installed, lock the first two courses in place by filling the trench in front and back with crushed stone.

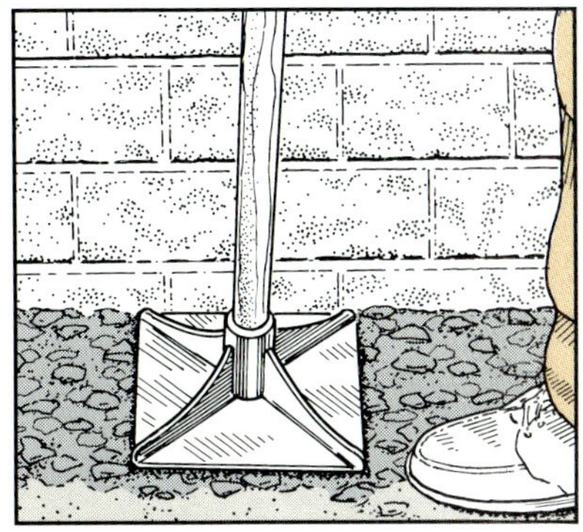

20 Firmly tamp the crushed stone in place and cover it with topsoil. Add backfill behind the wall, tamping as you go.

Once the trench is prepared for the blocks, make sure to check your reference string for square and level one more time. It's extremely important that this line be accurate and stable.

Laying the Blocks

The first course of blocks is by far the most important and laying it takes the most time. A little patience will go a long way because once the first course is firmly seated in the base, the other courses will practically fly up.

Begin by placing the first block into the gravel or stone. Rock it back and forth until it feels firmly seated (Fig. 10), then check it for level in both directions (Fig. 11). This may take awhile to level in place because, at first, removing or adding stone underneath will seem pretty awkward. But eventually it will start moving along. Once the first block is in place, put a framing square on top of the block and slide it over until the other leg hits the string (Fig. 12). By reading this leg of the square, you can establish the depth of the block relative to the string and then make sure that all ensuing base blocks are installed to the same depth.

Lower the second block into place and push it against the first (Fig. 13). Align both back edges, and then check for level and for depth. When satisfied, continue on with the other blocks. It's a good idea to level the entire course, every three or four feet, with a 4-ft. level (Fig. 14). This will tend to average out any minor differences in level between the blocks. Remember it makes more sense to undertake minor adjustments at this point than to let a slightly misaligned block go uncorrected. If a block rocks slightly on the first course, every course above it will rock too.

Cutting the Blocks

To make the block joints staggered, start the second course with a half block. First, measure and mark the centerline of the block on all four surfaces (Fig. 15). Then draw centerlines between these marks using a straightedge and a soft-lead pencil (Fig. 16).

Once all the lines are drawn on the block, score each with a mason's chisel and a mechanics hammer (Fig. 17) or a ball-peen hammer. Remember to always wear eye protection when cutting these blocks because the concrete chips can fly in totally unpredictable directions.

With all four edges scored, simply strike the block along the scored line and it should break. The process

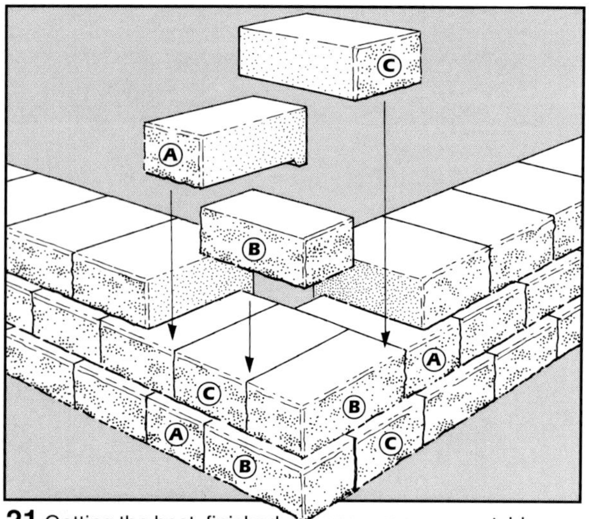

21 Getting the best finished appearance on outside corners takes a little work. For each course, three blocks must be cut. Begin by cutting blocks **A** and **B** into $^3/_4$ units. Place **A** in the normal block position against the last course block. Then remove the bottom lip from block **B** and place it at the corner of the course. Finally, take a full block (**C**) and remove enough of the lip so the block will fit properly in the space remaining. Alternate the position of these blocks on ensuing courses.

does take a little practice, and along the way you can end up ruining quite a few blocks before you finally get the hang of it. But eventually, the cutting goes quickly.

Once the half block is cut, slide it in place, making sure that the bottom retaining lip bears fully on the upper beveled edge of the blocks in the first course. Then continue adding the remaining blocks to the second course (Fig. 18).

Finishing Up

With all the blocks in place, backfill the trench, both in front of the blocks and behind them, with more gravel or stone (Fig. 19). Tamp the fill firmly in place (Fig. 20), and then add some topsoil to the front of the wall so the grass will grow. Also fill behind the wall, preferably with soil that has a lot of stone or gravel in it. The more stone and gravel, the better your drainage and the less likely that the drainage spaces between the blocks will clog.

On the job shown, a couple of straight walls were built to solve an erosion problem. But if you need to make an outside corner in your wall, the process is simple (Fig. 21). Just make sure to stagger the corner blocks in each course.

1 Use a framing square to lay out the stringer notches. Align riser and tread lengths on square with edge of stock.

2 After laying out the last tread, mark the bottom cutline. Subtract one tread thickness ($1\frac{1}{2}$ in.) from the bottom riser.

Building Wooden Porch Steps was written by Neal Barrett. Illustrations by George Retseck.

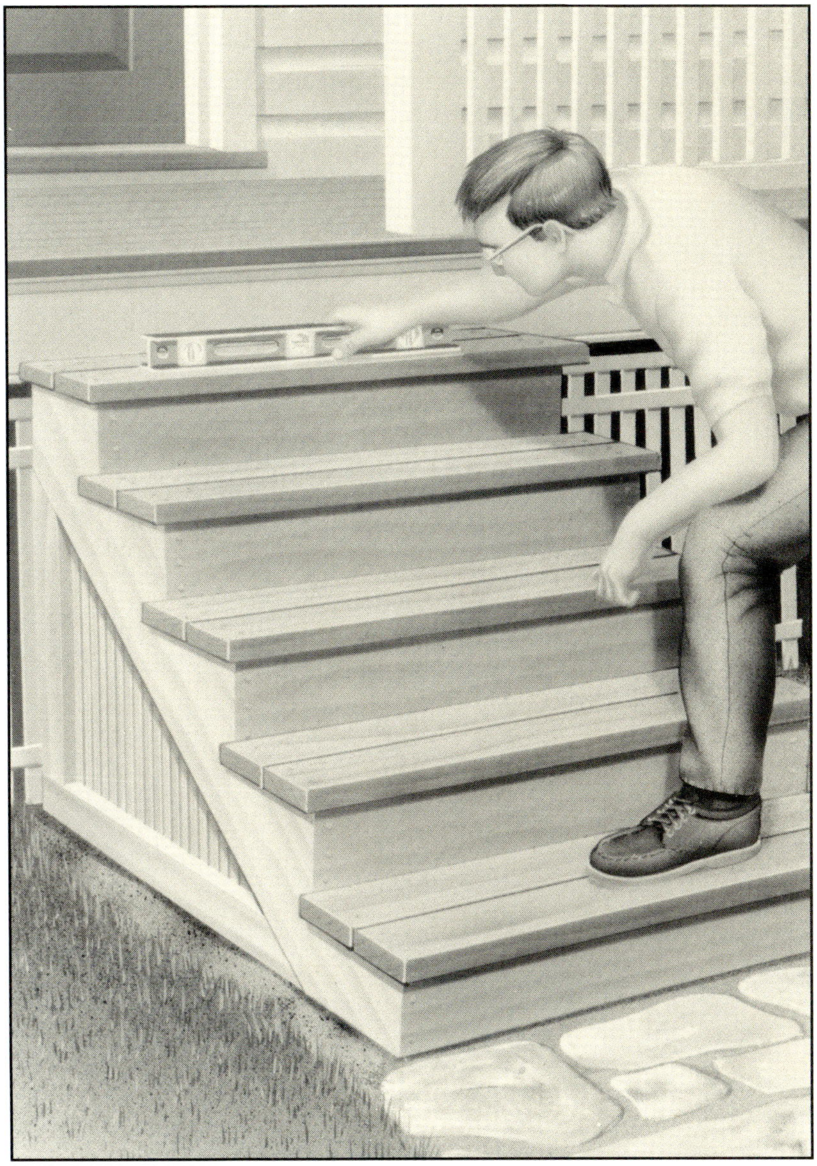

Building wooden porch steps

If you're intimidated by stair construction and your back porch steps have seen better days, consider yourself lucky. You have an opportunity not only to fix up the homestead, but to conquer the mysteries of riser height, tread width and stringer layout—all in one weekend.

The traditional style shown here features neat, mitered risers and beaded tongue-and-groove side panels, and is suitable for use either up to an entry or as an access to a porch or raised deck (see drawing on page 95). Except for the beaded side paneling, the structure is made from pressure-treated nominal 2-in. stock for long life out in the weather.

This free-standing design simply sits on a concrete or stone pad. If you don't have a pad, you can either pour one or set flat paving stones into the earth. Since the stair is constructed of pressure-treated material, you could even set it directly on the ground—just make sure that whatever foundation you choose is flat and level.

Stair Layout

A safe stair demands a uniform riser height (the distance between the treads) of between $6^1/_2$ and $7^3/_4$ in.—or as close to that as you can get. To calculate the height of your risers, measure the distance from your stair footing to your deck or porch surface. Divide that dimension by 7 to get an approximate number of risers. Round the resultant number to the next highest whole number and divide that figure into the deck height. If the resultant height is in the proper range, you've found your riser dimension. If it's too small, divide by the next smallest whole number.

In most cases, this type of stair is built so that the top tread is one step down from the porch surface. To do this, simply subtract one riser height from your overall layout. If you wish, however, your top tread could be left flush with the porch surface.

The width of your stair treads should fall between $10^1/_2$ and 12 in. In the installation shown, two 2x6s were used, spaced $^1/_4$ in. apart to yield an $11^1/_2$-in.-wide tread (this dimension may vary depending on the actual dimensions of your lumber). When laying out the stringer, make the cuts for the treads $1^1/_2$ in. less than the actual tread measurement. This way, each tread overhangs the riser below it by $1^1/_2$ in.

The width of your stair will, of course, vary with its location. For stairs wider than 48 in., plan on one or more center-support stringers.

Use a framing square to lay out the stringers. Place the square near one end of the 2x12 stringer stock and locate the tread cut length (overall tread minus $1^1/_2$ in.) on the blade (the long arm of the square) and the riser height on the tongue (the short arm of the square).

Adjust the angle of the framing square so that these two points are aligned with the edge of the board. Then, trace along the square's blades to lay out the top tread. Next, mark a perpendicular line at the back end of the top-tread layout line to yield the top plumb cut that defines the back edge of the stair.

For the remaining steps, hold the framing square so that the riser height on the tongue of the square intersects the point where the last tread cutline crosses the stringer edge. Adjust the square so that the tread dimension on the blade also crosses the stringer edge (Fig. 1).

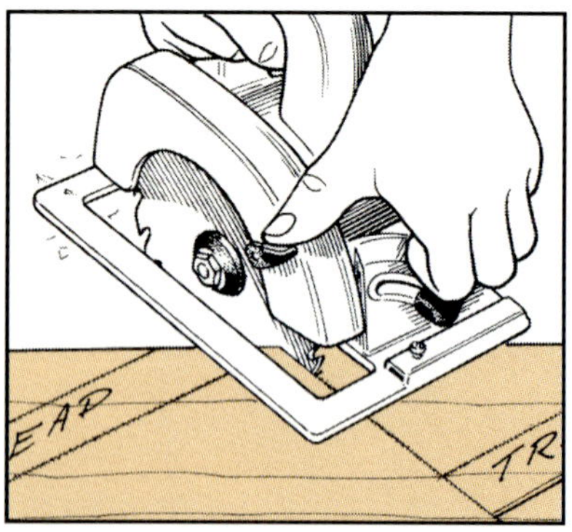

3 Begin the step cutouts with a circular saw set for a square cut. Follow layout lines and cut just up to intersecting lines.

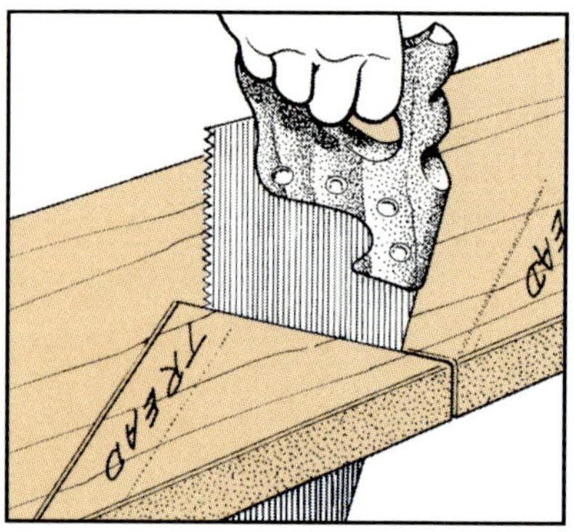

4 Finish cutouts with a handsaw. Hold saw vertically and cut into step corner. Use first stringer as a pattern for second one.

5 After marking inner and outer surfaces on both stringers, use a bevel gauge set to 45° for marking the mitered riser cuts.

6 Use a circular saw set to 45° to begin the riser cuts on the right stringer. Use a handsaw to cut the miters on the other stringer.

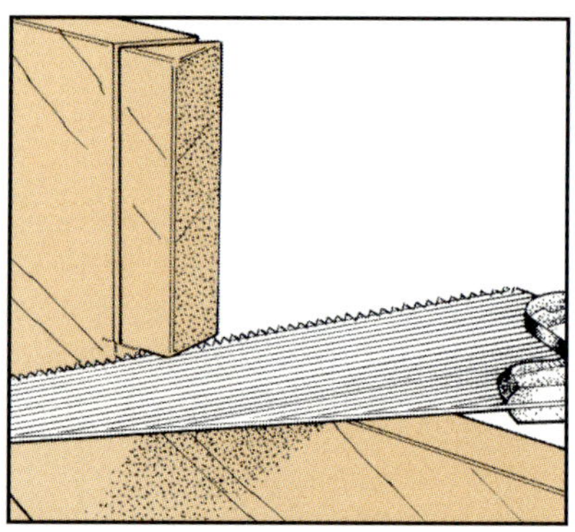

7 Remove the waste on both stringers with a handsaw. Hold the saw flat against the tread and cut into mitered corner.

Trace along the square to lay out each step shape. Lay out the bottom-riser cut on one tread thickness $1^1/_2$ in. less than the other riser cuts, and draw a line parallel to the tread lines from the bottom of this mark to indicate the bottom-level cut of the stringer (Fig. 2). This cut indicates the edge of the stringer that will sit on the concrete or stone footing.

Construction Basics

Use a circular saw to make the top and bottom cuts that define the stringer ends. Clamp each stringer between sawhorses to make the cutouts for the steps. Cut up to each layout line with the circular saw (Fig. 3). Then, use a handsaw, held vertically, to finish each cut (Fig. 4).

Once the first stringer is cut to shape, use it as a pattern to lay out the opposite stringer. Then cut the second stringer.

Clearly mark the inner and outer surfaces of the stringers. Support each stringer on its bottom edge, and use a bevel gauge set to 45° to mark the miter cuts for the risers (Fig. 5). Note that the risers are cut back toward the inside surface of each stringer.

Since a circular-saw blade can be angled in only one direction, you'll be able to use it to cut miters only on the right stringer, as you face the bottom of the stairs. Make the miter cuts just up to the tread line (Fig. 6), and use a handsaw to complete the cuts.

Cut the miters on the left stringer with a handsaw. Support the stringer in a vise, or clamp it to a workbench, to make the cuts. It's easier to make these cuts accurately if you clamp the stringer so that the risers are oriented vertically. With the layout lines clearly marked on the stringer sides, slowly cut down to the tread line. Finish the cut by extending the tread to the bottom of the miter (Fig. 7).

Side Framing

A great technique for completing the layout of the stair side is to use a large worktable or sheet of plywood as a template for the side. It's much easier to visualize the stair, and ensure square assembly, if the stringer is aligned with the square edges of the table or plywood. To use this method, make two marks on adjacent edges of the worksurface—one on the bottom edge equal to the sum of the tread cuts and one on the ver-

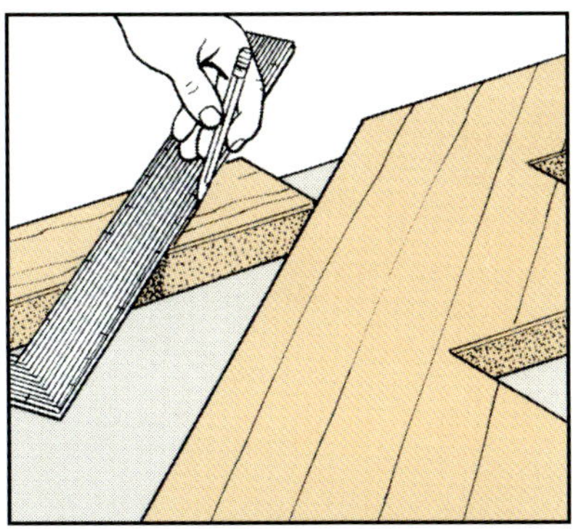

8 Use a square to lay out the angled cuts on the bottom 2×4 support. The angle of the cut is the same as the stringer angle.

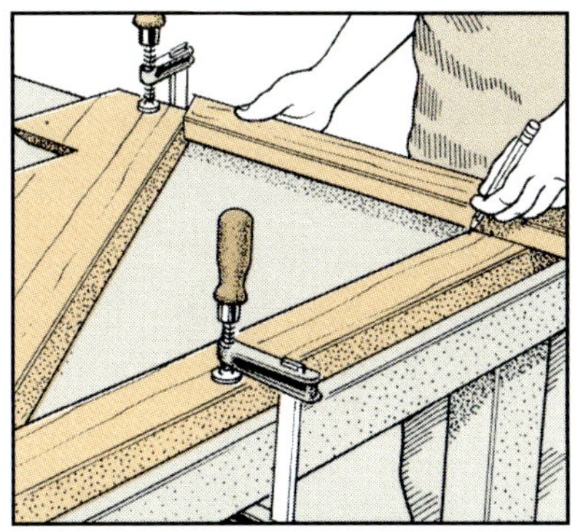

9 Clamp the side components to a square table or piece of plywood. Mark and cut the vertical support and clamp into place.

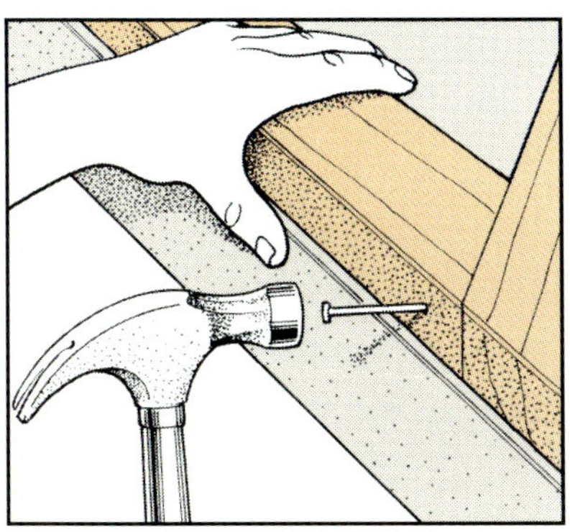

10 Use 10d or 12d galvanized nails to secure 2×4s to stringer. Prebore pilot holes to prevent splitting the wood.

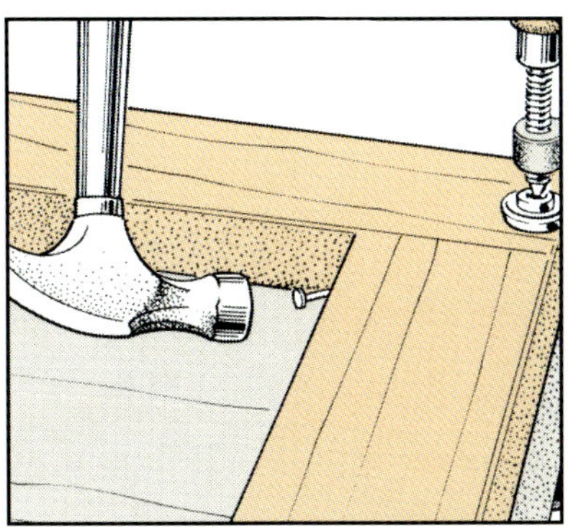

11 After boring the pilot holes, use 8d galvanized nails to toenail the bottom and vertical side 2×4 supports together.

12 Install $^5/_8$-in.-thick beaded fir to the inside surface of the stringer assemblies. Nail in place with 4d galvanized nails.

tical edge equal to the sum of the riser cuts. Align the stringer on these marks and clamp it in place.

Cut the bottom 2×4 support at an angle to meet the back edge of the stringer. This angle is the same as the angle of the tread cuts on the stringer. Use the framing square to mark the 2×4 (Fig. 8), then make the cut with the circular saw. Next, hold the piece in place against the stringer and mark its length at the end of the table or plywood.

The angle at the top end of the vertical 2×4 support is the same angle that yielded the riser cuts on the stringer. Lay out and cut the angle, then hold the piece in place against the stringer and mark its length against the bottom support (Fig. 9).

Position the two supports against the stringer and clamp them in place to maintain their position during fastening. It's a good idea to prebore holes for the nails in pressure-treated wood to reduce the chance of splitting. Use galvanized nails to fasten the bottom and vertical support to the stringer and to each other (Figs. 10 and 11).

Turn the assembly over so that the inside surface is exposed. Then, cut and nail strips of $^5/_8$-in.-thick beaded fir over the opening. This material is usually sold as porch ceiling or wainscoting, but is ideal for this application as well. Let the strips overlap the stringers and supports by approximately $1^1/_2$ in., and use 4d galvanized nails to fasten the strips (Fig. 12).

Assembling the Stairs

If necessary, use a circular saw and ripping fence to rip the riser stock to width. The risers shown were 7 in. wide, which required ripping 2×8s to the proper size. Remember that the bottom riser will be $1^1/_2$ in. less in width than the other risers.

While the ends of the risers must be mitered to meet the stringers, it's easiest to first cut the risers squarely to length. Then, go back and use the circular saw to miter each end. Clamp the stock to the saw horses before mitering (Fig. 13). By firmly clamping the stock, you free up both hands to control the saw cut.

13 After cutting the risers squarely to exact length, use a circular saw to make the 45° miter cuts on each end.

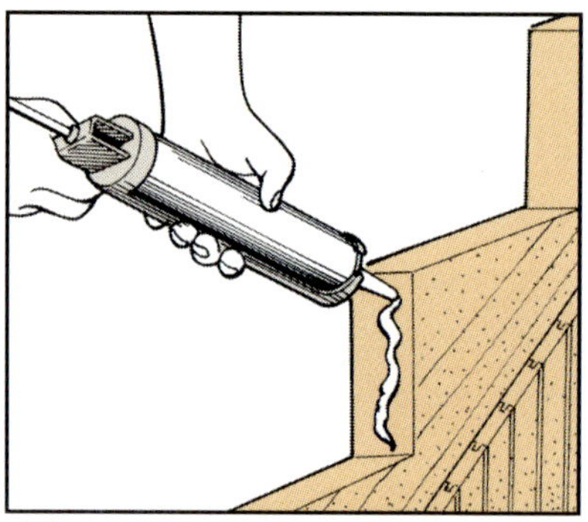

14 Apply pressure-treated lumber adhesive to the riser miter joints before nailing. Use 8d galvanized nails to fasten joints.

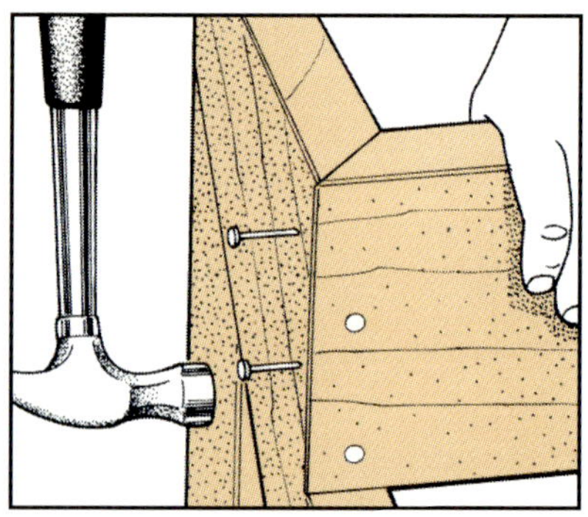

15 Drive nails from both directions when fastening the mitered risers to the stringers. Prebore to avoid splitting the lumber.

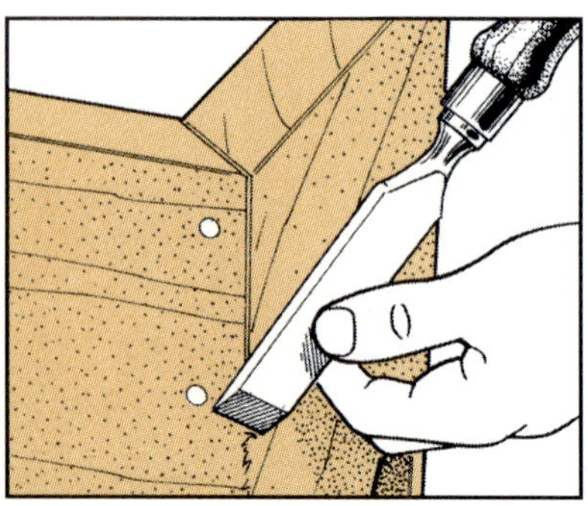

16 Use a chisel to slightly chamfer the sharp corners of each miter joint. Pressure-treated lumber should not be sanded.

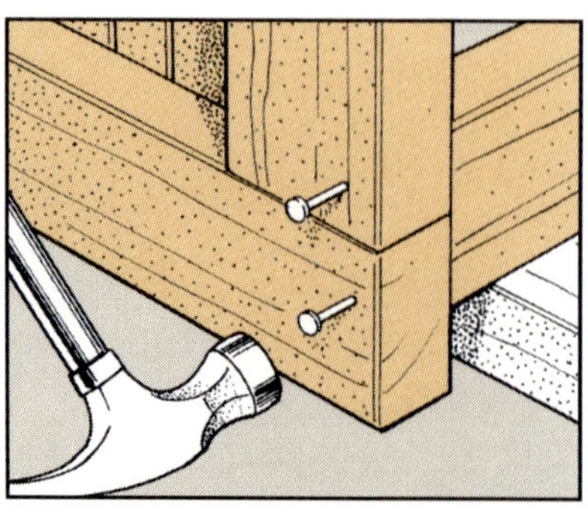

17 Use glavanized nails to fasten each side to the bottom back brace. Hold brace off the ground with $1^1/_2$-in. stock.

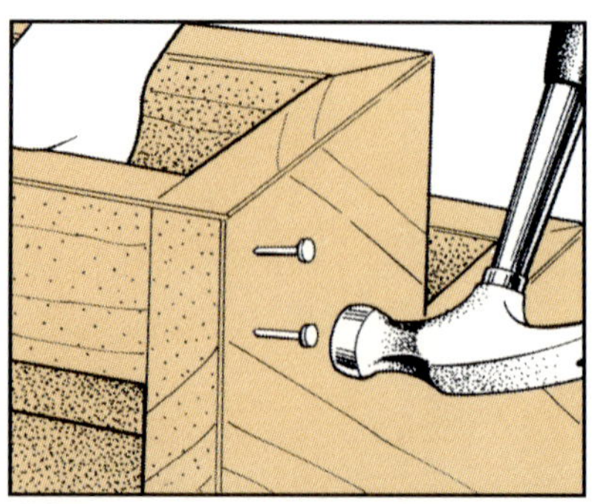

18 Install the top crossbrace flush with the top edge of the stringer. This brace helps support the back edge of the top tread.

Next, join the bottom riser to the two stringer assemblies. If you don't have a helper to support the stringers, temporarily clamp them to the side of a table or door while you attach the first riser. After this is attached to both stringers, the assembly will be self-supporting. Apply construction adhesive, preferably one designed for pressure-treated lumber, to the miter joints (Fig. 14). Use 8d galvanized nails to fasten the risers to the stringers (Fig. 15). After nailing, use a chisel to slightly chamfer the corner of each miter joint so it doesn't have such a sharp edge (Fig. 16).

Cut two horizontal 2×4 crossbraces for the open back of the stair. Shim the bottom brace $1\frac{1}{2}$ in. off the ground when you fasten it in place (Fig. 17). This provides clearance for any irregularities along the back edge of the footing that might cause the stair to sit unevenly. Nail the top brace even with the top edge of the stringer assembly (Fig. 18).

Next, cut two diagonal 2×4 braces 18 to 24 in. long with 45° miter cuts at each end. Install these between the bottom crossbrace and the stringer's vertical supports (Fig. 19).

Cut the 2×6 stock to length for the treads. Note that the treads should overhang the stringers on each end by about $1\frac{1}{2}$ in. Prebore holes for fastening each tread, then use $2\frac{1}{2}$-in. galvanized deck screws to attach the treads to the stringers. Use a $\frac{1}{4}$-in. shim to create a uniform space between the treads (Fig. 20). Fasten the inner tread boards to the risers by driving $2\frac{1}{2}$-in. galvanized deck screws through the back side of the risers into the back edge of the tread (Fig. 21).

Apply two or three coats of alkyd deck enamel, allowing each layer to fully dry before applying the next one. Take the time to cover all inside and bottom surfaces of the stair because all of the stair's parts will be exposed to moisture and, therefore, should be sealed.

Finally, slide your stair into place against the porch or deck. Use a level to check its position and, if necessary, shim the assembly with a cedar shingle to guarantee a firm base and a stair that doesn't rock.

19 Install 18- to 24-in.-long diagonal 2×4 braces between the bottom crossbrace and the side vertical supports.

20 Bore pilot holes and install the treads with $2\frac{1}{2}$-in. galvanized deck screws. Use a $\frac{1}{4}$-in. shim to space the boards.

21 Drive two or three screws through the back of the risers into the back edge of the rear tread boards for extra support.

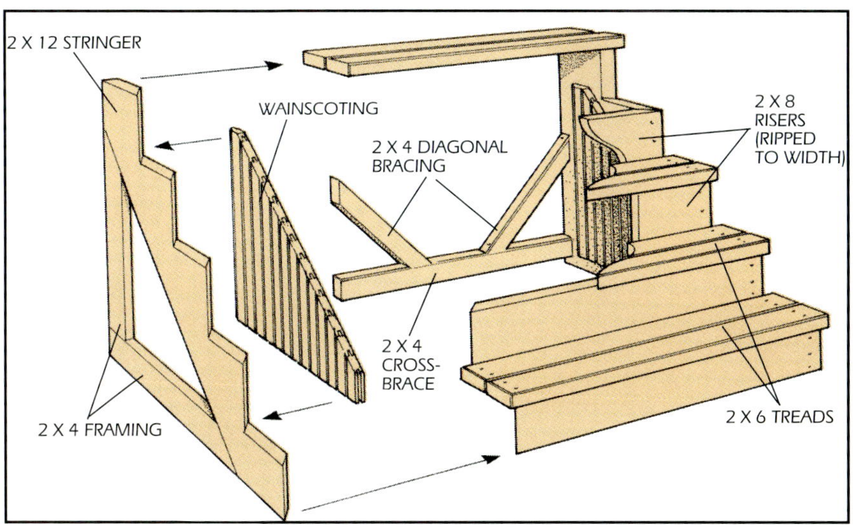

Free-standing stair components include stringers with tread and riser cutouts, double 2×6 treads, beaded tongue-and-groove side panels and 2×4 bracing to add rigidity.

For the best paint performance, wood siding should be primed on the front and back before installation. The redwood product used here (inset) came primed, and featured finger jointed construction. This provided the high performance of redwood at a lower cost.

1 Begin siding job by installing builder's paper at the bottom of the wall over the sheathing. Staple paper every 8 to 12 in.

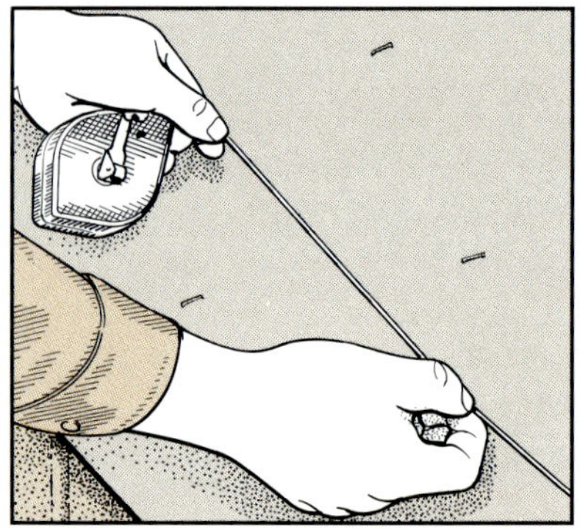

2 Determine the height of the baseboard trim at both ends of the wall and snap a chalkline between these two points.

Installing Clapboard Siding was written by Steven Willson. Illustrations by George Retseck.

Installing clapboard siding

One of the best things about siding is that usually it can be painted. This allows you to change the entire look and feel of your house for a relatively modest sum, especially if you do the work yourself. Replacing your siding, on the other hand, is not nearly such an easy or inexpensive job. Because of the large square footage that must be covered, the material is expensive. If you're working on a 2-story house, the job can be very time consuming and dangerous.

But if you are building something on the small side, like an addition, a free-standing garage or even a utility building for lawn and garden gear, you may well want to tackle the siding job yourself.

Keep in mind that these techniques will work for any type of wood clapboard siding. The most common varieties are redwood, cedar and pine. For the job shown, a relatively new redwood siding was chosen that comes in $^{1}/_{2}\times6$-in. fingerjointed boards up to 20 ft. long. This product is available in two grades—clear and all-heart wood—and can cost up to 25% less than top-of-the-line redwood siding (which usually runs between $2.50 and $3 per square foot). But it delivers the same structural stability, rot resistance and workability that have always made redwood the premium siding choice. While these boards can be covered with a clear finish, you may prefer to paint them for a more traditional look. This product is available uncoated or with an optional alkyd primer already in place.

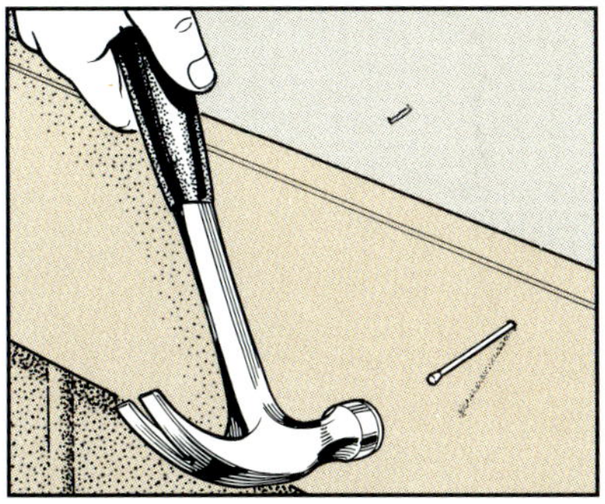

3 Cut the baseboard to length and attach it with galvanized nails. Set the nailheads and fill the holes with caulk.

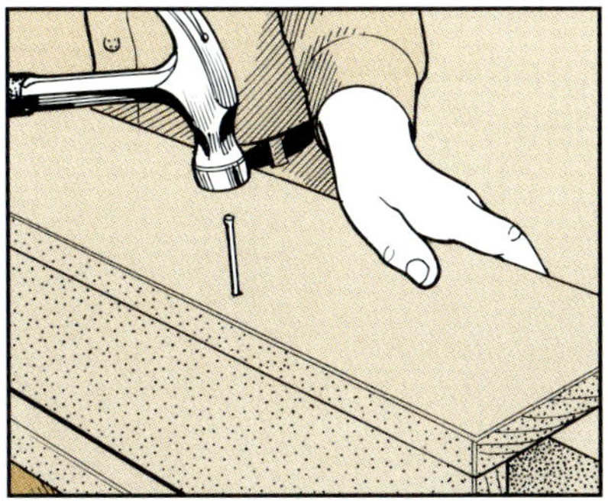

4 Cut all the corner board stock to length, and nail the boards together. Space galvanized nails about 6 to 8 in. apart.

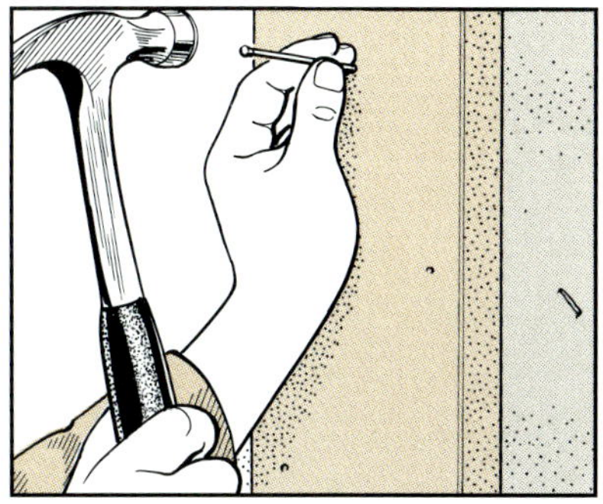

5 Lift corner boards onto house and attach securely. Drive nails into house corner studs, not just sheathing.

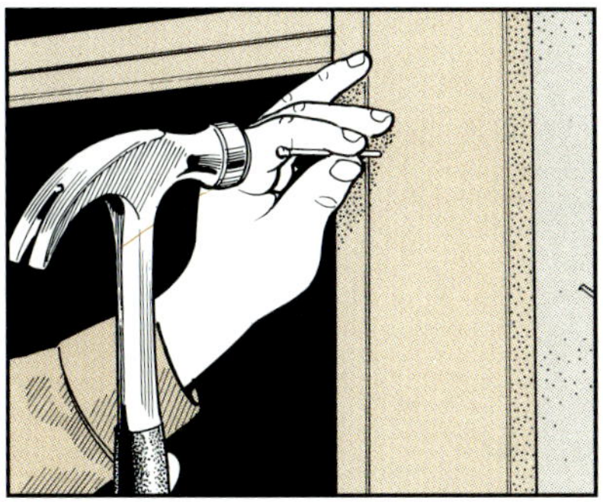

6 Nail trim in place around all windows and doors. Keep the trim as tight as possible to the window or door casing.

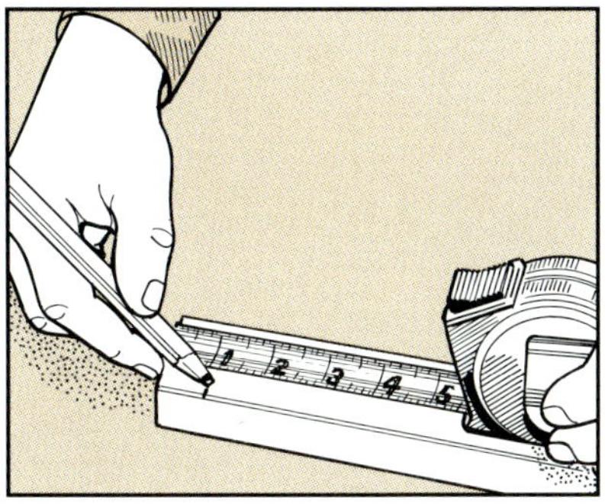

7 Begin marking the story pole at the 1-in. point. Then mark the rest of the pole every $4\frac{1}{2}$ in. from this first mark.

8 Once the story pole is laid out on one side, carefully transfer the marks to the other three sides using a square.

Getting Started

Your first step is to determine how much siding and other materials—builder's paper, staples, hot-dipped galvanized siding nails, trim boards and paint—you need. The best thing to do is simply draw a sketch of your building, along with all the pertinent dimensions, and take it to your local lumberyard. They'll show you the various product options available and help you decide what exposure would look best. For the job shown, a $4\frac{1}{2}$-in. exposure was chosen, which means that $4\frac{1}{2}$ in. of the surface of each board is exposed to the weather. They can also help determine the type of trim you should buy. The job shown used 5/4 stock in the following widths: 10 in. for the baseboards, 8 in. for the corner boards and rake boards, and 4 in. for the casing boards.

Nominal 5/4 thick boards actually measure about $1\frac{1}{16}$-in.-thick. By using this stock for the trim, the trimboards always projected more from the surface than the siding boards. This resulted in a crisp finished look and provided a good edge against which the caulk was applied.

Begin by stapling your builder's paper along the bottom of one wall over the sheathing (Fig. 1). Keep the paper smooth as you roll it out and be sure to use plenty of staples. A sudden gust of wind can easily tear off the paper before you have a chance to install any siding. Then, establish where your baseboard will fall and snap a chalkline to match the top of the baseboard (Fig. 2). Hold the board just below the chalkline and nail it to the wall using galvanized finishing nails (Fig. 3). Make sure to drive the nails into the wall studs, not just into the sheathing.

Once the baseboard is in place, get an accurate measurement for the length of your corner boards and then cut your stock to size and nail the boards together. Keep the joint flush and drive nails at least every 6 to 8 in. (Fig. 4). Make sure to spot prime any saw cuts. Then lift up the corner board, place it on the baseboard and nail it to the building (Fig. 5), again using galvanized nails. Install the rest of the baseboards and corner boards, then nail the casing boards around all the windows and doors (Fig. 6). If your building is only one story, you should nail your frieze boards in place now. But if you need scaffolding to reach a 2-story height, then wait and install them from your scaffolding.

Siding Boards

Once all the trim is in place, lay out the trim boards with course marks for the siding boards. To do this, first fabricate a story pole. This device is nothing more than a 2×2 that is marked to correspond to the proper course spacing of all the siding boards.

To establish the proper marks, first lay out the width of your course lap. In this case this was 1 in., so the mark was made accordingly (Fig. 7). Move the end of your tape measure to this line and then continue marking the story pole at the intervals that match your desired exposure. In the project shown, this was $4\frac{1}{2}$ in., so a mark was made every $4\frac{1}{2}$ in. above the first 1-in. mark. Once the story pole is marked on one

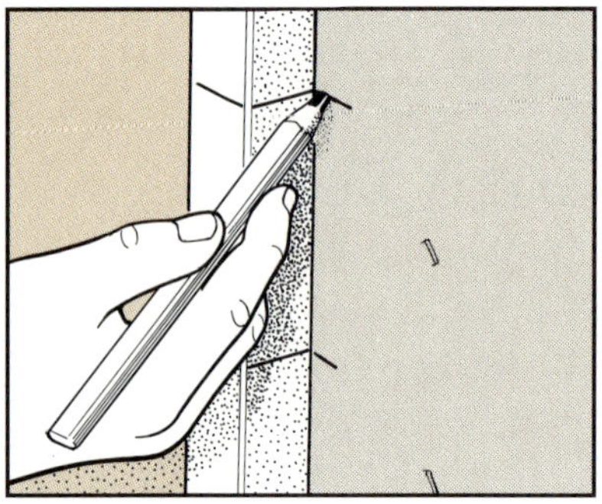

9 Place the story pole on top of the baseboard and against the corner board. Transfer the marks onto the paper.

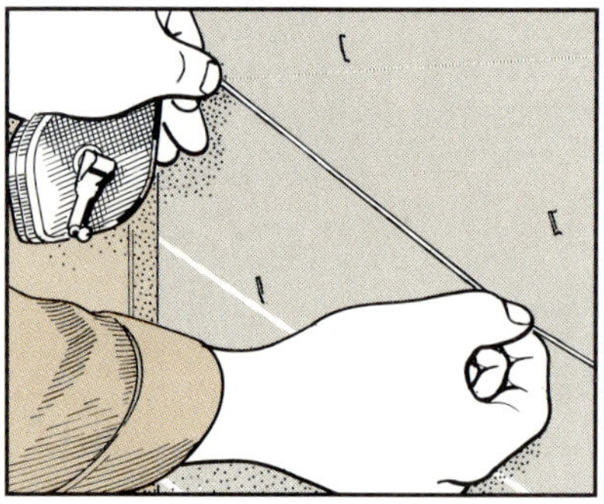

10 After marking both ends of the wall with the story board, snap a chalkline between the marks to locate the courses.

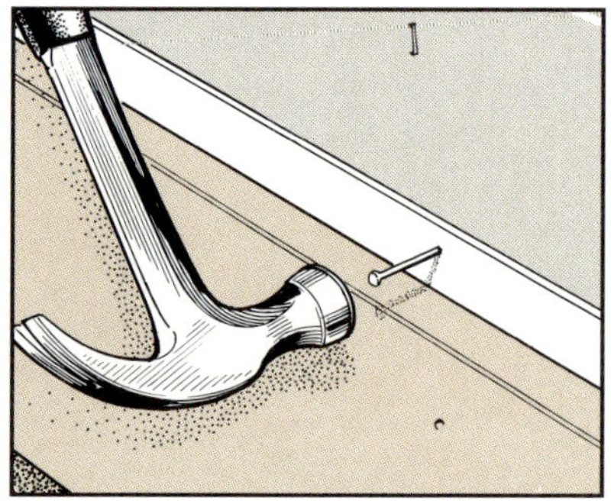

11 Cut 1 in. from the thin beveled edge of a piece of siding for a corner strip. Nail it on the wall just above the baseboard.

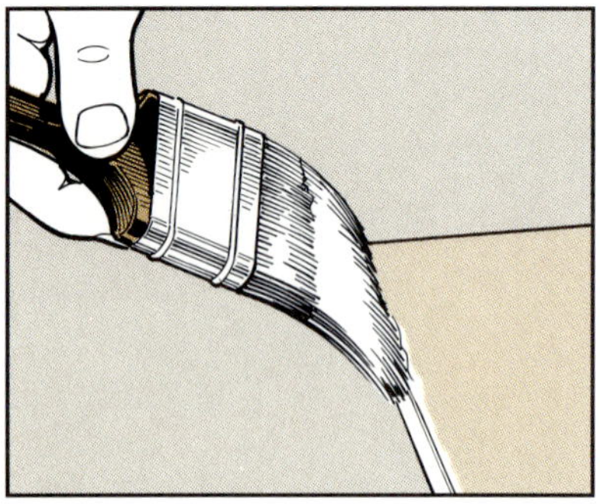

12 Cut the first piece of siding to fit, and remove any splinters. Then prime the cut with an oil or acrylic latex primer.

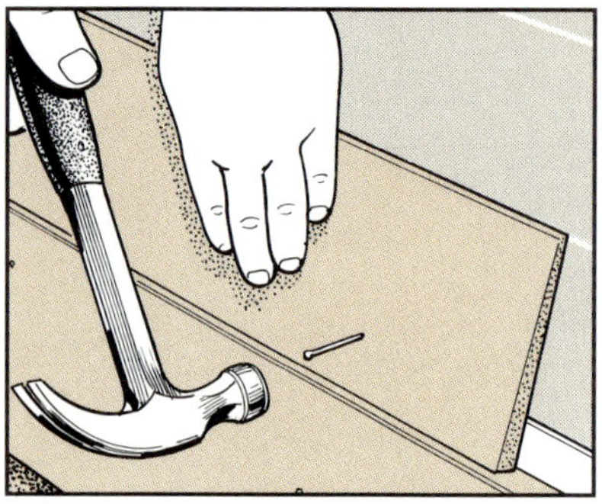

13 Nail the siding in place—about $1\frac{1}{4}$ in. above the bottom of the board—to just clear the starter strip.

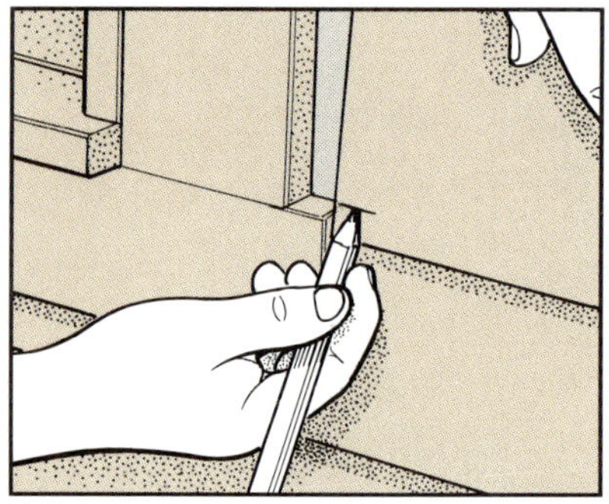

14 While not always practical, scribing is usually the best way to locate cutouts. Just hold the board in place and mark.

side, transfer these marks to all four sides (Fig. 8). Now the pole can be used in any position.

Next, transfer all the layout lines from the story pole to the builder's paper (Fig. 9). Make these marks at all the corner boards and casing boards. Then snap chalklines between all these marks to establish proper guidelines (Fig. 10). Be sure to stretch the string tight before you snap it.

Before you nail your first siding board in place, you must install a starter strip (Fig. 11). This is nothing more than a 1-in. piece ripped from the thin edge of a siding board. By nailing this piece at the bottom of the wall, the first full siding board will be held away from the wall at the same angle as all the other boards. Once this board is in place, cut your first siding board to length (if necessary) and coat any cuts with primer (Fig. 12). Then nail the board on the wall. Keep the nail above the starter strip and make sure to nail into the wall studs (Fig. 13). If the end of a board misses a stud, you can nail the end into the sheathing only, as long as the sheathing is plywood. If you have nonstructural sheathing, you must cut the siding to fall on a stud.

When you come to obstructions like windows and doors, you need to fit the siding boards to the trim. A quick way to do this is by scribing the end of the board (Fig. 14) and then making the cut. If scribing isn't practical, simply measure the cutout and mark the board accordingly.

One of the biggest frustrations of working with any wood siding is the splitting that can occur when you drive a nail too near the end of a board. To avoid this, never nail closer than 2 in. to the end of a board (Fig.

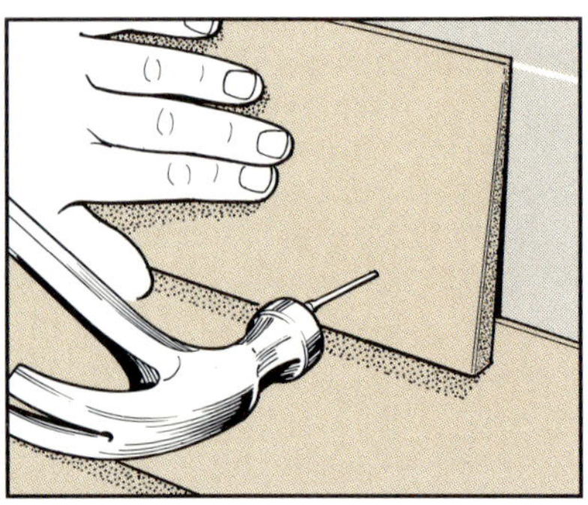

15 Nail directly into wall studs behind sheathing. To avoid splitting, keep nails at least 2 in. from the end of the board.

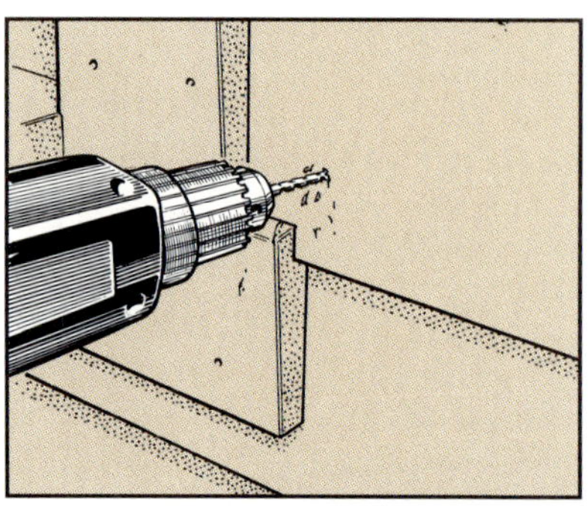

16 If the board end falls where there's no stud, bore a pilot hole in the siding and drive a nail only into the sheathing.

17 Once all the trim and siding is installed, make sure to set any projecting nailheads with a nailset and hammer.

SCAFFOLDING SYSTEM

A simple scaffold made up of planks and sawhorses is all you need. It's cheap, quick to assemble and not very dangerous.

But if you are working two or three stories above the ground, you need a way to get up there that is not only safe and economical but that also provides enough room to do what needs to be done. One of the best scaffolding systems is the one shown here, commonly called the *pump jack system.* All that's involved is making some double 2×4 posts and sliding some specialized hardware on each. (The poles should be spaced between 8 and 10 ft. apart.) A brace goes on the top of each pole, and the pump jack mechanism goes on the bottom. Between the pumps you install full-size 2×12 planks.

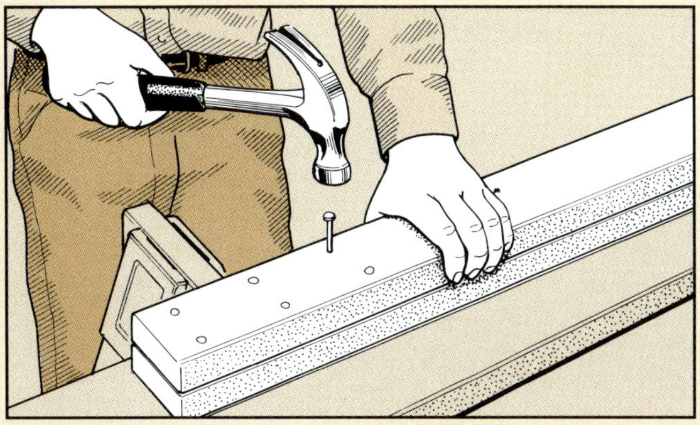

Construct the poles by nailing together two 2×4s from both sides. Use 12d common nails driven in pairs every 4 or 5 inches.

The top brace is attached to the house or roof and keeps the pole from falling. The bottom fixture supports the scaffolding boards. Its clever, foot-operated pump mechanism is what moves you and the scaffolding up and down the pole.

These systems are commonly available at rental outlets and when installed and operated properly, they're very safe. If you are uncomfortable with heights, you really should consider hiring someone else to do the work.

Slide the pump mechanism and top braces over the pole. Then stand the pole in place and nail the top braces to the house.

Place planking on the pump mechanism. Then push the pump down and up with your foot to achieve the desired height.

15). If you have to nail closer, simply prebore nail clearance holes (Fig. 16). Avoid driving the nailhead into the siding. This last blow usually does the splitting.

Once all the siding is in place, make sure to set all projecting nailheads on the trim boards (Fig. 17) and fill the holes with caulk. Then apply caulk to all the joints between the siding and the trim (Fig. 18). This step is very time consuming but yields a big reward by drastically improving the weather tightness of any building. Make sure all openings are filled, and wipe off any excess caulk with a putty knife to achieve a smooth, professional surface (Fig. 19).

Once everything is caulked, paint the siding with two coats of paint (Fig. 20). Some people prefer alkyd paint for the exterior, but premium latex paint works just as well and is much easier to clean up.

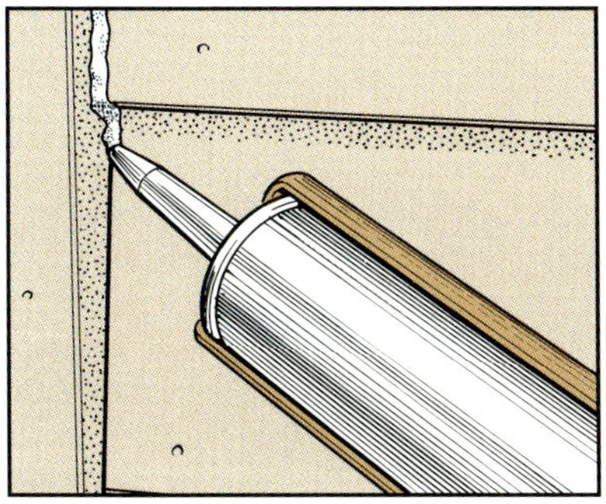

18 Thoroughly caulk all the joints between the siding and trim boards. Be sure to use a high-quality exterior caulk.

19 Using a stiff putty knife, force the caulk into the joints and smooth out the surface to create a seamless finish.

20 Starting at the top of each wall, paint the entire surface with acrylic latex paint. When dry, apply a second coat.

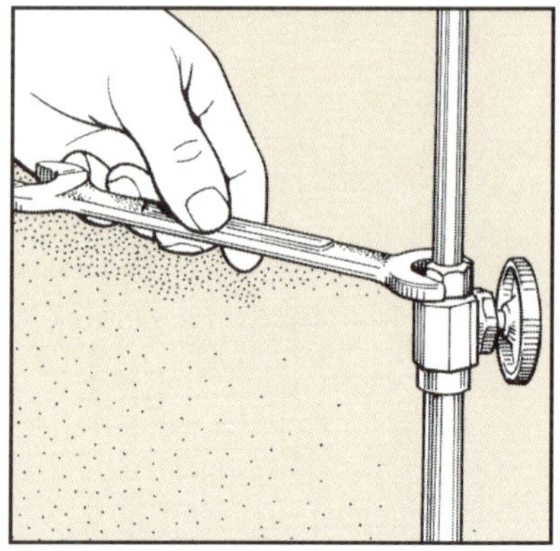

1 Shut off the water to the sink, then loosen the compression fittings that hold the sink supply lines to the shutoffs.

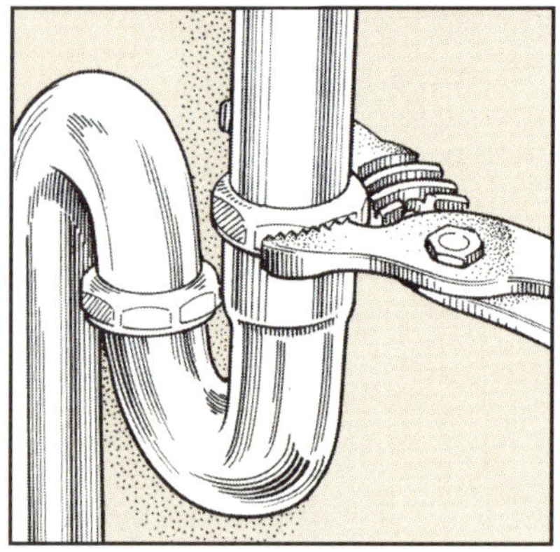

2 Use slip-joint pliers or a pipe wrench to loosen the slip nut that holds the sink tailpiece to the waste line trap.

Countertop facelift

There are some relatively inexpensive steps to kitchen renovation you can take that will give your kitchen some new life. One option, especially if you want to do the work yourself, is to resurface your countertops with new plastic laminate—without removing the old tops. The technique shown here will help you avoid much of the inconvenience of complete countertop replacement, but you can still count on having your kitchen out of commission for at least a day or two. If this is your first foray into the world of plastic laminate work, it is a good idea to purchase a piece of laminate and experiment with the application techniques before you tackle the countertops.

Plan Ahead

Before beginning this project, carefully inspect your countertop to make sure that it is a candidate for being relaminated. The original laminate material must have a smooth finish, rather than the sculpted, uneven surface that some laminates offer. Next, check that the laminate is firmly bonded to the substrate over its entire surface. Any bubbles or loose edges will make the counter unsuitable for recovering. If there are any small cracks or pits in the counter surface, they can be filled with an auto-body filler (such as Bondo) and then sanded flush with the surface.

Bring a sketch of your countertop layout, with dimensions, when you go to purchase the laminate. The material is usually available in a wide variety of sizes, and a sketch can help in planning the best sizes to purchase for minimizing waste.

When it comes to picking your adhesive, a user-friendly water-based contact adhesive is the best choice.

Countertop Facelift was written by Neal Barrett with illustrations by George Retseck.

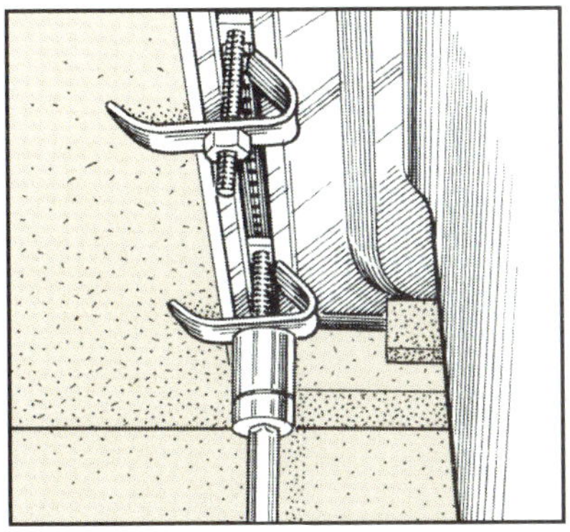

3 Remove the clips that hold the sink to the countertop, using either a screwdriver or nut driver, depending on fastener.

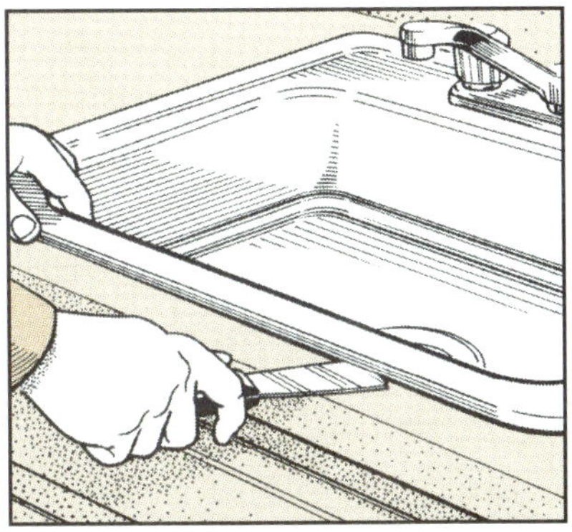

4 Most sinks are set in a bead of caulk or putty. To loosen the bond, carefully work a putty knife around the rim of the sink.

5 Lift the sink from the countertop and store it in a safe place where the pipes and fittings will not be damaged.

6 Begin by sanding the entire countertop with 120-grit paper. This rough surface lets the contact adhesive hold better.

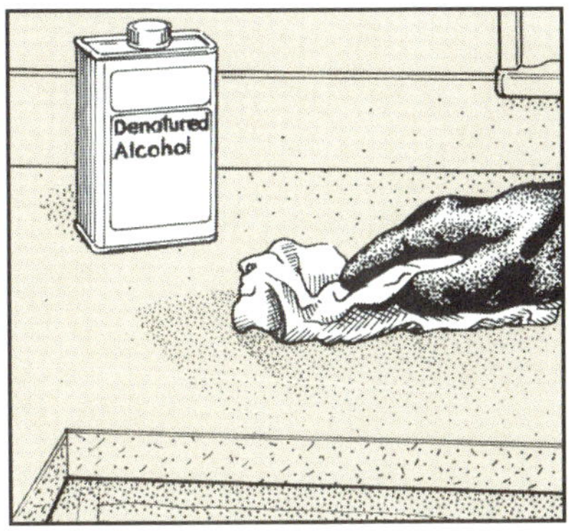

7 Brush away sanding dust, then wipe all surfaces with denatured alcohol to remove any grease or other contaminants.

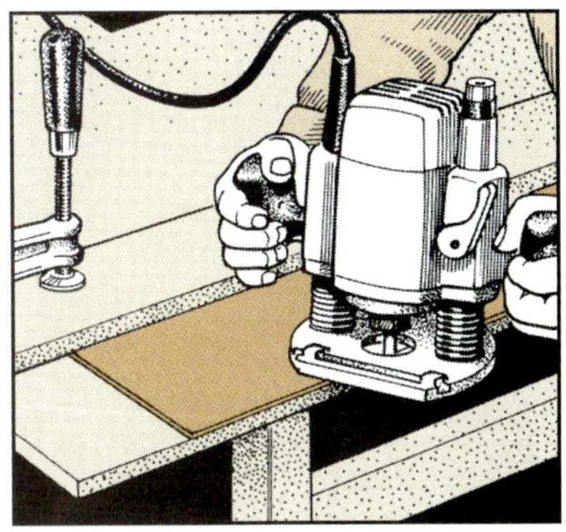

8 Use a router and a flush trimming bit to make any seam cuts on the laminate. Be sure to clamp the stock to a straightedge.

Getting Started

The first step in preparing the countertop is to remove the sink. Use the local shutoffs to turn off the water to the sink, then loosen the nut on each shutoff that holds the sink supply lines (Fig. 1). Loosen the slip nut that holds the sink tailpiece to the trap (Fig. 2), and remove all the clips that fasten the sink to the countertop (Fig. 3). Most sinks are set in a bead of plumber's putty or caulk. To loosen the bond of this setting medium, carefully run a flat putty knife between the sink rim and the countertop surface (Fig. 4). When the sink is loose, lift it from the counter and store it in a safe spot with all the applicable hardware (Fig. 5). Stuff a rag into the open end of the drain trap and cover the open ends of the sink supply lines to keep them clean while you work.

Next, check the entire counter surface for any holes, pits or cracks and fill them with auto-body filler. When dry, sand these patches flush with the surface, then lightly sand the entire counter surface with 120- or 150-grit sandpaper (Fig. 6). Thoroughly remove all sanding dust from the counter, then wipe the surface with denatured alcohol to remove any residual oils, soaps or other contaminants (Fig. 7).

Lay out the sizes of your countertop pieces on the laminate material, allowing an overhang of $^1/_2$ in. on all edges. There are several methods for cutting plastic laminate, but the most practical in this instance is to use a sabre saw fitted with a fine-tooth blade, like a metal-cutting blade. Support the laminate well on both sides of the cut and proceed slowly. A small amount of chipping near the blade is normal.

If your countertop requires a seam, the pieces must be cut perfectly straight. The preferred method of doing this is with a router and a ball-bearing flush trimming bit. Securely clamp the laminate to a piece of plywood or flakeboard that has a straight edge. Make sure the laminate overhangs the edge by about $^1/_8$ inch. Then use the router to flush trim the laminate to the edge (Fig. 8). Trim the mating piece in the same manner to yield a nice, tight joint.

After cutting the joints, place the pieces together to check for fit. If there are any small gaps, you can use a mill file to gently remove material for the tightest possible fit. Then, lay the laminate on the countertop in its desired position and trace the joint line directly onto the old counter (Fig. 9). This line serves as a guide for the laminate after the adhesive is applied.

The next step is to spread the adhesive on both the laminate and the countertop. Most adhesives can be spread with either a brush or a roller. Generally speaking, a roller is the faster method, and the one

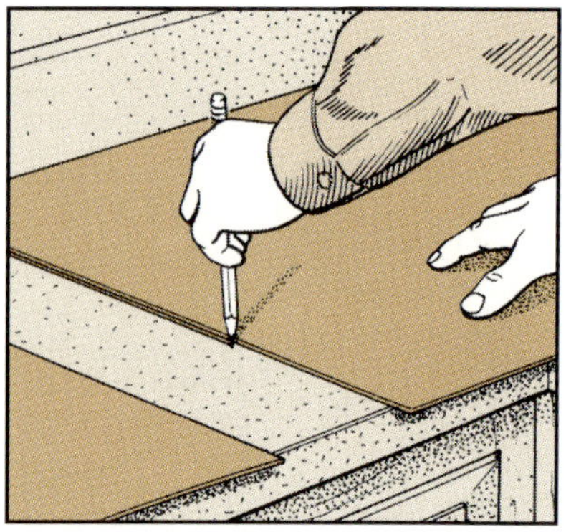

9 Before applying any adhesive, lay the laminate in place and mark any seam lines directly onto the countertop.

10 Pour out the contact cement on the counter and spread it evenly with a roller made especially for contact cement.

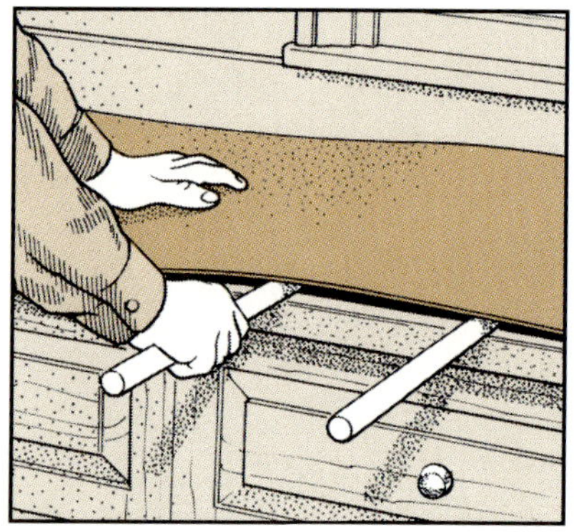

11 To perfectly position the laminate, support the piece on a series of 1-in.-dia. dowels spaced 12 to 16 in. apart.

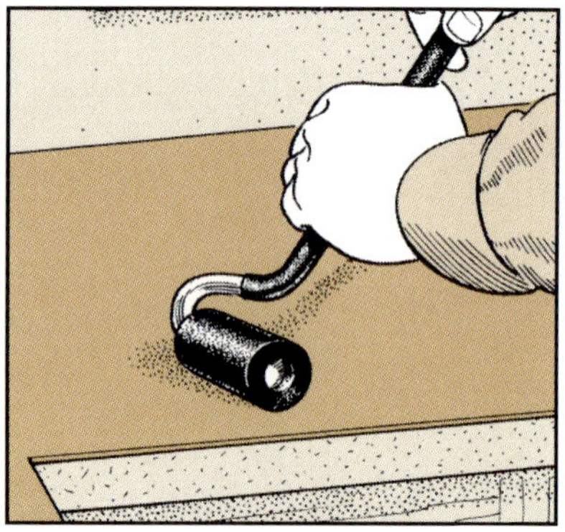

12 Roll the entire surface to ensure a good bond with the old counter, using a rubber J-roller or pastry rolling pin.

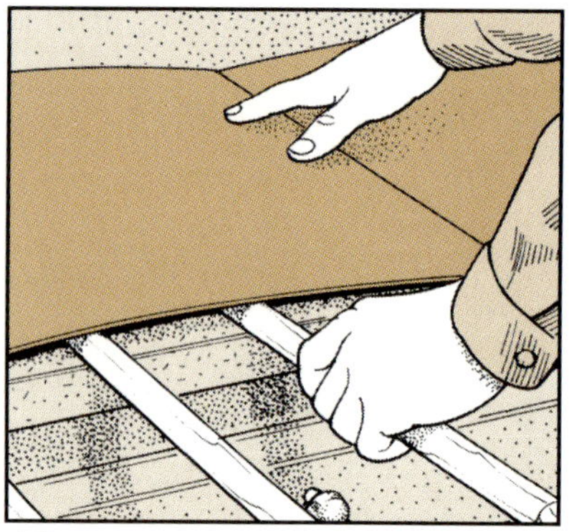

13 When installing the second piece of a laminate, always position the seam edge first. Then remove the closest dowel.

14 Use a router with flush trimming bit to carefully cut off the overhanging laminate on all the exposed edges.

that gives the most even coverage. There are special roller covers sold just for contact cement. They have a nubby, carpetlike appearance and are sold in paint stores and home centers.

Lay the laminate, bottom side up, on a large, flat surface that has been covered with old newspapers or plastic sheeting. Pour a small amount of contact cement onto the laminate and spread it with the roller. Continue in this way until all of the laminate is covered with adhesive. Next, move to the countertop and spread the adhesive there using the same technique (Fig. 10).

Contact adhesive must be allowed to dry until it no longer feels sticky when touched with your finger. Under most circumstances, this takes about 30 minutes. When the adhesive is dry, you can install the laminate.

Installing Laminate

Since the adhesive bonds instantly when the laminate touches the counter, you must have a way of positioning the material without allowing the two surfaces to touch. To do this, use a series of 1-in.-dia. dowels, spaced 12 to 16 in. apart along the length of the counter. Since the adhesive is dry, the dowels can be placed between the counter and laminate without sticking—and they allow careful placement of the laminate over the counter without any contact between the two.

Carefully position the first piece of laminate using the seam mark as a guide. Then, beginning at one end, remove one dowel at a time to bring the laminate onto the counter (Fig. 11). Lightly smooth the laminate with your hand as you remove the dowels to avoid trapping any air and creating bubbles. Use a rubber roller (a rolling pin can substitute) to roll over the entire surface and ensure a good bond (Fig. 12). Move on to the next piece of laminate, again using the dowels to position the piece. Pay extra attention to the alignment of the pieces at the joint. Be sure to first remove the dowel closest to the joint, then work your way back from there (Fig. 13). Again, roll the piece to provide a complete bond.

Use the router with a flush trimming bit to trim the laminate flush with the countertop edge (Fig. 14). At those points where the countertop returns to the wall, and the router cannot reach all the way into the corner, use a mill file to trim it flush.

Drill an access hole of approximately 1 in. dia. in the sink cutout for entry of the router bit. Then use the router to flush trim the laminate in the cutout area (Fig. 15). Use a mill file again to trim the laminate against the back side of the cutout if the router cannot reach all the way to the edge. Also use the file to trim inside the corners where two pieces of laminate meet (Fig. 16).

15 Drill an access hole inside the sink cutout area. Then use the router to trim the waste flush to the edge of the cutout.

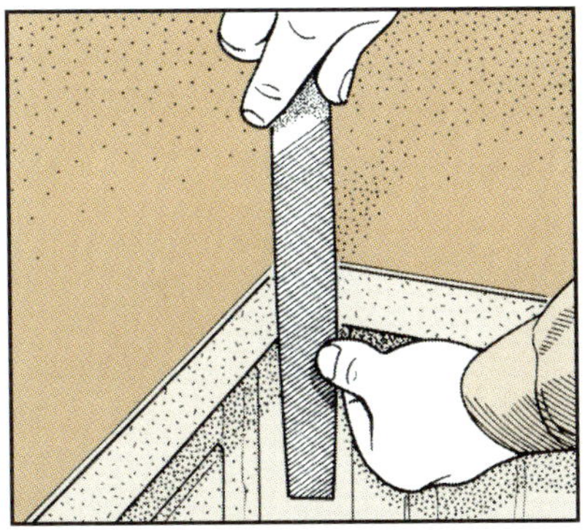

16 Use a mill file to square the inside corners of the countertop edges. Keep the file perpendicular to the counter.

17 Apply laminate to strips of 1/4-in.-thick hardboard to create the new backsplash. Trim the edges flush with a router.

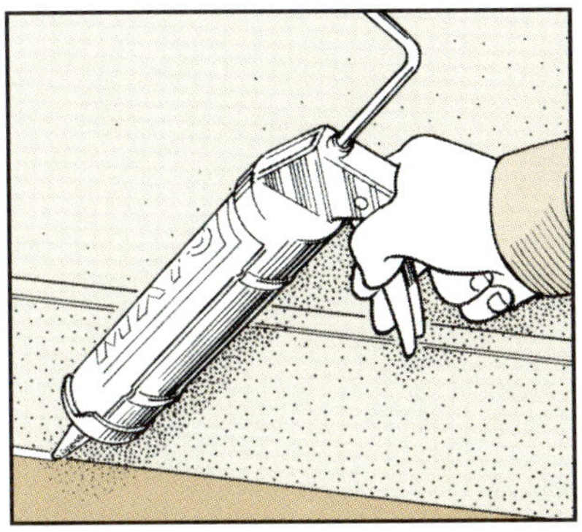

18 Apply clear silicone caulk to the back of the new backsplash and to the counter where the new backsplash will be placed.

19 Push the new backsplash onto the old and hold it in place with clamps made from scrap plywood and spring clamps.

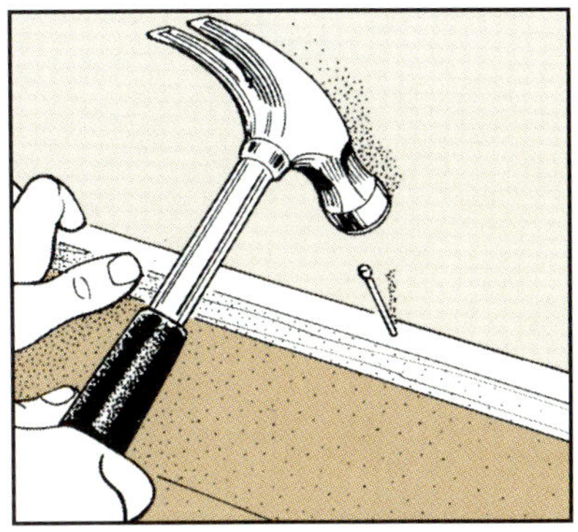

20 Cut strips of hardwood to use as backsplash caps. Then bore pilot holes and attach the caps with 8d finishing nails.

21 Attach hardwood edging to the front of all the countertops with finishing nails. Set nailheads and fill holes with wood filler.

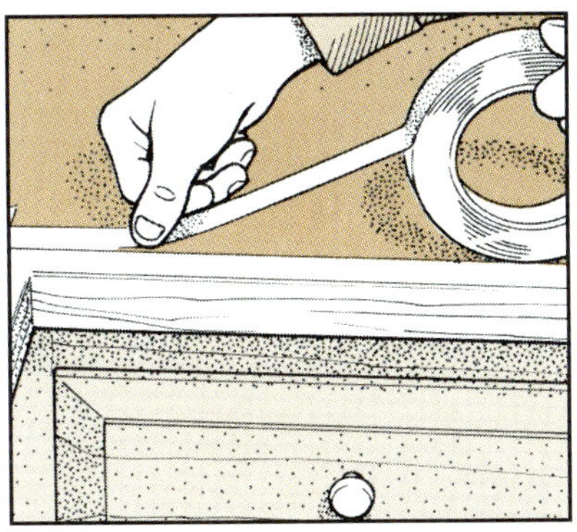

22 Before applying a finish to the hardwood edging—or backsplash caps—protect the laminate with masking tape.

23 For the best protection, apply three to four coats of polyurethane to the edging and caps before using your countertop.

Cut strips of 1/4-in.-thick hardboard to width for the backsplash. If you wish, you can leave these at rough length at this point, and trim them to finished length after lamination. Cut your strips of laminate to overhang the hardboard by 1/2 in. on all sides. Apply the contact cement to all parts, then trim the strips to finished length using a miter box or table saw.

To apply the strips to the backsplash, use clear silicone adhesive. The silicone can also be used to seal the joint between the backsplash and the countertop. Run a small bead of silicone along the back edge of the countertop, then apply a wavy bead along the backsplash (Fig. 18). Position the strip, then use some homemade clamping jigs to temporarily hold the strip in place until the silicone sets (Fig. 19).

Trimwork

Rip strips of 3/4-in.-thick hardwood to width for the countertop edging and backsplash cap. Drill pilot holes for No. 8d finishing nails (5/64 in. dia. is ideal) and nail the strip to the edge (Fig. 20). Use a nailset to drive the nails below the wood surface and fill with matching wood filler (Fig. 21). Carefully sand the filler when dry. To finish these strips, first protect the adjacent laminate surfaces with masking tape (Fig. 22). Brush on three coats of polyurethane (Fig. 23).

1 First, remove all broken glass from the sash. Note: Wear heavy-duty work gloves and safety goggles for protection.

2 If the old putty is hard and diffficult to remove, you can soften it by gentle heating with a hair dryer or heat gun.

Glass Replacement was written by Rosario Capotosto. Illustrations by George Retseck.

Glass replacement

Like many other jobs, repairing broken glass is simply a matter of following a few basic procedures. You'll find everything you need at your corner hardware store.

The following techniques cover most of the window types found in homes: single-glazed wood sash, insulated double-glazed wood sash and steel-casement and sliding aluminum sash windows.

Very often, the glass must be replaced from the exterior side of the window. If your job is within easy reach, you can replace the glass with the window in place. For hard-to-reach windows, however, it's safer to remove the entire sash.

Single-Glazed Wood Sash

For the single-glazed wood sash, the standard window in most homes, the glass must be replaced on the exterior side.

If the pane is merely cracked, start the job by removing the putty or glazing compound. But if the pane is broken, be sure to wear goggles and heavy-duty gloves and remove the shards carefully (Fig. 1). If standard putty was used, it'll probably be rock hard. Soften the putty with a heat gun set at a low temperature. Keep the gun moving to avoid scorching the wood or cracking any of the adjacent panes (Fig. 2).

Then, remove the softened putty with a putty knife (Fig. 3). When the wood frame is relatively clean, use needle-nose pliers to pull out the old glazier's points.

After the putty, points and remaining chips of glass have been removed, scrape the sash down to bare wood with a chisel held perpendicularly to the wood surface (Fig. 4).

Next, seal the bare wood with linseed oil, thinned exterior house paint or primer (Fig. 5). Allow this coat to dry completely. Then, to determine the exact

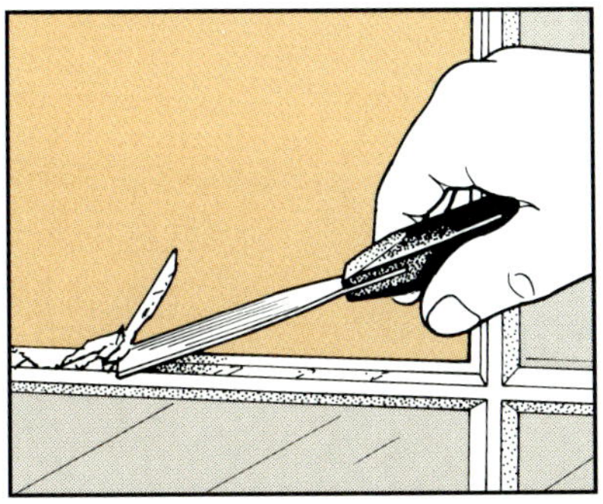

3 Use a putty knife to clean out the old putty or glazing compound. Be careful to avoid cutting into the wood frame.

4 After the glazier's points are removed, scrape the sash down to bare wood using a perpendicularly held chisel.

5 Coat the bare wood with linseed oil, thinned exterior house paint or primer to seal it. Then, let the sealer coat dry.

6 Use a straightedge and glasscutter to cut the glass. Lubricate the cutter wheel and score the glass with only one pass.

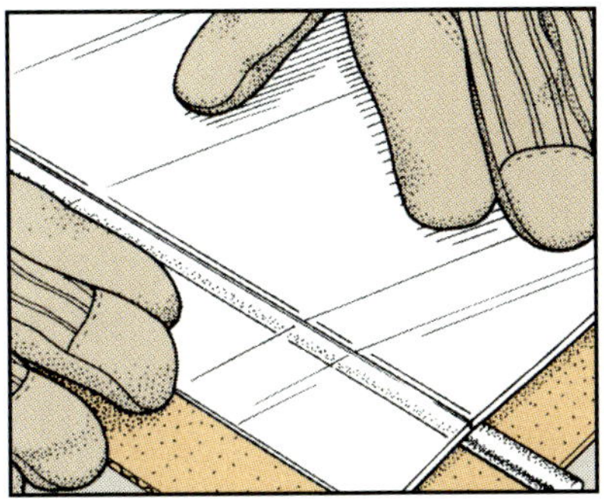

7 Place the score line over a dowel and apply pressure on both sides of the glass. This will snap the two pieces apart.

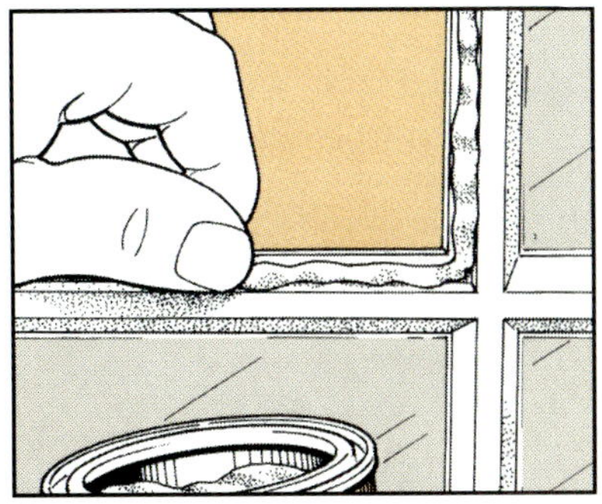

8 Lay a small bead of glazing compound around the inside face of the sash rabbet to both cushion and seal the glass.

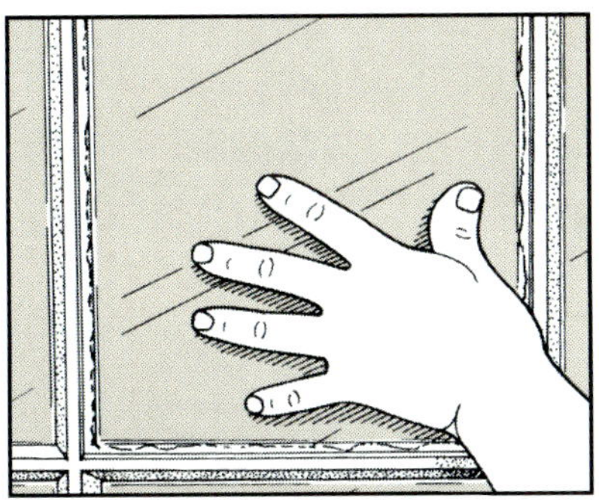

9 Place the new pane of glass in position and then press it evenly all around to achieve a tight, gap-free seal.

10 Using the tip of a putty knife, position the glazier's points against the glass and then press them into the wood.

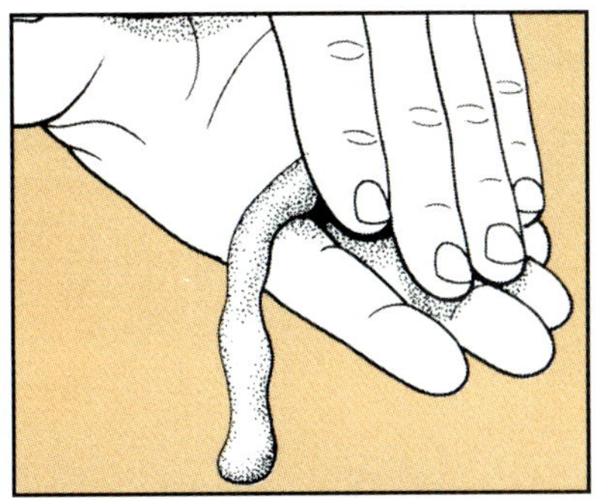

11 Glazing compound is much faster to work than putty. Shape it into a rope by rolling it between your palms.

size of the replacement pane, measure the opening and subtract $^{1}/_{8}$ in. from each dimension.

To cut glass to size, place the glass on a firm surface, padded with cardboard or newspaper. Use a felt-tipped pen to make the cutting-line marks on the glass. Then, lubricate the cutting wheel of the glass cutter with kerosene or a light spray lubricant. Align a straightedge with the cutting line. Hold the cutter between your index and middle fingers, backed by your thumb. Place the cutter wheel about $^{1}/_{8}$ in. from the far edge of the glass and draw the cutter toward you in a single, firm stroke (Fig. 6). Place a dowel under the score line and press down on the glass in order to make a clean break (Fig. 7).

Once the glass has been cut, apply a thin bead of glazing compound along the inside face of the sash rabbet to provide a cushion and seal for the glass (Fig. 8). Smooth the compound with a putty knife and press the glass firmly into the opening (Fig. 9).

Next, install glazier's points against the glass. Press the points into the wood with a putty knife (Fig. 10).

Roll some of the compound between your palms to form a rope shape approximately $^{3}/_{8}$ in. in diameter (Fig. 11). Lay the compound along the edges of the pane and press it firmly in place with your thumb (Fig. 12). Smooth the compound with a putty knife. Hold the knife at an angle and draw it along the compound to form a neat, triangular bead (Fig. 13).

Let the compound cure for about one week before painting it. Allow the paint to overlap the glass pane by about $^{1}/_{8}$ in.—this will provide a good seal between the compound and the glass (Fig. 14).

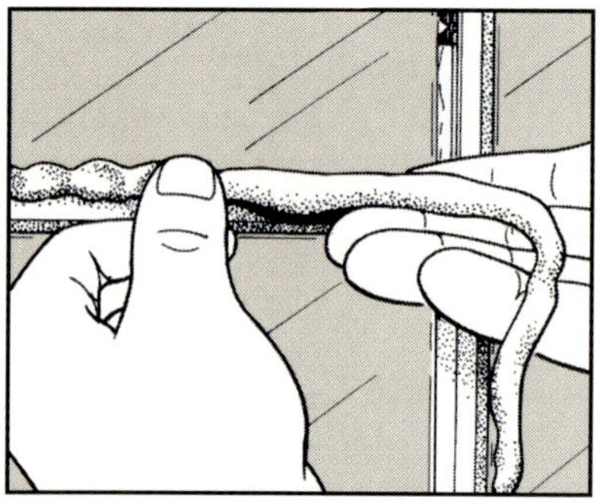

12 Apply the rolled-out glazing compound over the glazier's points and press it firmly against both glass and sash.

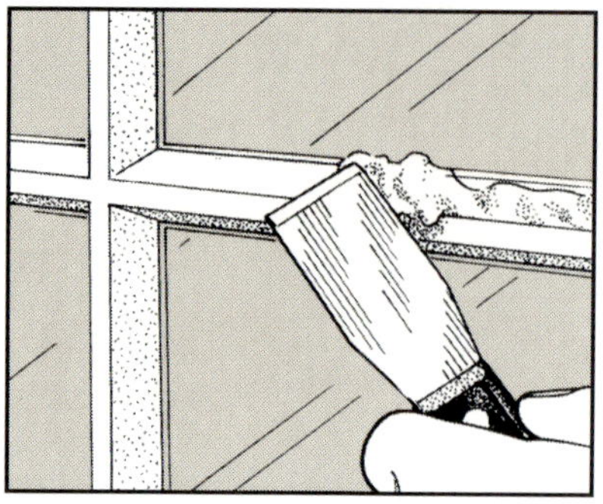

13 Hold the putty knife at an angle as you draw it across the compound to create a neat, triagular 45° bevel.

14 Let the compound cure for about one week before painting. Extend the paint onto the glass to further seal the joint.

Double-Glazed Wooden Sash

A double-glazed pane is typically a factory-sealed unit that consists of two panes separated by a metal spacer. If the pane is installed with compound, replace it by using the technique described for single-glazed windows. The replacement double-glazed pane, however, must be obtained from the window manufacturer.

If your window panes aren't bedded with compound, chances are they're held in place with wood strips that are nailed or stapled to the inside of the sash.

Begin by prying away the wood strips with a putty knife (Fig. 15). Avoid damaging the strips—you'll want to use them again.

After the strips have been removed, use a utility knife to cut between the glass and the silicone caulk that seals the glass on the outside of the window. Have a helper stand inside to catch the glass as it falls from the sash (Fig. 16). Then, with a utility knife or chisel, scrape away the old silicone (Fig. 17).

To install a new pane, first place a $^1/_4$-in. bead of nonlatex, nonacrylic silicone sealant around the face of the sash rabbet (Fig. 18). Push the glass in place with equal pressure all around so the silicone squeezes out around the edges (Fig. 19).

Install and nail the wood retaining strips, making sure not to nail too close to the glass. Use a piece of cardboard to protect the glass (Fig. 20). Next, trim any excess silicone with a utility knife, leaving a $^1/_8$-in. bead around the perimeter.

15 Use a putty knife to pry out the wood strips that hold the double pane. Be careful not to damage the wood.

16 After cutting the seal between the pane and wood, press glass away from the frame. Helper inside catches the pane.

17 With a chisel, scrape any remaining sealant from the frame. Hold the tool so that it's perpendicular to the surface.

18 Begin installing the new double-glazed pane by applying a fresh bead of silicone sealant around the wood frame.

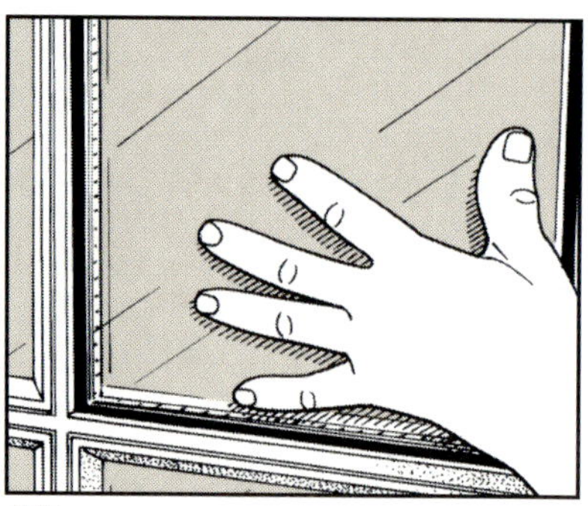

19 Press the new pane into the sash. Apply even pressure to seat it firmly and allow excess silicone to squeeze out.

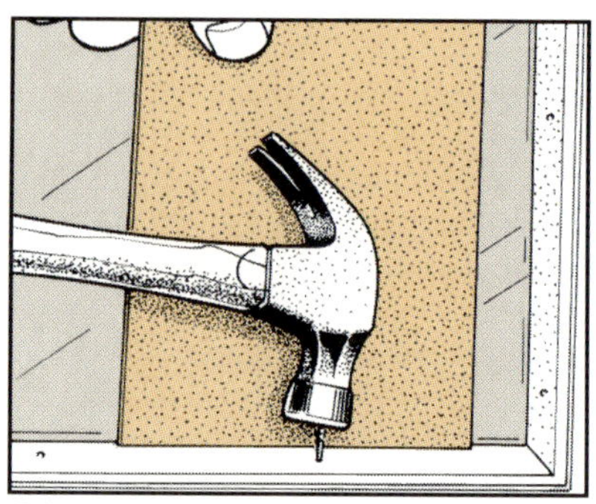

20 To renail the wood strips, place cardboard against the glass for protection and then slide the hammer along.

21 After removing broken glass, putty and clips, use sandpaper to remove rust on the metal frame. Prime bare spots.

22 Lay a thin bead of compound around the frame and insert the glass. Press the glass firmly into the compound.

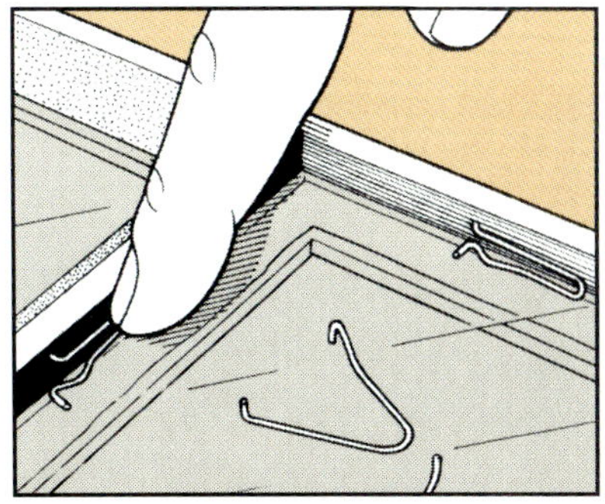

23 Insert the spring clips into holes in the sash. Then, apply and trim the compound as described for wood sashes.

Steel-Casement Window

If you're replacing glass of a vintage metal sash in which the pane is set in compound or putty, the procedure is the same one as described for the single-glazed wood sash. Instead of glazier's points, however, you'll find spring clips holding the pane in place.

First, remove all broken glass, chip out the putty or compound, and then carefully pull out the spring clips with a screwdriver or pliers. Use sandpaper to clean away any rust or loose paint on the frame (Fig. 21).

Cover bare spots with metal primer, followed by a coat of paint. When the paint is dry, lay a cushion bed of compound along the frame, then position the new pane in place. Press the pane gently and uniformly until the compound squeezes out evenly to the edge of the frame (Fig. 22).

Insert spring clips into the holes in the sash to secure the glass (Fig. 23). Then, pack compound evenly around the frame and bevel it to a triangular bead with a putty knife.

24 Pull the vinyl sealing spline from aluminum sash. Insert a knife at one corner in order to pry up end of spline.

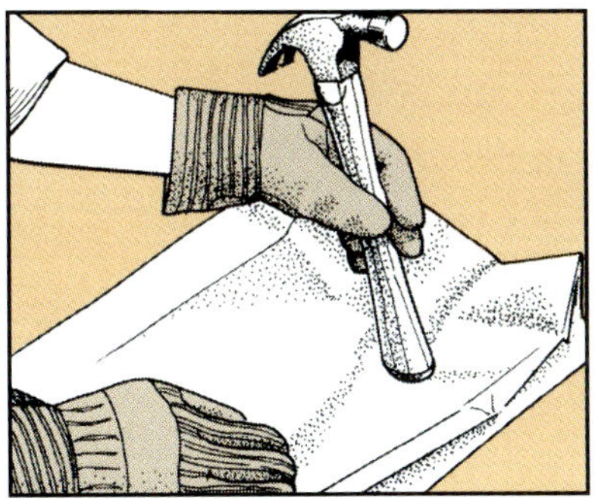

25 If the glass isn't free, wrap the sash with newspaper and gently tap around the perimeter to break the cement seal.

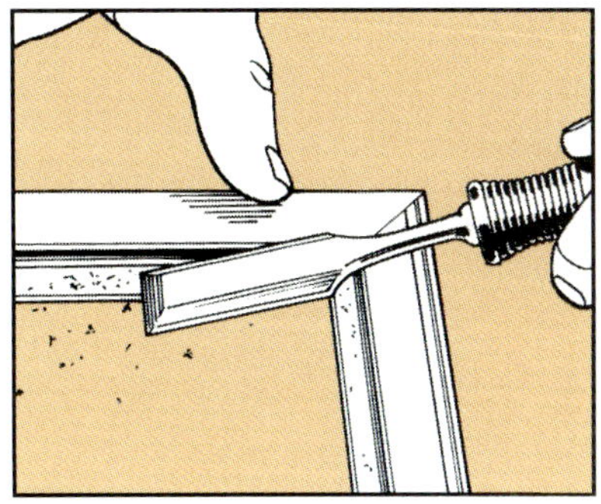

26 Use a chisel to scrape off any traces of the old cement. Then, finish cleaning the surface with an abrasive pad.

Sliding Aluminum Sash

In the most common type of aluminum sash, the glass is held in place with a bead of cement and a vinyl spline. To replace the pane, first lift the sash out of the window frame, then pry out the spline using a knife to get a start at the corner (Fig. 24).

If the pane remains cemented to the frame, wrap some newspaper around the sash and gently tap to break the glass free (Fig. 25). Use a sharp chisel and an abrasive pad to remove all traces of cement and thoroughly clean the sash (Fig. 26).

Buy or cut a piece of glass that's the same thickness as the original. Cut the glass about $^{1}/_{16}$ in. less than the opening. Apply a thin bead of Duco household cement to the frame, then lay in the glass (Fig. 27).

27 Apply a thin bead of cement around the ledge of the window frame. Then, lay the glass in place and press to seal.

28 Replace the vinyl spline by pressing it with a small block of wood. Miter the ends of the new spline to fit corners.

To replace the four spline pieces, start at one corner and press the spline in with your thumb. Then, use a $^{1}/_{4}$×2×8-in. strip of plywood to work the spline under the lip of the frame (Fig. 28).

1 To prepare for acid etching, first remove oil and dust from glass by wiping with alcohol. Then, allow to dry.

2 Peel backing from stencil material and apply to glass. Apply vinyl slowly while smoothing out bubbles and wrinkles.

Etching glass

If you've ever stopped to admire an etched-glass door, window or mirror, you know the effect is both unique and stunning. The combination of clear polished glass with a delicately contrasting frosted geometric or pictorial design enhances just about any setting. What you may not know, however, is that you can etch glass right in your own home or shop with a few simple, easy-to-master techniques.

When choosing glass to etch, keep in mind that the best material to work with is 1/4-in.-thick plate glass or laminated safety glass. Standard 1/8-in.-thick window glass can be used, but the results will not be as good. Thinner glass is more likely to break when placed under the mechanical stresses of diamond-burr

Etching Glass was written by Neal Barrett with illustrations by George Retseck. Dover publications (180 Varick St., New York, NY 10014) offers a variety of books on period and cultural designs in the Dover Pictorial Archive Series. The Woodworkers' Store (21801 Industrial Blvd., Rogers MN 55374) sells a kit—No. 68544, that includes all the supplies you need to begin etching including cream, cleaner, brush, gloves and predesigned stencils. For those who prefer to work with their own designs, individual supplies are available from art suppliers and local stained-glass studios or through the mail from Sunshine Glassworks, Ltd., 240 French Rd., Buffalo, NY 14227. You will need etching cream, an acid-resist stencil material, a disposable brush, heavy rubber gloves and eye protection. For sandblasting, a 4-mil sandblast resist is available from Sunshine Glassworks in 12-in. squares and rolls. The most readily available tools for diamond burr etching are made by Dremel and Foredom and sold through woodworking and carving supply dealers. The sewing pattern tracing paper used here was Dritz Trace-B-Gone tracing paper which is sold in fabric stores.

3 With your drawing taped in place and carbon paper underneath, trace your pattern with a sharp pencil.

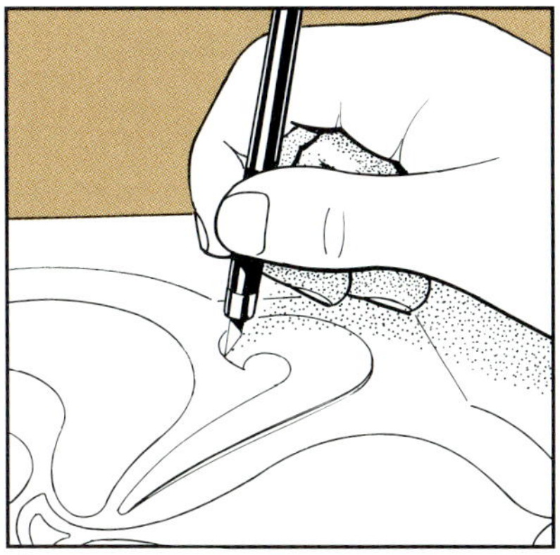

4 Use a sharp razor knife to cut the stencil. A swivel-blade knife is best for patterns that have many curved lines.

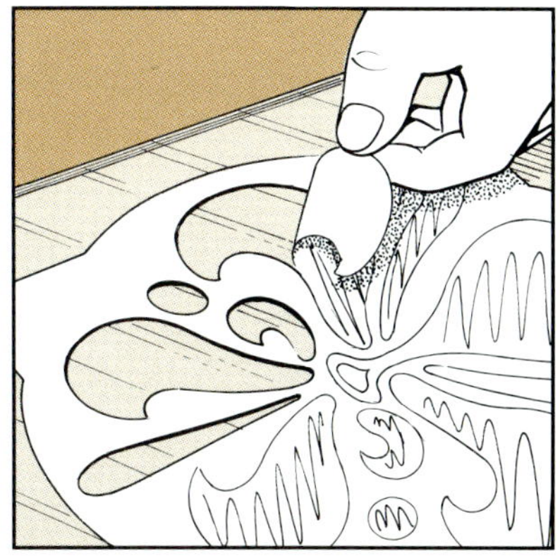

5 Carefully peel away the stencil in the areas to be etched. Examine the cuts and fix any wavy lines or ragged edges.

6 With newspaper or a plastic sheet under the work, apply acid cream to the glass and let it stand for 10 minutes.

7 Rinse away the cream with plenty of cold water. Don't rinse into a porcelain sink, to avoid etching the sink's surface.

8 After etching and rinsing, remove the stencil to reveal the finished pattern. Then, clean the surface with glass cleaner.

engraving and sandblasting. If you wish to work with $^1/_8$-in. glass, the best technique is acid etching.

The only type of glass that should not be etched is tempered glass. Tempered glass has been heat treated in a way that creates great tension within the material. When the surface is etched, the internal stresses may cause the glass to shatter. Generally, tempered glass is labeled as such in a corner of the pane.

If you are planning to etch a door or window with double-glazed panes, you should check with the window manufacturer to see if you will void any warranty by etching. In this case, it might be better to etch another panel and mount it over the insulated pane.

While you're in the planning stage, consider whether the lines and areas you draw will be etched into the glass surface or whether the background will be etched and the design left clear. Often the ultimate use of the panel will be the deciding factor in this regard. When the design is to serve as a decorative embellishment on a window or mirror, the design itself is etched to maintain broad transparent areas. For increased privacy, however, etch the background and leave the design in clear glass. Experimentation is the best way to decide which results you want to achieve.

Acid-cream Etching

This technique uses an acid to erode the surface of the glass. Because it requires little in the way of special tools, the process provides a relatively inexpensive option for etching glass. The acid is a dilute form of hydrofluoric acid in a cream-like consistency. It's brushed on the surface of the glass over a vinyl stencil, then washed off to reveal the etched pattern. While this technique is the easiest and least expensive, it's also the most limited in the results that can be achieved—diamond-burr engraving and sandblasting both offer more control over the depth and texture of the etching.

Begin by thoroughly cleaning the glass surface with denatured alcohol (Fig. 1). Peel about 1 in. of the backing paper from the vinyl stencil material and carefully adhere this edge to the glass in the desired area. Slowly pull the backing off the vinyl while you smooth the vinyl to the glass with the other hand (Fig. 2).

Be sure to eliminate any bubbles or wrinkles in the stencil material as you go. The vinyl should extend beyond your intended design area at least 2 to 3 in. in all directions to adequately protect the glass. If you are working on a panel within a wood or metal frame, protect the frame from contact with the acid cream.

9 Apply the sandblasting stencil material to the glass and use a plastic squeegee to ensure a good contact.

10 Place carbon paper under your drawing, and transfer the design to the stencil material with a sharp pencil.

11 Use a sharp razor knife to cut the stencil material to the lines. Then peel away the areas to be sandblasted.

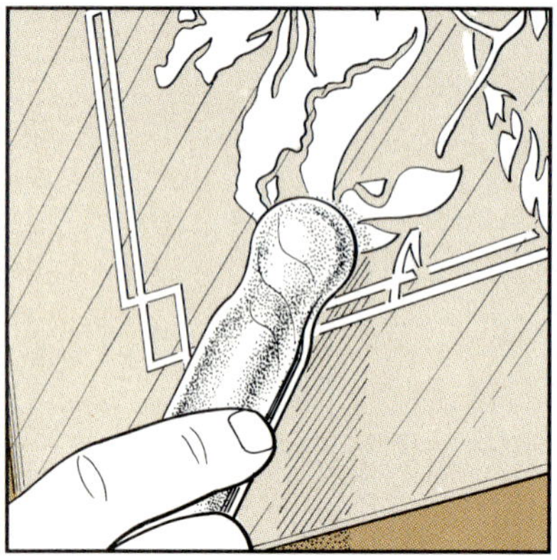

12 Check that the stencil makes good contact with the glass. Use rounded screwdriver handle to press edges to glass.

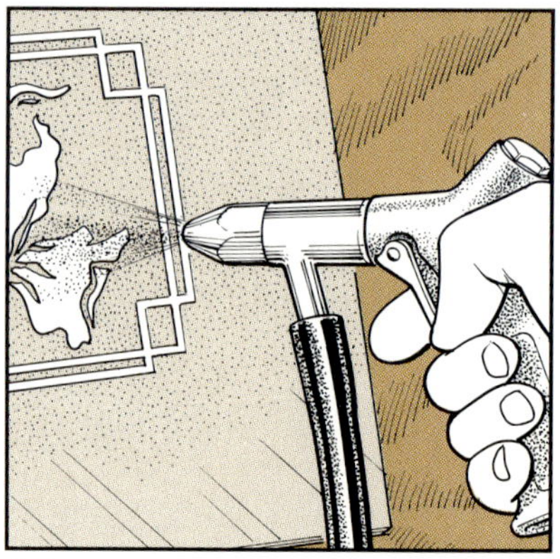

13 Prop up the work and make a series of overlapping passes with the sandblaster. Wear a respirator and goggles.

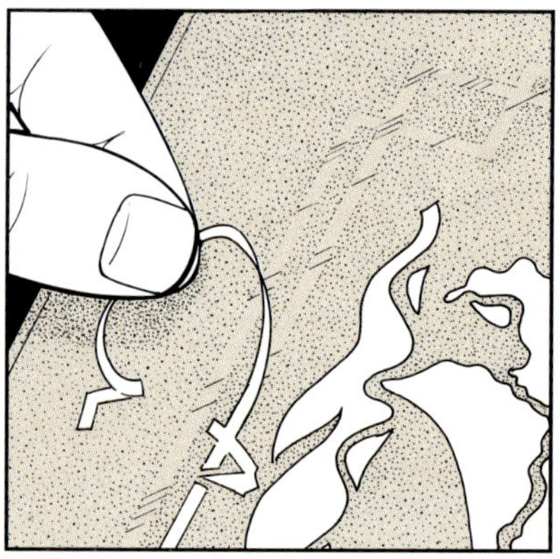

14 When you're satisfied with the results, remove the remaining stencil material and clean the glass surface.

Use masking tape to fasten your full-size drawing to the glass, with carbon paper (carbon side down) between the drawing and the stencil material. Carefully trace your pattern with a sharp pencil to transfer it to the stencil (Fig. 3).

The best way to cut the stencil is with a sharp razor knife. When your design incorporates straight lines, use a straightedge to guide the knife. For designs that involve many curved lines, the best tool is a swivel-blade razor knife. These knives, available at most art supply stores, allow you to change the direction of the cut without rotating the knife, resulting in a smoother edge (Fig. 4).

After you have cut the stencil, carefully remove the resist material in the areas that are to be etched. Examine the stencil and make any adjustments to fix wavy or ragged edges (Fig. 5).

Place several layers of newspaper or a polyethylene sheet under the work to protect your worktable, and be sure to wear heavy rubber gloves and eye protection when you work with the acid cream.

Use a brush to apply a thick coat of cream on the exposed glass surface, lapping it about $^1/_2$ in. over the cutout stencil edges. Brush the cream over the glass in several directions to ensure complete coverage of the design (Fig. 6). Leave the cream on the glass for about 10 minutes, then wash it off with plenty of cold water. Do not rinse into a porcelain sink as the acid may etch the sink's surface. Instead, wash the cream into a large plastic basin first, diluting it with lots of water (Fig. 7). If possible, use a hose to wash off the cream outdoors.

Examine the design to be sure the etching is even and complete, and reapply the cream if necessary. When you are satisfied with your results, peel off the resist material and clean the panel with glass cleaner (Fig. 8).

Sandblasting

If you already own an air compressor, you're well on your way to having the equipment you need to etch glass by sandblasting. You also need a sandblaster—a spray-gun-type tool that uses compressed air to drive the abrasive particles under pressure. Tool dealers that sell air compressors usually carry sandblasters as well. If you'd rather not buy the equipment, it's usually available through rental outlets for use on a short-term basis.

The blasting medium used for glass etching is either silicon carbide or aluminum oxide. Different textures can be achieved by using either finer or coarser grits. These materials should be available where you buy or rent the sandblaster.

In its preparatory stages, the technique of sandblasting glass has much in common with the acid-etch method. The method of preparing the glass panel is almost identical, although the resist medium is different.

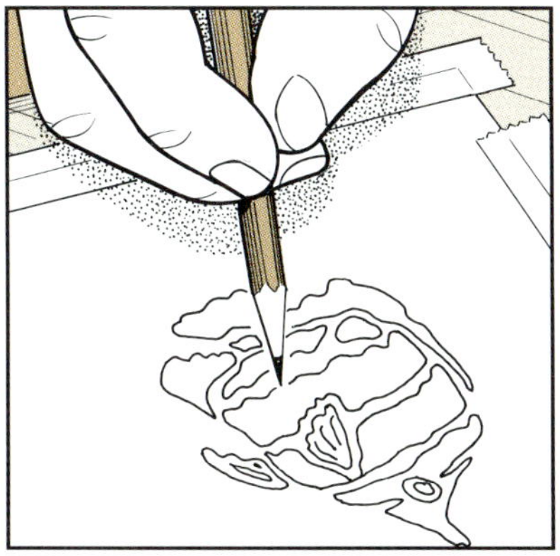

15 After taping your design over the wax transfer paper, trace your pattern carefully to mark the glass.

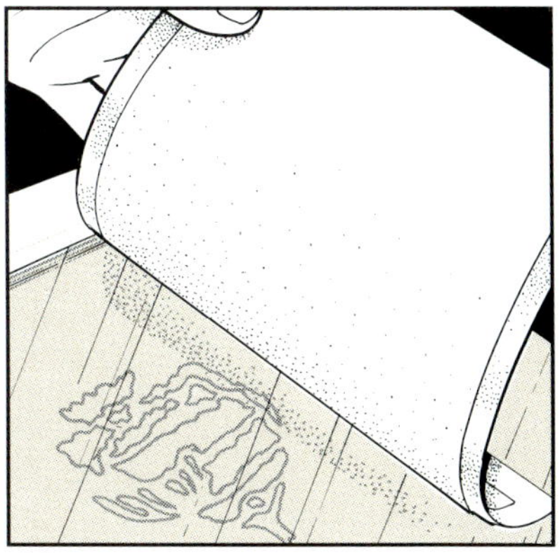

16 With the pattern attached at one edge, examine the tracing. Check for missing or incomplete lines.

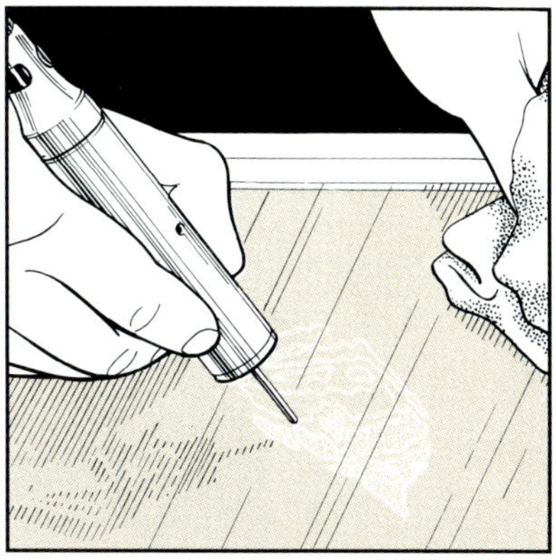

17 Use a flexible-shaft tool with a diamond burr to engrave the design. Be careful not to smudge the wax lines.

Apply the resist to the glass in the same manner as described for the acid technique. Here, though, it is even more important to eliminate any bubbles in the material. Use a plastic squeegee to smooth the resist onto the glass as it is applied (Fig. 9). If any bubbles remain, the sandblasting material could tear the resist at those points, ruining the design.

Using carbon paper, trace your design onto the stencil material (Fig. 10). Then, use a razor knife to cut to the lines and remove the stencil material in the areas that are to be etched (Fig. 11). Use the rounded end of a screwdriver handle or a similar hard, smooth tool to press the stencil along the pattern lines to ensure good contact (Fig. 12).

Sandblasting offers the possibility of quite varied and interesting techniques, such as shading, texture variation, and multilevel etching. For the beginner, however, a single-level etching is an appropriate place to start.

Sandblasting is, by its very nature, a messy process, and professionals generally use specially designed cabinets to control the dust and recover the blast media. A viable alternative is to work outdoors with a heavy dropcloth behind the work to catch the dust.

It is extremely important that you use a good-quality respirator that fits properly. Goggles that completely protect your eyes are also necessary. The dust produced by the blasting process is hazardous if inhaled or allowed to contact the eyes, so these precautions are vital.

Again, if you are etching a design on a door or window pane, protect the frame from the blast stream, as the painted surface can be damaged by the abrasive particles.

To proceed with the blasting, prop your stencil-covered glass panel in front of the dropcloth. Holding the blasting gun about 4 to 6 in. from the glass, and with the compressor set at 30-psi to 40-psi pressure, make a series of passes over the glass. Begin at the top edge of the panel and overlap your blast pattern slightly with each pass to be sure that you cover the entire surface to be etched (Fig. 13). It is usually necessary to go over the entire panel several times to etch the surface evenly.

Wipe the dust off the glass, and carefully examine the panel to see if the etching is even and complete. Repeat the process if necessary. Then remove the resist material and clean up the glass (Fig. 14).

Diamond Burr Etching

The third technique for etching uses diamond burrs to engrave a pattern directly into the glass surface. The burr is driven by a flexible-shaft grinder. These units have a motor of 1/5 to 1/8 hp, connected by a flexible shaft to a handpiece which holds the burr. Diamond burrs come in a variety of sizes and configurations. The most useful shapes to start with were a conical-shaped and a ball-shaped tip, each about $^{5}/_{32}$ in. in diameter. The best shape to use depends on the design you are engraving.

The first step in this process is to transfer your design onto the glass surface. If you wish, you can draw directly onto the glass using a thin wax pencil. It's best, however, to make a full-size drawing first and then trace this onto the glass. To make the tracing, use a waxy tracing paper such as that used to transfer sewing patterns onto fabric. When you trace over this paper, a wax line is transferred to the glass. Tape your pattern to the glass panel with the transfer paper beneath, and trace the design with a sharp pencil (Fig. 15). Then, lift the paper to check that you have a clear pattern to follow (Fig. 16).

Wear a dust mask and eye protection when you engrave. Begin by using the edge of the conical diamond burr to engrave the outlines of your design into the glass surface. Note that the waxy image traced onto the glass is rather delicate, so you must be careful not to smudge the design as you work (Fig. 17).

After the outlines are cut into the glass, proceed to fill in the body of the design. At this point, use a sponge or rag to spread water over the glass surface as you work. The water both cools the cutting tip to prolong its life and keeps the glass dust from becoming airborne. The water makes it a little more difficult to see the engraved surface, so periodically wipe the surface dry to check your progress.

One of the nice features of this technique is that it gives you the ability to manipulate details of the design in terms of texture and depth of cut.

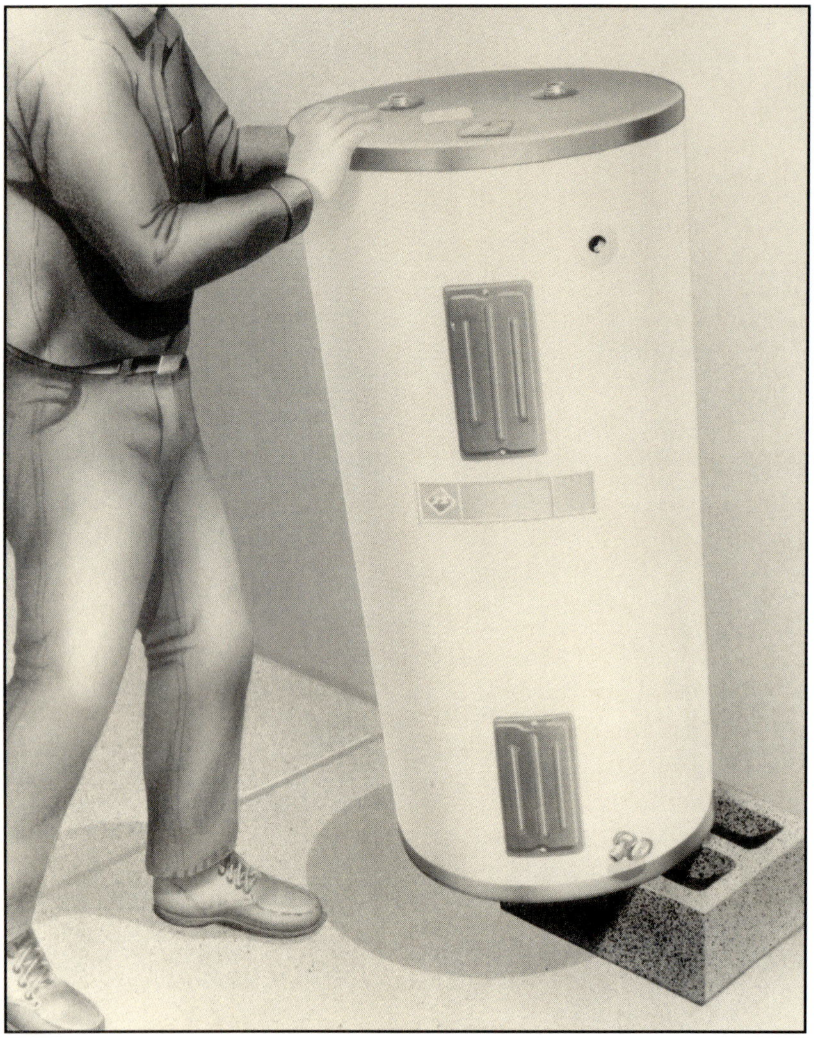

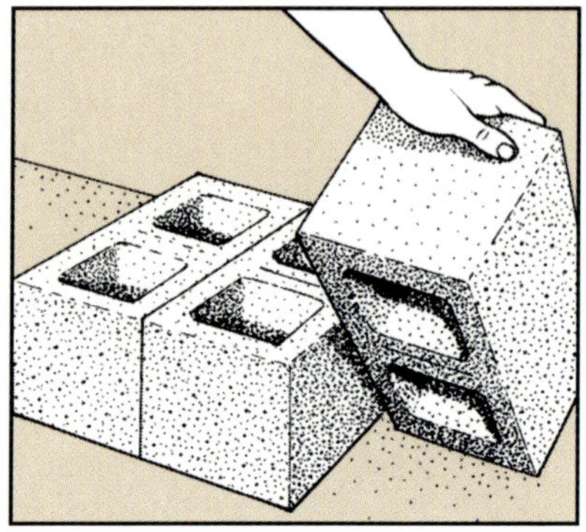

1 Create a platform for the tank on the floor using concrete blocks. This platform protects the tank from water damage .

2 Slide the tank onto the blocks and center it. Align the drain toward the front and make sure the tank doesn't rock.

Installing an Electric Water Heater was written by Steven Willson. Illustrations by George Retseck.

Installing an electric water heater

A water heater, especially an electric model, is a very simple device. Unheated water enters one side of the tank. The water is heated by a couple of electric resistance elements that extend from the side of the tank into the middle of the water. Then on demand the water exits the other side of the tank. Installing an electric water heater involves both plumbing and electrical work.

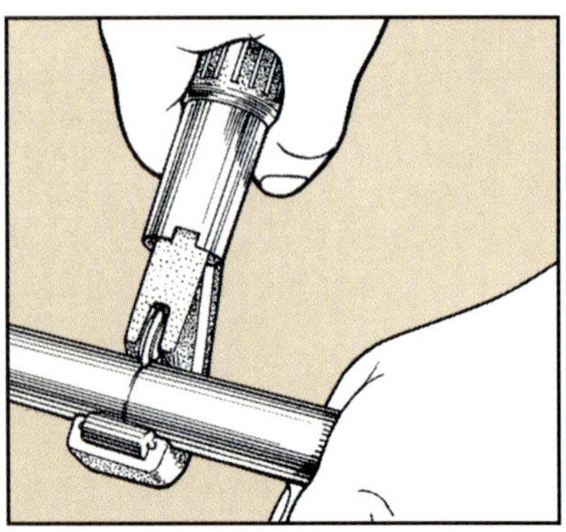

3 Begin installing the cold water copper tubing by cutting a piece to length. Use a standard tubing cutter for the cut.

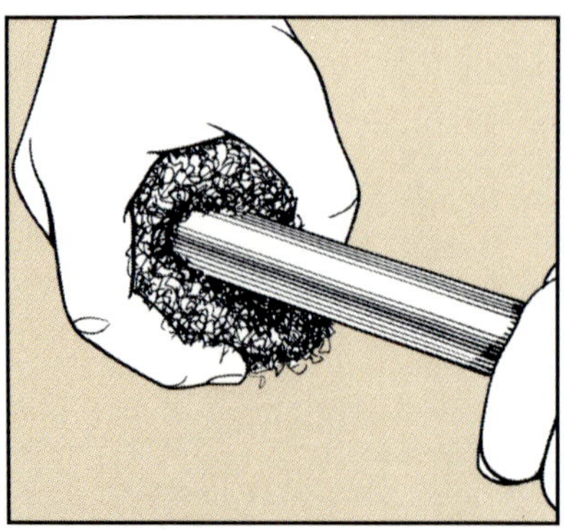

4 Once the tubing is cut, clean the end with a steel-wool pad. Make sure to clean at least a 1-in.-long section of tubing.

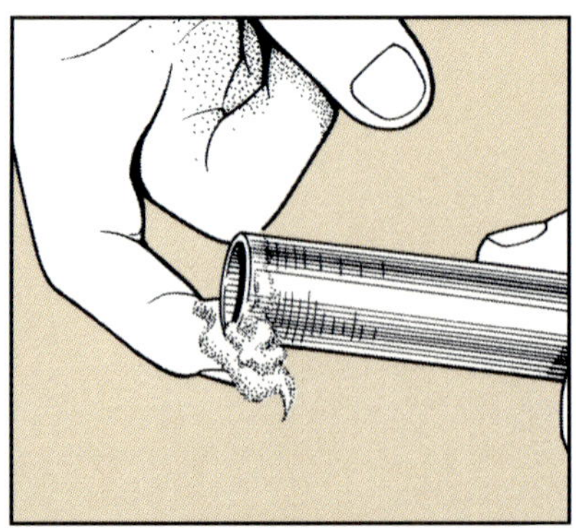

5 Apply paste flux to the polished end of the tubing with your fingertip. Make sure to cover the entire perimeter.

Getting Started

Plan your installation on paper first. This is a great way to minimize the number of fittings you need and the number of trips to the hardware store to buy the things you forgot.

The job shown involved replacing a tank and moving its location as a part of a larger remodeling job. If you're just putting a new tank in the same place, you'll have even less work to do. Begin by removing the tank from its box and reading all the product literature that comes with it. Make sure to incorporate any specific manufacturer instructions into your plans, especially if not doing so voids the product warranty. Select a convenient spot for the tank and place two or three concrete blocks on the floor (Fig. 1). These blocks help prevent damage from minor floods and make getting at the drain much easier.

Next, slide the tank on top of the blocks making sure to keep the drain faucet to the front (Fig. 2). Rock the tank back and forth slightly to make sure the blocks don't move. If the blocks do move, or the tank rocks on top of the blocks, reposition everything until the tank is stable.

Soldering Basics

Soldering copper tubing and fittings is really one of the easiest building skills to acquire. All you need (besides the tubing and fittings) are a propane or Mapp gas torch (a Mapp torch is preferred because it burns hotter and melts lead-free solder better). You will also need a tubing cutter, some paste soldering flux, several pads of steel wool, a wire bush to clean the ends of the fittings and some lead-free solder. All of these items are commonly available at local hardware stores and home centers.

The rules are simple: The mating surfaces must be cleaned thoroughly and covered with flux, the tubing cuts have to be absolutely square and the fittings can't be bent or distorted.

The place to begin is by cutting a 6- to 8-in.-long piece of $^{3}/_{4}$-in.-dia. tubing for the cold water entrance line on the tank. Use a tubing cutter, not a saw, and keep the wheel square to the pipe as you work (Fig. 3).

Next, clean the end of the tubing with a piece of steel wool (Fig. 4). Rub clean an area of at least 1 in. long and make sure that only a bright copper color can be seen when you're done. Then cover the cleaned area with some soldering flux (Fig. 5) and put the piece aside.

You can also use steel wool to clean the inside of all your fittings, but it's much more convenient to use a simple wire brush designed for the purpose. Just insert the brush into the end of the fitting and turn until the surface is clean (Fig. 6). Add flux to the inside of the fitting (Fig. 7), and then slide the fitting over the end of the tubing piece.

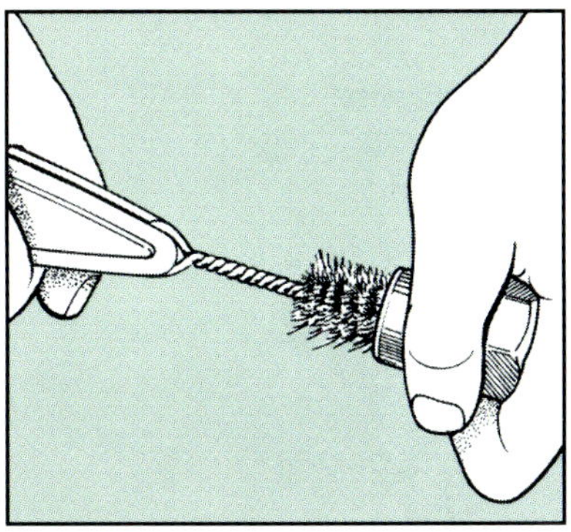

6 Clean the inside of a female pipe adapter with a wire brush. Make sure the entire inside surface is clean.

7 Add flux to the inside of the adapter fitting. Spread it liberally and then slide the fitting onto the end of the tubing.

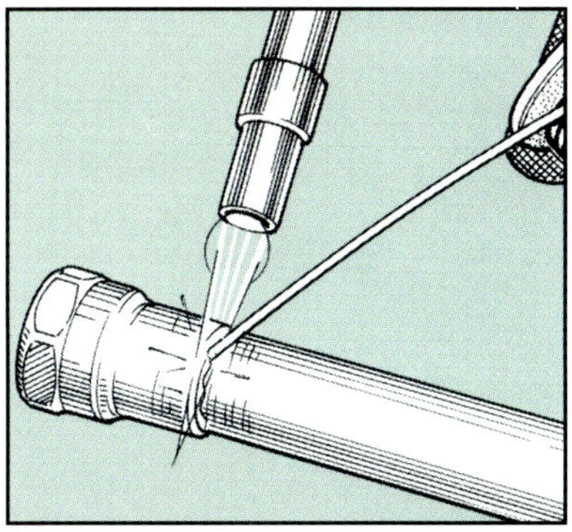

8 Heat the joint until the flux burns. Then add solder and keep heating until it melts and runs out the bottom of the joint.

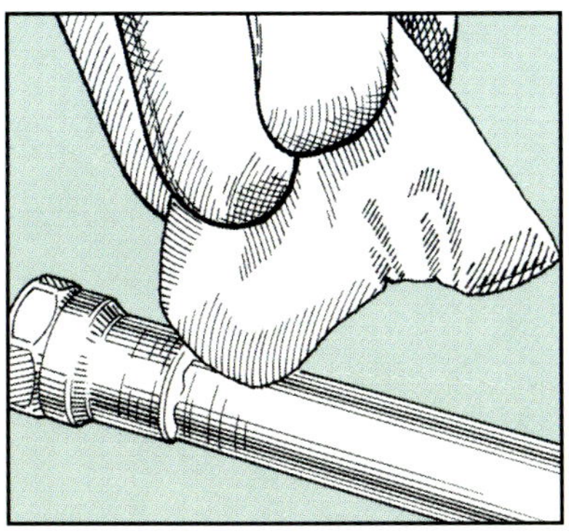

9 Once the joint is full, remove the torch. Then wipe the joint clean with a soft rag to remove any excess solder before it dries.

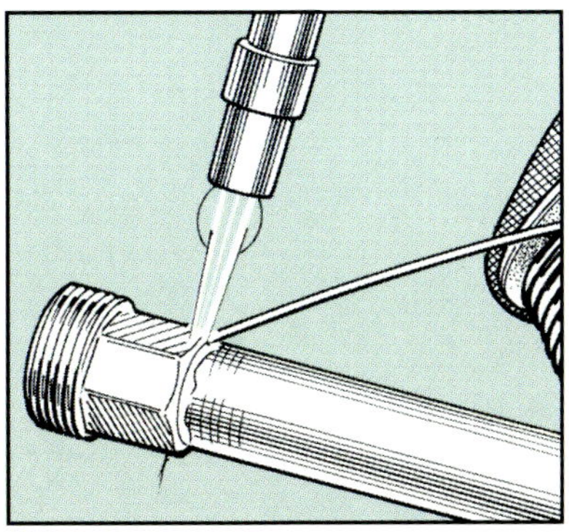

10 Solder the male side of a union to the other end of the tubing after you've cleaned the mating surface thoroughly.

11 Use Teflon tape to seal the pipe threads on the tank nipple. Imbed the tape in a clockwise direction.

Begin heating the joint by turning on the torch and adjusting the flame so the inner blue flame is about 3/4 in. long. Bring the tip of the flame to bear directly on top of the joint and heat this area until the flux melts and burns out.

As soon as the flux disappears, touch the top of the joint with some solder (Fig. 8). If the tubing is hot enough, the solder will melt right away. If not, simply lift off the solder, keep heating the joint and try again. Once solder starts to melt, keep pushing the solder into the joint until it drips out the bottom. This means the joint is full. Immediately remove the flame and wipe off any excess solder with a soft rag (Fig. 9). Be sure to wear heavy gloves to prevent burns.

In the installation shown, it was decided to put a union fitting on both the cold and hot lines as they left the tank to enable the tank to be moved easily. To install these unions, simply clean all the tubing ends and fittings as before, add some flux and solder the parts together (Fig. 10). Once this assembly is complete and cool to the touch, put some Teflon thread-sealing tape onto the tank nipple threads (Fig. 11) and tighten the adapter in place (Fig. 12). Join the two halves of the union together (Fig. 13) and tighten the nut firmly.

Next, clean and flux a shutoff valve for the cold side and slide it over the tubing end (Fig. 14) and solder it in place. Once the tubing is cut, clean the end with a steel-wool pad.

T&P Valve

The T&P valve (temperature and pressure relief valve) is a safety device that creates a pathway for the water to escape if the pressure inside the tank builds to a dangerous level for any reason. It's important that the valve you buy is rated the same as your water heater. The product literature for both will describe what's required. Simply match the ANSI (American National Standards Institute) rating numbers of both.

To begin the installation, temporarily thread the valve into the tank and take a measurement between the bottom of the valve and the floor (Fig. 15). Deduct 4 in. from this measurement and cut a length of tubing to match. Once your measurement is taken, remove the valve and coat the threads with Teflon tape (Fig. 16) and reinstall it in the tank (Fig. 17). Then solder a male adapter onto the tubing, let it cool and cover the threads with Teflon tape (Fig. 18). Finish up by threading the drain assembly into place and tightening securely with a wrench (Fig. 19).

Electrical Power

A water heater always requires a separate 220-volt circuit and, in this case, a 30-amp circuit breaker and 10/2 (with ground) circuit cable. Bring in new cable, from a joist-mounted junction box, to the new tank location by boring holes through the middle of overhead joists and run the cable along the side of the joist.

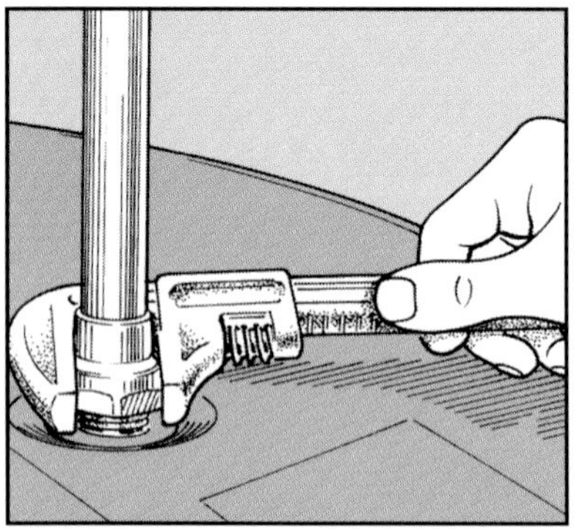

12 Thread the tubing and adapter assembly onto the tank and then tighten firmly in place with an adjustable wrench.

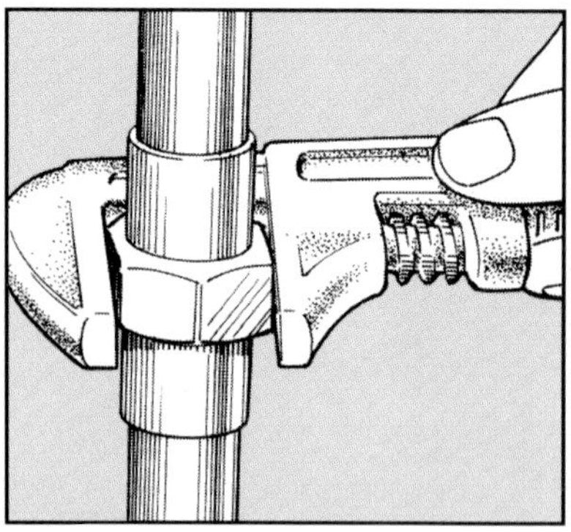

13 Solder a short length of tubing onto the nut side of a union. Then join the two halves with the nut. Tighten it firmly.

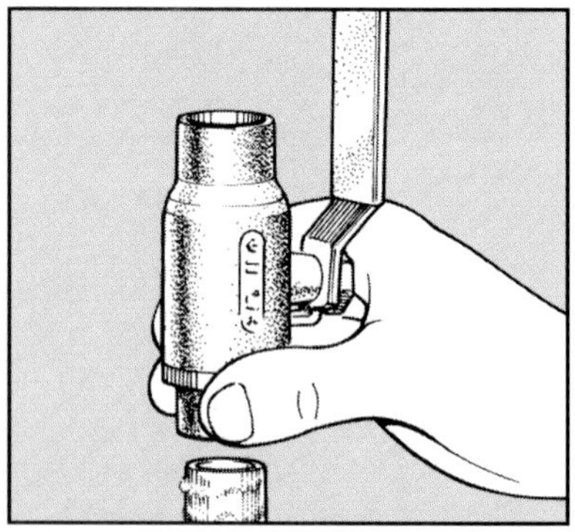

14 Clean the tubing and the ball valve, and apply flux to them both. Slide the valve over the tubing and solder together.

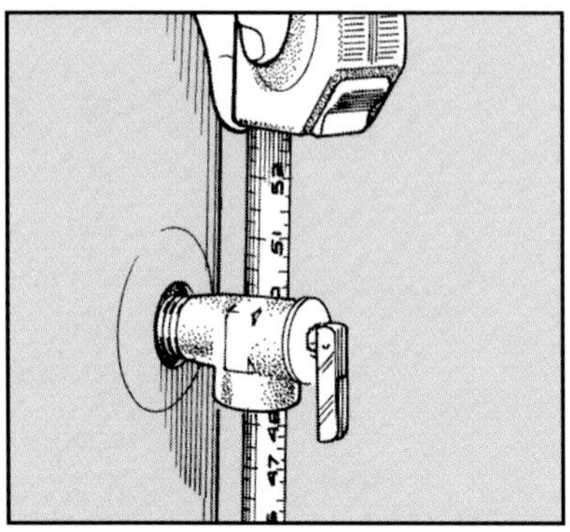

15 Temporarily install a temperature and pressure relief valve and measure from the bottom of the valve to the floor.

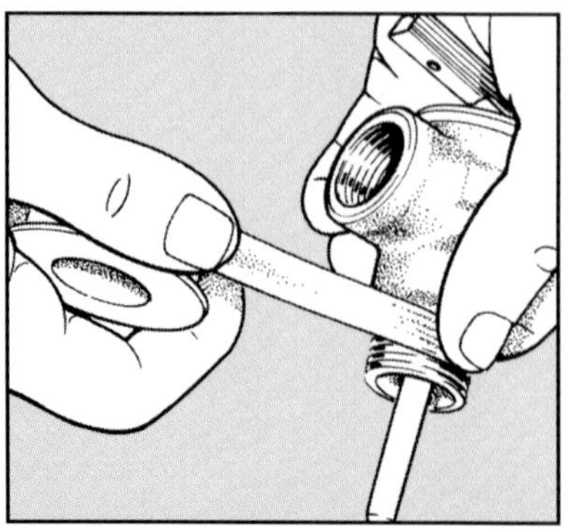

16 Remove the temperature and pressure relief valve. Then cover the threads with Teflon tape, streching it in place.

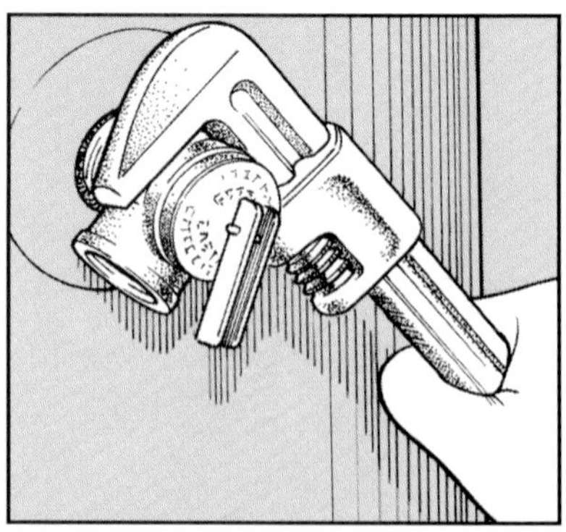

17 Reinstall the valve in the tank using an adjustable wrench. Make sure that the open end of the valve points down.

To gain access to the electrical wires in your tank, remove the covering plate on the top (Fig. 20) and pull out the black and white wires that you find there. Then remove the knockout plug from one cable hole using a screwdriver and hammer (Fig. 21) and slide a conduit connector into the hole (Fig. 22). Firmly attach the connector by threading its nut in place from inside the tank opening.

Next, measure the distance from the top of the tank up to the joists above and add about 4 in. so the conduit can be attached to the side of a joist or a piece of blocking nailed between two joists. Once the conduit is cut, slide the free end of the cable into the top of the pipe (Fig. 23) and pull the cable out the bottom. Then fish the cable end through the connector and into the tank opening and slide the conduit into the connector (Fig. 24). Tighten it in place with the connector screw (Fig. 25) and attach the ground wire from the cable to the grounding screw inside the tank opening. Join the two white wires with connectors and the two black wires together with connectors (Fig. 26). Replace the covering plate and your installation is done.

Check your work by first filling the tank with water and making sure that there are no leaks in your plumbing job. Remember to close the drain valve before turning on the water. Only when the tank is full should you turn on the circuit breaker and send power to the heating elements. If you turn on the elements before the tank is full of water, they will be ruined and will have to be replaced.

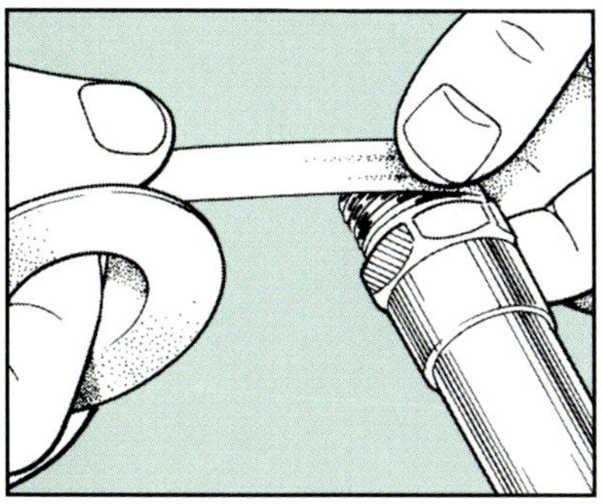

18 Cut the relief valve tube to length and solder a male adapter to one end. Cover the adapter threads with Teflon tape.

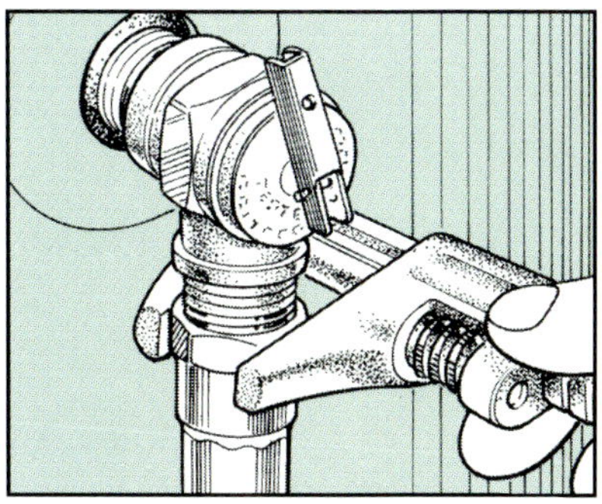

19 Thread the drain tube into the relief valve and tighten. The open end of the tube should be 3 to 4 in. above the floor.

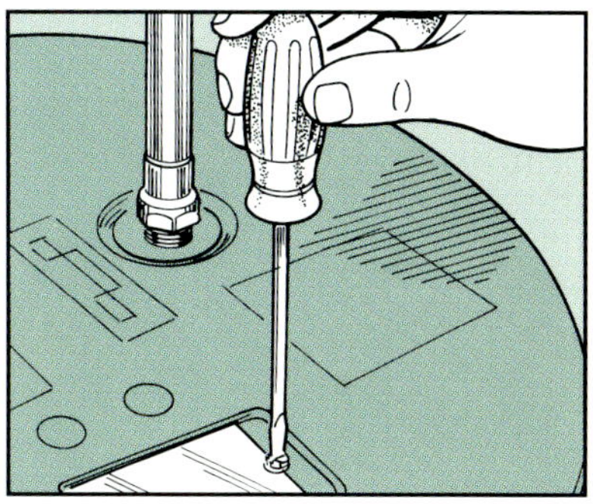

20 Remove the cover plate that protects the electrical wires. Usually just one screw holds the plate in place.

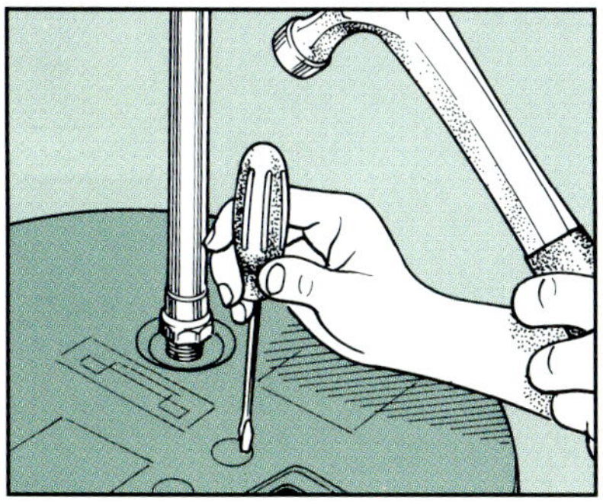

21 Locate a knockout on the top of the tank and force it down with a screwdriver and hammer. Break it off with pliers.

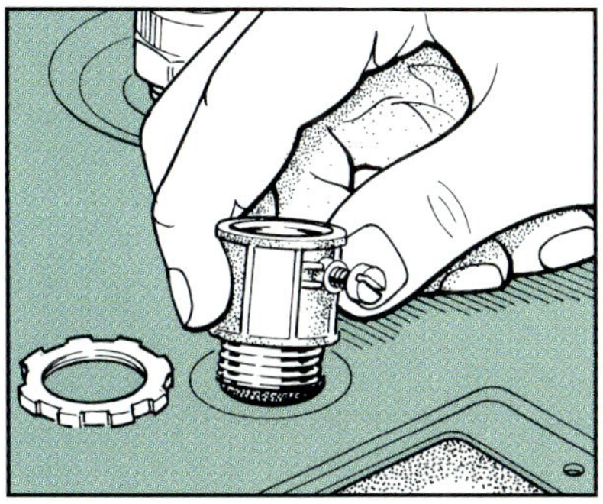

22 Slide the threaded end of a conduit connector into the knockout hole and tighten it in place with the connector nut.

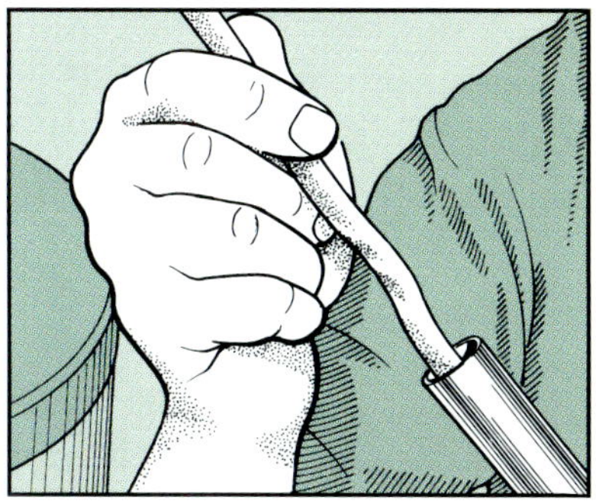

23 Cut a piece of conduit to length and slide it over one end of the electrical circuit cable. Avoid damaging the insulation.

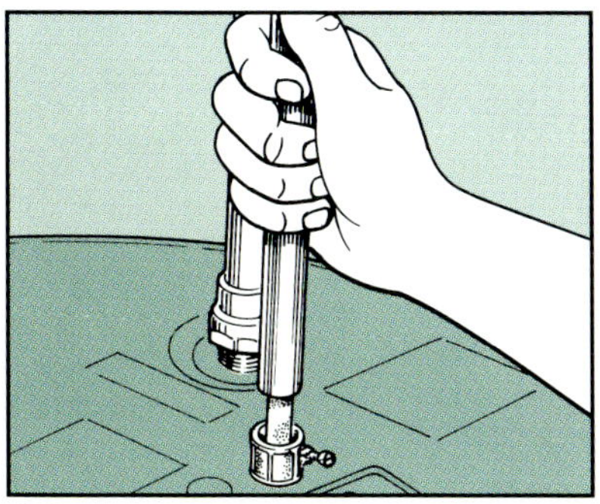

24 Feed the cable through the connector and into the tank opening. Then slide the conduit completely into the connector.

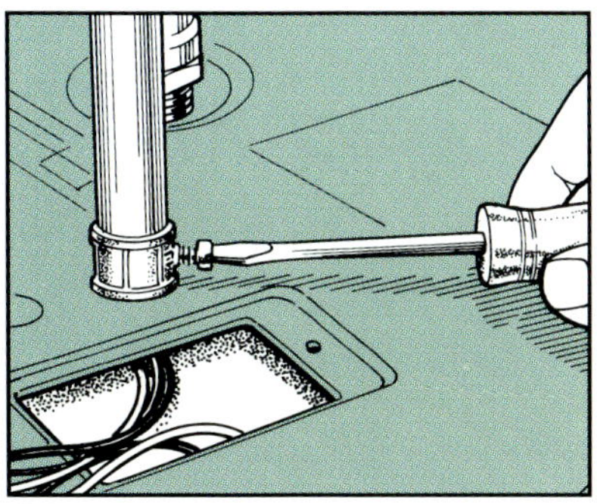

25 Fasten the top of the conduit to the floor framing above. Then attach it to the connector with a setscrew.

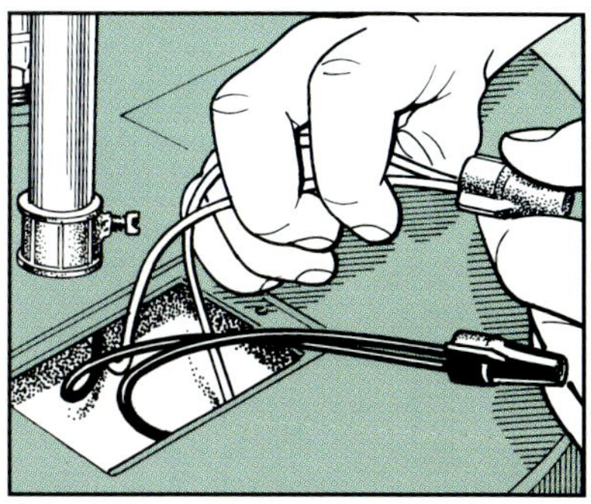

26 Attach the cable ground wire to the ground screw. Then join the white wires and black wires with wire connectors.

Installing a hot water dispenser

Instant soup may be fast, but only after you've heated the water on your stove top. Even microwave ovens take a minute or so to do the job. If you really want instant soup—and coffee, tea, hot cereals and just about anything else that uses small quantities of hot water—you're in the market for a hot water dispenser.

Instant hot water dispensers deliver water that's at least 50°F hotter than that served up by your water heater, at a rate of up to 60 cups per hour. The daily operating cost is roughly equivalent to that of using a 40-watt light bulb.

The heart of a hot water dispenser is a small tank that contains a heating element. The faucet, when turned on, feeds water from the tap to the tank where it's heated to its thermostatic limit. When the faucet is again turned on, cold water from the supply tube enters the tank, pushing heated water up through a second tube and through its spout.

Hot water dispensers are easily installed in the fourth deck hole of a kitchen sink. To bore a new hole in a stainless-steel sink, use a 1¼-in. holesaw, though an electrician's knockout punch would make a cleaner cut. If you have a porcelain or enameled sink, you may be able to bore a hole through the counter next to the sink and position the dispenser's spout over the sink basin. Be sure to place the faucet well back, however, so that dangerously hot water is kept beyond the reach of small children.

You'll need at least 20 pounds of static water pressure. Your water supplier will be able to tell you what the pressure is in your neighborhood.

Your electrical hookup will depend, in large part, on local code requirements, and an electrical permit may be required. While it is possible to pull power from a small appliance circuit, keep in mind that many kitchen circuits are already hard-pressed.

Installing a Hot Water Dispenser was written and photographed by Merle Henkenius. Several brands of hot water dispensers are on the market, with models ranging from \$90 to \$170. The installation shown used an In-Sink-Erator model H-770 (Emerson Electric Co., 4700 21st. St., Racine, WI 53406).

Under-the-sink Wiring

Many codes stipulate a dedicated circuit for the dispenser, or, at the very least, that it share a circuit with another dedicated appliance such as a food disposal. Most codes also require that a circuit terminating inside the sink cabinet must be switched. This can be accomplished with a switched receptacle, a 2-gang box where one side contains a receptacle and the other side houses a single-pole switch, or separate switch and receptacle boxes.

The installation shown has a dedicated 15-amp circuit with a grounded, switched receptacle. Assuming that there is basement access, start by boring a 5/8-in. hole through the sink base-cabinet floor and down through the subfloor (Fig. 1). Then, pull 14/2 (with ground) cable between the service panel and cabinet. Feed the cable into the cabinet and strip roughly 10 in. of sheathing from it (Fig. 2).

Encase the wiring within the cabinet in conduit. The easiest choice is flexible conduit, pushed several inches through the hole in the cabinet floor. Join the receptacle box to the conduit with a box connector (Fig. 3). Then, mount the box to the cabinet wall using wood screws or coated drywall screws (Fig. 4).

To wire a switched receptacle, connect the black (incoming) hot wire to the brass hot terminal on the switch and the white neutral wire to the silver terminal on the receptacle. Then, run a black jumper wire from the other switch terminal to the brass receptacle terminal (Fig. 5).

To ground the receptacle and box, join the circuit ground wire with two green pigtails, using a twist connector. Then fasten one pigtail to the green terminal on the receptacle and the remaining pigtail to the metal box, using a grounding clip or grounding screw. Finally, mount the cover plate and turn the switch to the OFF position (Fig. 6).

At this point, you can complete the electrical circuit at the panel or install the dispenser first, rather than cart tools back and forth.

Installing the Unit

First, install a self-piercing saddle valve on the cold water supply riser. A self-piercing saddle valve allows you to tap into the water piping without shutting off the water. If your code doesn't allow this fitting, or if your waterlines are made of galvanized iron, you'll need to shut off the water, drill the tap hole in the pipe wall and install a saddle valve over the hole.

Fasten the saddle valve to the riser, using a screwdriver to tighten it down (Fig. 7). To pierce the riser with a self-piercing saddle valve, thread the tap clockwise all the way, then back it out all the way, allowing water to flow through the valve. Make sure to place the valve high enough on the riser to reach the

1 Bore a 5/8-in. hole through the cabinet and floor, into the basement. Feed cable from the panel through this opening.

2 Strip about 10 in. of sheathing from the cable. Then strip 5/8 in. of insulation from the end of each wire.

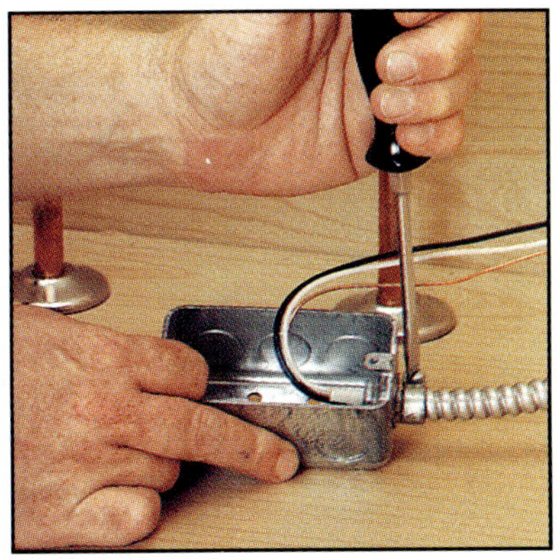

3 Feed the wires through the flexible conduit and connect the conduit to a metal duplex box with a box connector.

4 Mount the duplex box to the cabinet wall near the tank location. Use wood screws or coated drywall screws.

5 Run a jumper from switch to receptacle. Join black circuit wire to brass terminal and neutral wire to the silver terminal.

6 Install the switched receptacle in the box and fasten the cover plate. Do not plug in the unit until it's charged with water.

new faucet's factory-installed supply tube. Then, screw the heater unit's hanger bracket to a cabinet wall and hang the heater on the bracket (Fig. 8).

If you're removing an old spray hose from the fourth sink hole, use a basin wrench or small adjustable wrench to thread the hose from its faucet port. Then loosen the jamb nut securing the spray's deck fitting and remove the assembly (Fig. 9). Wrap Teflon tape around a $^1/_8$-in. threaded plug and tighten the plug into the faucet spray port (Fig. 10).

With the deck hole ready, straighten the faucet tubing and feed the tubing through the sink's deck hole (Fig. 11). While a helper holds the faucet in position from above, slide the slotted mounting washer onto the factory-installed screw and tighten the assembly in place (Fig. 12).

With the faucet secured, carefully bend its $^1/_8$-in. supply tube to meet the port of the saddle valve. Then, slide the valve's compression nut and ferrule onto the supply tube and insert the tube into the valve port (Fig. 13). Lubricate the ring and threads with

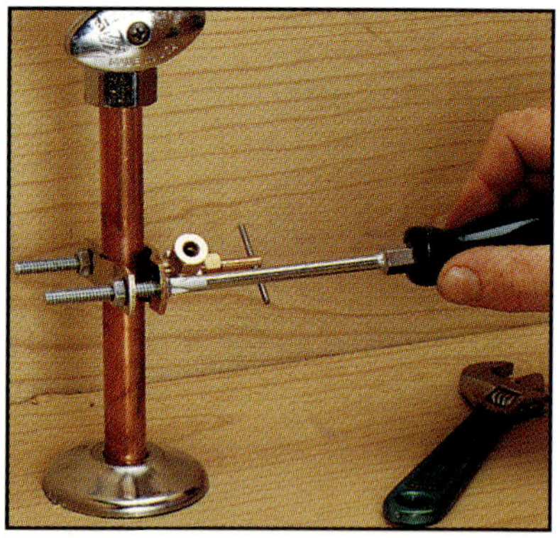

7 Mount the self-piercing saddle valve on the cold water riser pipe by drawing up the saddle bolts evenly.

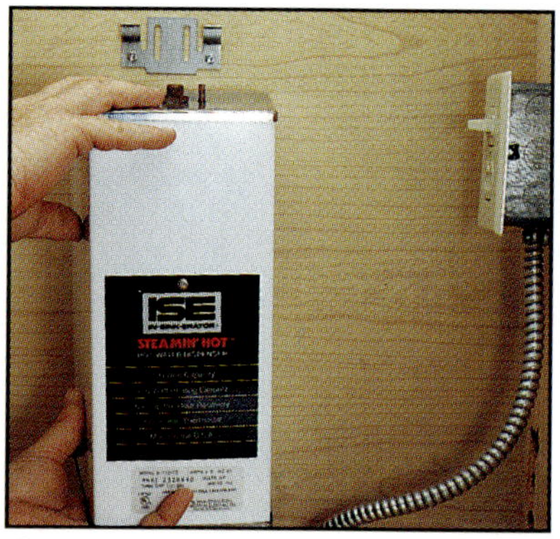

8 Screw the hot water dispenser's mounting bracket to the cabinet wall and hang the tank on the bracket.

9 Disconnect the old spray hose at the faucet port. Then, loosen the spray hose jamb nut and lift out hose and deck fitting.

10 To seal the faucet port, wrap Teflon tape around a $^1/_8$-in. threaded plug and then tighten it into the faucet port.

11 Straighten the supply tubes attached to the heater faucet and insert through the sink's deck hole from above.

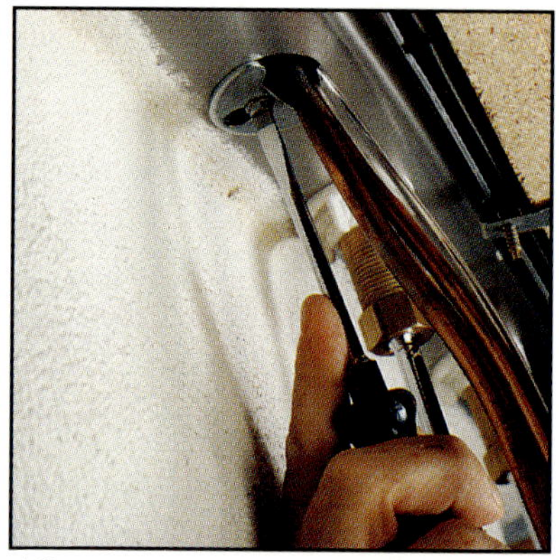

12 Use the factory-installed fastening screw and mounting washer to fix the water-heater faucet in the hole from below.

13 To connect the water supply, slide the saddle valve's compression nut and ferrule onto the supply tube. Lubricate and tighten.

14 Fasten the two remaining copper tubes to the tank with compression nuts and ferrules. Don't overtighten the nuts.

15 Slide the plastic tube over its copper tank nipple and secure it with a spring clip or hose clamp.

liquid soap or petroleum jelly and tighten the nut hand-tight, plus two full turns with a wrench.

If your plumbing system is plagued by water-borne sediment, you may wish to turn the water on at this point and bleed a cup or two through the faucet into a container. Otherwise, leave the water off until you make the heater tank connections.

With the supply tube connected, you'll see two remaining copper tubes and a plastic tube extending from the faucet. One copper tube supplies the cold water to the tank and the other supplies hot water to the faucet. The plastic tube leads to the expansion tank. Trim all tubes to length.

Connecting to Power

If working within the service panel seems beyond your reach, it may be. If you can complete the rest of the installation yourself, a service call by a licensed electrician to install a new circuit breaker and make the connections won't cost that much.

If you decide that you can also do the work yourself, take a few simple precautions. To begin, always shut off the main disconnect switch before opening the panel. From here on, touch only one metal surface at a time with the screwdriver while grasping only the handle. Whenever possible, use only one hand. Avoid touching the panel cabinet while working inside the panel.

After throwing the main disconnect to the OFF position, remove the screws securing the panel cover and pull the cover free. Next, punch out one of the available knockout plugs in the side or top of the panel and install a box connector. Strip about 18 in. of sheathing from the cable and feed it through the connector. Then tighten the screws that bind the cable to the connector (Fig. 16).

Attach the white neutral and bare wire ground to the neutral/ground bus, or to the separate neutral and ground buses, if your panel is so equipped. Just cut the wires to length, trim about 5/8 in. of insulation from the neutral wire and feed each under an available lug on the appropriate bus. Finally, tighten these lugs firmly with a straight-blade screwdriver (Fig. 17).

To connect the hot side of the circuit, strip 5/8 in. of insulation from the black wire and tighten it under the terminal screw on a 15-amp breaker. Then, without touching the hot-bus bar, hook the back end of the breaker over its panel tab and press the slotted front end over its hot-bus prong (Fig. 18).

Next, break a slot from the face of the panel cover (Fig. 19) and replace the cover. Finally, turn on the new breaker and main disconnect switch.

16 Install a box connector in one of the panel's knockouts and secure the cable with the connector's fastening screws.

17 With main switch off, secure the white and bare wires under terminal lugs on the neutral/grounding bus. Tighten firmly.

18 Secure the black, hot wire under the log of a 15-amp breaker. Then press the breaker onto its hot-bus prong.

19 Use pliers to twist a breaker-slot plate from the panel cover. Then, replace the cover and energize the panel.

Charging the Dispenser

As with any appliance containing an electric heating element, don't turn the power on before filling the tank completely. Energizing a dry element will cause it (or its one-time fuse) to fail in a matter of seconds.

To properly charge the system, turn the self-tapping saddle valve in completely, then out completely. With the water on, hold the faucet open. After about one minute, water will purge all air from the tank and begin flowing through the spout.

When you're sure the tank is fully charged, plug in the unit and turn on the switch inside the cabinet. It will take roughly 15 minutes to heat the first tankful of water. During this time, you should expect some steaming, hissing and rumbling. When the heater shuts off, carefully bleed the hot water and steam through the faucet, then allow the unit to reheat. You may need to repeat this procedure several times before the system settles into steady operation.

The model installed here is preset to heat the water to 190°F. Those living in high altitudes may need to turn the temperature down slightly to keep the water from boiling.

1 Shut off the circuit that powers the old ceiling fixture, and remove the lamp's diffuser to access the mounting plate.

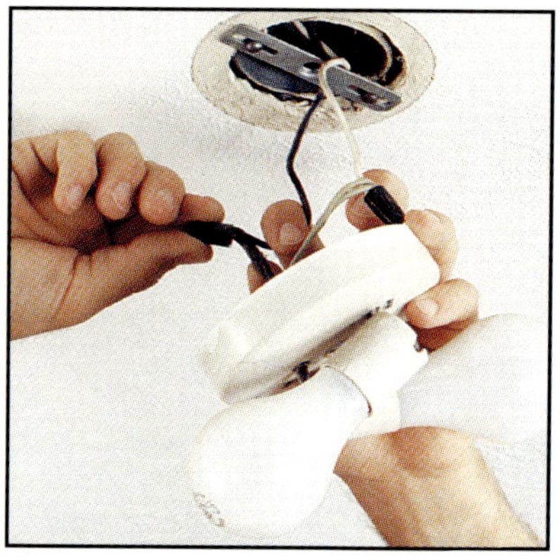

2 After removing the screws that hold the fixture mounting plate in place, twist off the wire connectors and set the unit aside.

3 If the mounting plate was secured by a threaded nipple, remove the mounting bracket from the fixture box.

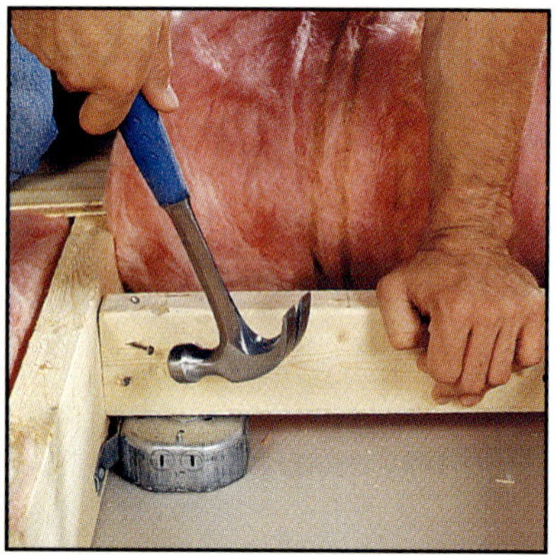

4 Install a 2×4 brace to support the weight of the fan. If you don't have attic access, use a retrofit fan box kit.

5 With the brace in place and leveled, use a drill/driver to firmly attach the box to the brace with wood screws.

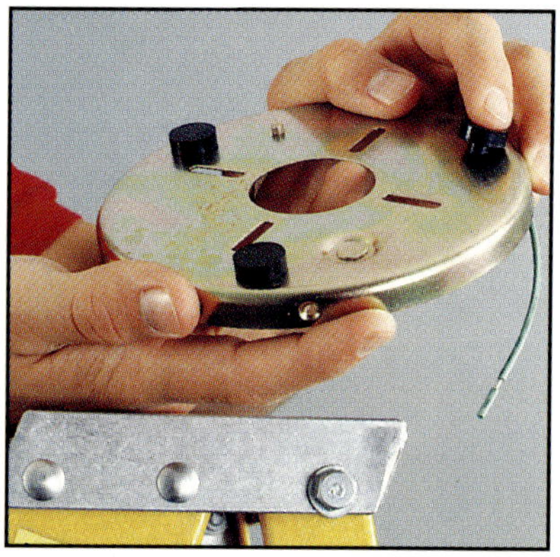

6 The fan installed here has three rubber vibration-absorbing pads that fit in holes in the fan mounting plate.

Installing a ceiling fan

Most folks install a fan to create a cooling effect during the warmer months. However, a ceiling fan is also an excellent means for circulating air during the winter. It's especially good at moving warm air from the ceiling to the rest of the room. This not only makes the room more comfortable, but you may be able to take the thermostat down a notch, as well.

Ceiling fans and light kits are available separately so you can mix and match styles and models to suit the look you're after.

Before You Start

Your ceiling light will be wired in one of two ways—with the power originating at the switch, or with the power routed first to the ceiling box and then through the switch.

The wiring configuration of your room may have the power originating at the switch, with a 14/2 switch leg that brings current to the ceiling fixture. If your room has the power routed first to the ceiling box, there will be a switch loop extending to the switch box. The wiring connections to the fixture at the ceiling box differ only slightly in each case, and the manufacturer's instructions will provide wiring diagrams for both configurations.

If you have only a 2-wire switch leg, you can control the light and fan from the wall, but not each independently—the wall switch powers both. If you'd like to control the fan and light separately at the wall, you need to pull a new 3-wire cable from the fixture to the switch box and install a second switch.

In the installation shown, the existing 2-wire switch leg and switch was used and pull-chain switches on the fan and light fixture were used for independent control.

Installing a Ceiling Fan was written and photographed by Merle Henkenius. The installation shown used a Hunter fan (Model EMB-03, Hunter Fan Co., 2500 Frisco Ave., Memphis, TN 38114), priced at about $100, and a light kit, priced at about $20. *Ceiling Fan Wobbles* was written by Norman Becker. Illustration by George Retseck.

7 Drive screws through the mounting plate and box, and into the 2×4 brace until the plate rests against the ceiling.

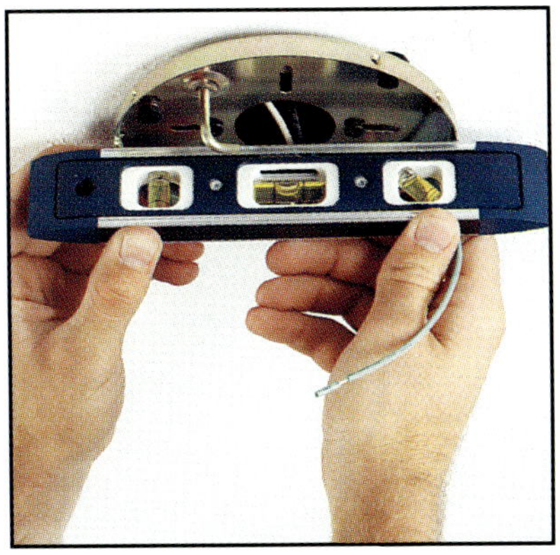

8 Use a small level to check that the plate is level in both directions. Tighten the screws into the brace and adjust the plate.

9 With mounting plate firmly attached, install two of the three screws in the plate side for holding the motor assembly .

10 With the fan components on the floor, attach the motor cowling to the fan canopy with the screws provided.

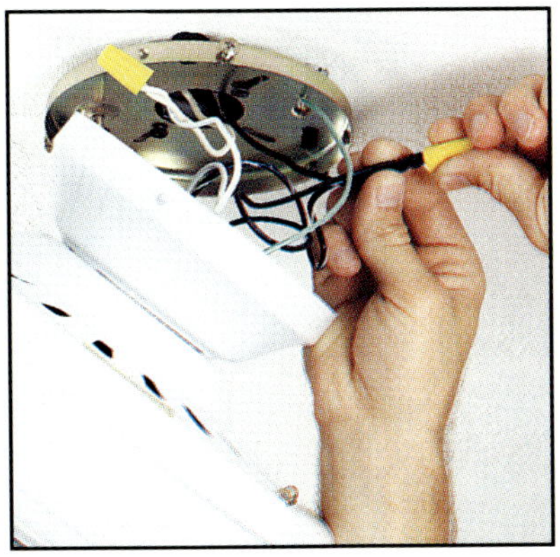

11 Hang the assembly from the mounting plate using a wire hook. Then, attach like-colored wires with wire connectors.

12 Hold the assembly in place on the mounting plate. Add the third mounting plate screw and tighten all firmly.

Removing the Old Fixture

Start by shutting off the power to the ceiling fixture circuit at the service panel. Then, remove the diffuser from the old fixture (Fig. 1). This will reveal either a brass nut on a threaded nipple or two machined screws at the outer edges of the base. Remove the nut or the screws that secure the base to the ceiling box. This allows the fixture to drop away from the box, exposing the wire connections. Undo the wire connectors that join the like-colored wires and remove the fixture entirely (Fig. 2). If the fixture base was secured by a threaded nipple, you'll find it attached to a box bracket. Remove the bracket from the box as well (Fig. 3).

Securing the Box

In all cases, you'll need to beef up the support for the ceiling box so it can safely handle the weight of the fan. Most electrical codes require one of two options. You can either install a wooden brace between ceiling joists and screw the existing box to the brace, or install a code-approved fan box that's designed to be able to carry the extra weight.

Access to the box will have a lot to do with your decision. With attic access, the simplest approach is to brace the box. Clear the insulation away and cut a 2×4 brace to bridge the joist space. Position this brace so that it rests on top of the box, level it, and nail or screw the brace to the joists (Fig. 4). Then, from below, use wood screws to secure the box to the brace (Fig. 5).

If you can't reach the box, such as when working through a first-floor ceiling in a 2-story home, a specialized retrofit fan box will be easier. These special-purpose boxes have a heavy threaded joist support that is designed to be fed through the existing box opening. When positioned, you simply rotate the bar, which drives pronged ends against the adjacent joists. Retrofit fan-support boxes are available where you buy your fixtures, and cost about $12.

Installing the Fan

The Hunter fan that is shown here has rubber bushings and grommets at the most vibration-prone locations to help reduce noise when the fan is running. If you're installing a similar fan, be sure to insert the rubber bushings into the holes in the mounting plate. These three bushings act as vibration-absorbing cushions (Fig. 6).

With the wooden brace in place and the box secured to it, attach the fan mounting plate with extra-long 4-in. screws, driven through the holes in the back of the box and into the brace (Fig. 7).

13 After mounting the blades on their metal brackets, screw each bracket in its place on the motor assembly.

14 To install the light kit, remove the two screws that hold the bottom cap onto the switch housing and take off the cap.

15 Using the same screws and tapped holes, install the light kit adapter ring on the bottom of the switch housing.

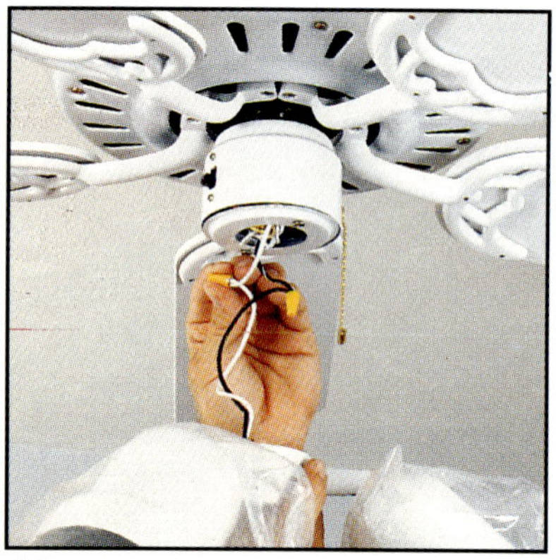

16 Lift the light kit and join the white leads with a wire connector. Then join the kit's black lead to the remaining lead.

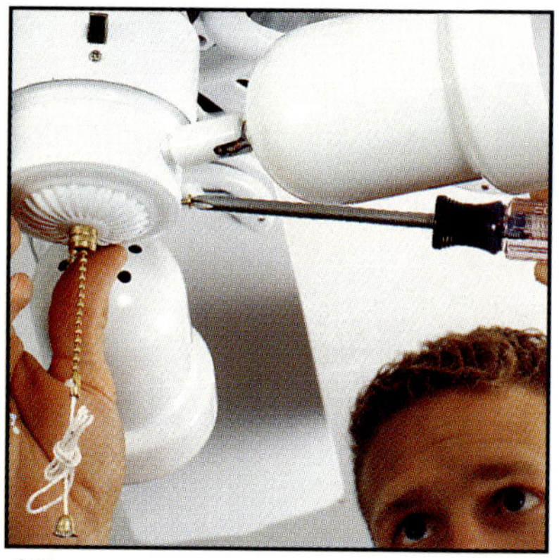

17 Screw the light kit to the switch housing and install the bottom cap, which contains the light's pull-chain switch.

18 Set pull-chain switches so the light is on and the fan is off. Wall switch will control light while pull chain controls fan.

Use a drill/driver to drive the screws just until the plate makes contact with the ceiling. Then, to assure a perfectly level installation, hold a torpedo level across the plate (Fig. 8) and finish each screw manually while checking that the plate is level.

With the mounting plate installed on the ceiling and leveled, and the switch-leg wires pulled through the plate opening, install—but don't tighten—two of the three brass screws in the sides of the plate (Fig. 9). Then screw the fan's metal canopy to the motor cowling (Fig. 10).

Make a short hook out of stiff wire and use the hook to hang the canopy/motor cowling assembly from the ceiling plate. Temporarily hanging the motor assembly in this way allows you to make the wiring connections without also having to hold the motor assembly. The hook makes the connection a one-person job.

To make the electrical connections, simply join like-colored wires with twist connectors—white to white and black to black (Fig. 11). Then, join the circuit ground wire to the fixture's grounding pigtail and to a separate pigtail bonded to the metal box. If your circuit is an older, ungrounded type, ignore the fixture's green grounding pigtail.

With the wiring connections made, remove the assembly from its temporary hook and position the canopy against the ceiling plate. Align the slotted holes in the canopy with the two brass screws already started in the mounting plate. Install the third screw after the canopy is in place to complete the connection (Fig. 12). Because these three screws hold the fan to the ceiling, draw them down tightly.

With the motor assembly in place, mount each wooden fan blade on its metal bracket. Each blade receives three screws, each fit with a rubber grommet. With the blades and brackets ready, screw the brackets to the motor assembly using two screws in each bracket (Fig. 13).

Installing the Light

To access the wiring that powers the light kit, loosen the screws that hold the cap on the fan's switch housing (Fig. 14). With the cap removed, you'll see a bundle of wires. Of these wires, two will be labeled for use with the light kit. One will be white (neutral) and the other, black, red or blue (hot).

Before wiring the lamp, however, install the adapter ring included with the fan kit (Fig. 15). The adapter serves as a reducing ring for the lamp housing. Attach the adapter ring with the screws provided.

Pull the two labeled wires through the adapter ring, lift the lamp and make the wiring connections. Join the two white wires with a wire connector and the fixture's black wire to the remaining labeled wire (Fig. 16). Because painted fixtures scratch easily, leave the plastic protectors on until after the lamp is wired. Finally, fasten the light kit to the fan with the two screws provided for this purpose (Fig. 17) and thread vibration-resistant bulbs into the fixture. In most cases, 60-watt bulbs are the maximum. Anything brighter poses a fire hazard.

Final Adjustments

With the fan and light kit installed, return power to the circuit and test your work. If you turn the switch on and nothing happens, don't panic. The pull-chain switches are probably in their OFF position. The fan will have four positions—OFF, plus three speeds. The light will simply have an ON/OFF switch. Set these as you prefer. You can opt to have the light controlled by the wall switch and the fan switched at the pull chain. By doing it this way, the fan won't start every time you turn the light on and you save wear and tear on the fan motor (Fig. 18).

Your fan will have the capacity to spin in both directions, and can be switched accordingly. Look to the side of the switch housing for the directional switch. Because the fan blades are canted slightly, rotation in one direction will move air upward, in the other, downward.

A ceiling fan can wobble for a variety of reasons. Check that the blades are not warped or out of balance. Fasten a clothespin to a blade and see if it corrects the problem.

Ceiling Fan Wobbles

There are several reasons why a ceiling fan wobbles when operating. The fan blades could be out of balance, out of track or warped. The wobble could also be caused by the air turbulence that results from the blades being closer than 6 in. from one side of a sloped cathedral ceiling or ceiling beam.

You can check to see if the fan blades are out of balance by clipping a spring-type clothespin halfway between the tip and the blade iron on the leading edge of one blade. Turn on the fan to LOW speed and see if the weight stops the wobble. Try each blade to determine if it needs more weight. If the closepin stops the wobble, it should be replaced with thin adhesive-backed lead-weighted tape, which is available through the fan manufacturer's service center.

Check to see if one or more blades are out of track. Using a yardstick, measure the distance from the ceiling to the tip of each blade. The distance should be equal for each blade. If it isn't, contact the nearest manufacturer's service center about correction or warranty replacement. If the blades are not out of track, try swapping blades to correct the problem. Switch the position of two adjacent blades while leaving the other two in their original positions. While the blades are off the fan, lay them on a flat surface to see if they are warped. If so, then replace the blades.

OFF
ON
7-8
3-4
3-8
1-4
1-8

Making power tool jigs

Imagine drawing a straight line. Better yet, go ahead and draw one—freehand. Pick up a pencil, put the point on a piece of paper and move the point across the paper as straight as you can. Now take a look at your line. Is it really straight, straight enough, or is it downright crooked? Of course, you could practice drawing straight lines, and, after awhile, you may see an improvement. No matter how good you get, though, the odds are your lines will never be perfect. Whether you like it or not, no two will be the same.

The solution, of course, is to use a ruler. Because a ruler is made perfectly straight, you can draw as many lines as you like, each one as accurate as the next.

A ruler, of course, is a tool. But it's a very distinct and important kind of tool. It doesn't cut, or join material, and it supplies no extra power to get the job done faster. Its value lies in its ability to constrain an activity so that it can be reproduced over and over again with consistency and accuracy.

In woodworking, tools of this nature are used all the time. When they're used in conjunction with tools such as saws or drills, they're called *jigs*. Like the ruler, their purpose is to constrain the action of the tool so that it performs its role consistently. The accuracy is built into the jig.

Sometimes, jigs are built right into the tool you buy. A table saw's fence and miter gauge are jigs, and the ball-bearing pilot on some router bits is a form of jig that works in concert with the stock edge to guide your cut uniformly.

While some jigs can be bought—such as doweling jigs and router fences—most woodworkers make their own.

Custom-made jigs have several real advantages over making do with what's available. First of all, you can make a jig to suit a specific repetitive job, such as cutting decorative tops on picket fence slats or tapering a set of table legs uniformly. Second, you can build the jig when you need it, usually out of a few scraps of wood left over from your last project. Also, making your own jigs is a fascinating creative exercise that brings you in touch with your tools and how they help you get the job done. By combining jigs with a power tool, you multiply the tool's usefulness and become involved with tool design and construction. Finally your finished work will be a greater source of pride because your tool making skills and inventiveness play as important a part as do your woodworking skills.

While many jigs are specific tools unique to one job only, there are some woodworking tasks, like crosscutting and boring straight holes, that occur in just about every project you take on. To this end, here is a set of jigs that you can make yourself and that provide increased accuracy and consistency for the most common operations. As a basis for the jigs, three of the most popular power tools have been chosen—a circular saw, a drill and a router.

All of the jigs are made from ordinary birch plywood, combined with a few small pieces of hardwood or softwood. In addition to ordinary bolts and screws available at any hardware store, special knobs have been incorporated to make the jigs easier to adjust and use.

The jigs range from sophisticated to simple. Each one, though, is designed to make a basic operation go a little easier. In fact, you may even find yourself using the first jig you make to help build the next. For example, you can use the crosscut platform to cut your stock to size for the jigs that follow, and use the horizontal boring jig to bore aligned holes in the simpler drill jigs.

Keep in mind that the designs and specifications suit the particular power tool models used. Be sure to check to see if the designs require modifications to fit the tools you own. After you've checked out the sampling, your own creative juices will start to flow and you'll no doubt discover new uses for some of the design features implemented here. By designing and using jigs, you realize the full potential of your power tools—right in your own shop.

Making Power Tool Jigs was written by Thomas Klenck. Knobs are available from The Woodworkers' Store, 21801 Industrial Boulevard, Rogers, MN 55374. The bushings for the self-centering drill jig are available from Woodworker's Supply, 1108 N. Glenn Rd., Casper, WY 82601.

Circular saw jigs

Text and photographs for *Circular Saw Jigs* by Rosario Capotosto. Technical art by Eugene Thompson.

ADJUSTABLE CROSSCUT JIG

When you bought your portable circular saw, you probably thought you had *the* tool for basic woodworking chores. Then you saw the pros with the chop saws—power miterboxes that cut with fraction-of-a-degree accuracy and production-line consistency.

Well, there is another solution. The crosscut jig is designed to do just about anything a standard power miterbox will, with a few extras just for fun. It will cut miters from 45° left to 45° right, and handle stock up to $1^1/_2$ in. thick.

Its large capacity means you can work with panels as wide as $16^1/_2$ in.—a figure that compares well with full-size radial-arm saws. The jig dimensions shown fit the Porter-Cable $8^1/_4$-in. saw (model No. 368-1). If you own a different saw, you'll have to modify the jig to suit your baseplate size and blade location.

Building the Jig

Start by cutting the plywood base to size, and then glue and nail the 1×4 base frame members in place. Position the middle frame member so it straddles the kerf position. Next, cut the stock to size for the guide rails and support blocks, and secure the support blocks from beneath with screws (Fig. 1). While the support blocks may be made out of hardwood or softwood, use hardwood for the guide rails. Cut the rabbets in the rail members (H, J and K) as shown in Detail 2 on the drawing (page 127).

After attaching the support blocks to the base, temporarily screw the narrow rail assembly (G and H) in place. Locate the miter-fence pivot point by first measuring the distance from the edge of your saw's base to the center of the blade. Then, measuring from the inside edge of the narrow rail assembly, mark the blade center position on the jig base. Use a square and rule to locate the blade position (Fig. 2). Bore the pivot hole 8 in. from the adjacent base edge as shown.

Position the wide rail assembly and lay your saw on the rails. Adjust the wide rail so the saw slides freely without excessive side play, and screw the rail to the supports (Fig. 3). Then, remove both rail assemblies.

1 After assembling the jig base, use glue and screws to attach the guide rail support blocks to both ends of the base.

2 Mark kerf by measuring saw blade-to-base edge distance from left guide. Place pivot on kerf, 8 in. up from base edge.

3 Use your saw to position right guide rail accurately. Then, bore pilot holes and attach right rail assembly with screws.

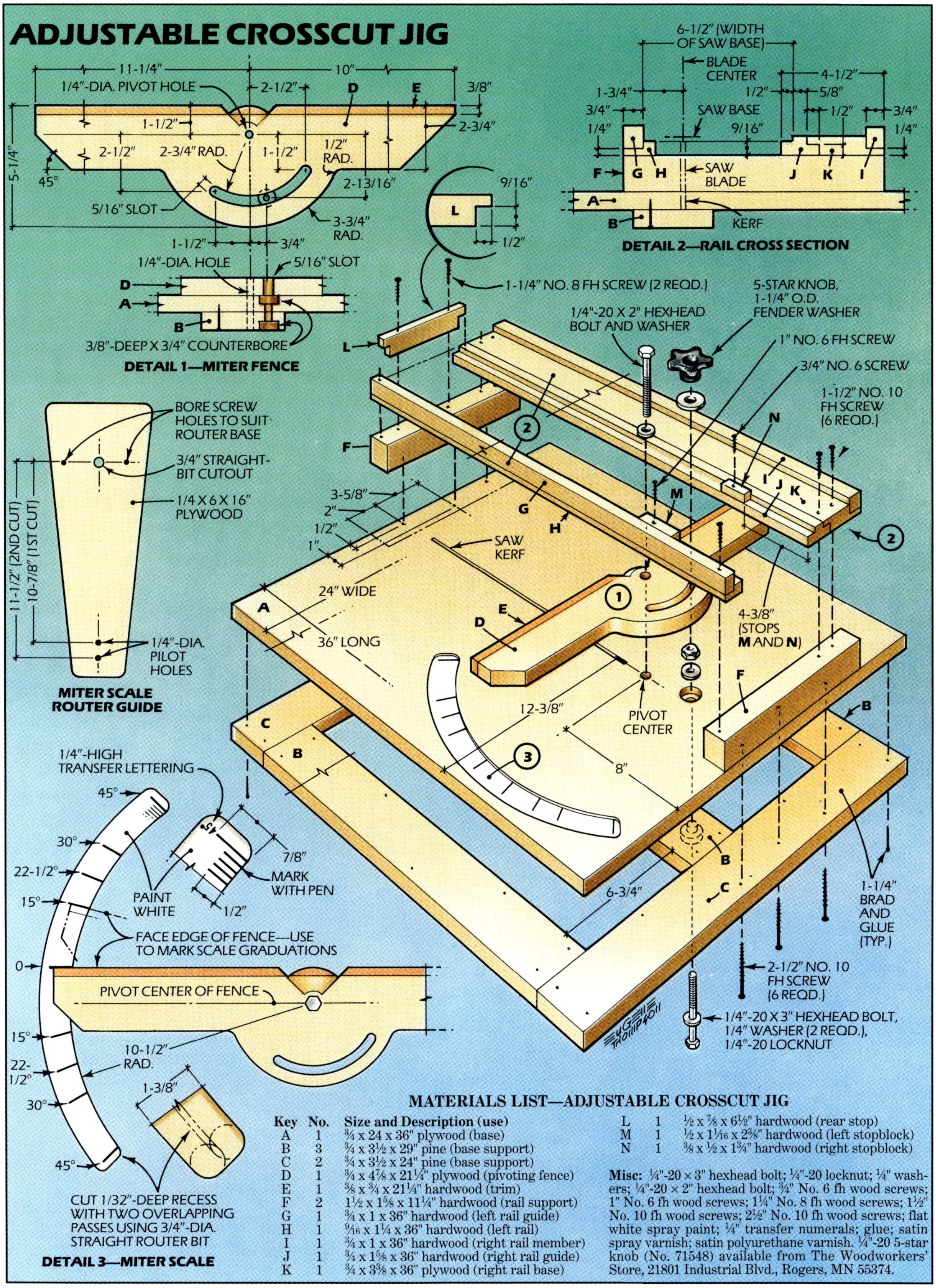

MATERIALS LIST—ADJUSTABLE CROSSCUT JIG

Key	No.	Size and Description (use)
A	1	¾ x 24 x 36" plywood (base)
B	3	¾ x 3½ x 29" pine (base support)
C	2	¾ x 3½ x 24" pine (base support)
D	1	¾ x 4⅞ x 21¼" plywood (pivoting fence)
E	1	⅜ x ¾ x 21¼" hardwood (trim)
F	2	1½ x 1⅝ x 11¼" hardwood (rail support)
G	1	¾ x 1 x 36" hardwood (left rail guide)
H	1	5/16 x 1¼ x 36" hardwood (left rail)
I	1	¾ x 1 x 36" hardwood (right rail member)
J	1	¾ x 1⅝ x 36" hardwood (right rail guide)
K	1	¾ x 3⅜ x 36" plywood (right rail base)
L	1	½ x ⅞ x 6½" hardwood (rear stop)
M	1	½ x 1 1/16 x 2⅜" hardwood (left stopblock)
N	1	⅜ x ½ x 1¾" hardwood (right stopblock)

Misc: ¼"-20 x 3" hexhead bolt; ¼"-20 locknut; ¼" washers; ¼"-20 x 2" hexhead bolt; ¾" No. 6 fh wood screws; 1" No. 6 fh wood screws; 1¼" No. 8 fh wood screws; 1½" No. 10 fh wood screws; 2½" No. 10 fh wood screws; flat white spray paint; ¼" transfer numerals; glue; satin spray varnish; satin polyurethane varnish. ¼"-20 5-star knob (No. 71548) available from The Woodworkers' Store, 21801 Industrial Blvd., Rogers, MN 55374.

4 After roughing out the curved slot in the fence, use a router, straight bit, guide bushing and template to finish slot.

5 Use a shopmade guide to rout the recess for the miter scale. Guide has two pivot centers to rout recess in two passes.

6 Mask the area surrounding the miter-scale recess and apply flat white spray enamel. You could also use a paintbrush.

7 Install the fence and use it to mark graduations in the recess. Use a protractor clamped to the fence to measure angles.

8 To make the kerf in the base, first clamp two temporary support walls to the rails. Lower the saw and move it along the rails.

9 Install stops to limit forward travel of saw. Make blade-clearance cut in fence by repeating cuts through fence pivot range.

Miter Fence and Scale

To build the miter fence, first glue a hardwood strip to the edge of a $\frac{3}{4}$-in.-thick plywood board that's slightly larger than the overall size of the fence. Lay out the cutting lines as shown, and mark the pivot hole. To make the curved slot, first bore $\frac{5}{16}$-in. holes at each end of the slot and then use a sabre saw to rough out the slot. Install a $\frac{5}{16}$-in. straight bit in your router and attach a template guide bushing to the base. Cut a template for the curve that's dimensioned to suit your guide bushing's offset. Tack the template to the miter fence and trim the slot with the router (Fig. 4).

Rout the $\frac{1}{32}$-in.-deep recess for the miter scale by first mounting your router to the shopmade miter-scale router guide shown in the drawing. Use a $\frac{3}{4}$-in. straight bit in the router. Bore two pivot holes in the guide—one $10\frac{7}{8}$ in. from the router bit center and the other $11\frac{1}{2}$ in. from the bit center. Then, make two overlapping passes—one from each pivot center—to form the $1\frac{3}{8}$-in.-wide recess (Fig. 5). Mask the area around the recess and spray two coats of flat white enamel paint (Fig. 6).

To lay out the scale graduations, first install the miter fence and tape a protractor to the fence so it's aligned with the pivot center. Use a $\frac{1}{4}$-in.-thick strip to raise the protractor above the pivot bolt head. Then, place a wood block on the base so one corner nearly touches the protractor while lying precisely on the blade centerline. Using the corner of the block as a reference point, rotate the fence 1° at a time and trace a line on the scale recess (Fig. 7). After applying transfer-type numerals, coat the graduations with satin spray varnish.

Bore and counterbore the hole for the lock-knob bolt and locknut, and install the fence and the guide rails. Cut and install the rear stop. Then, lock the fence at 0°.

Final Touches

To make the saw kerf in the base, temporarily attach two boards to the rails to form high walls. Fully extend the circular saw blade, raise the blade guard and lash it in place. With the rear of the base against the rear stop and the saw tilted so the blade clears the base, turn on the power and slowly lower the saw until it rests on the rails (Fig. 8). Stop the saw and unlash the blade guard. Then, turn on the power and make a slow pass to complete the kerf. Stop the kerf at the point where the fence meets the base. With the saw at this point, install the two forward stopblocks.

To cut the blade-clearance recess in the fence, simply run the saw up to the stopblocks while adjusting the fence through its range (Fig. 9).

Finish the crosscut jig by first removing the guide rails and the pivoting fence. Then, apply two coats of satin polyurethane varnish to the components, and reassemble the jig.

10 After boring the pilot holes in the guide rail, tack the pieces together and align them with a square.

11 Remove the hardwood block excess by making a cut with your saw. The cut edge now indicates saw kerf position.

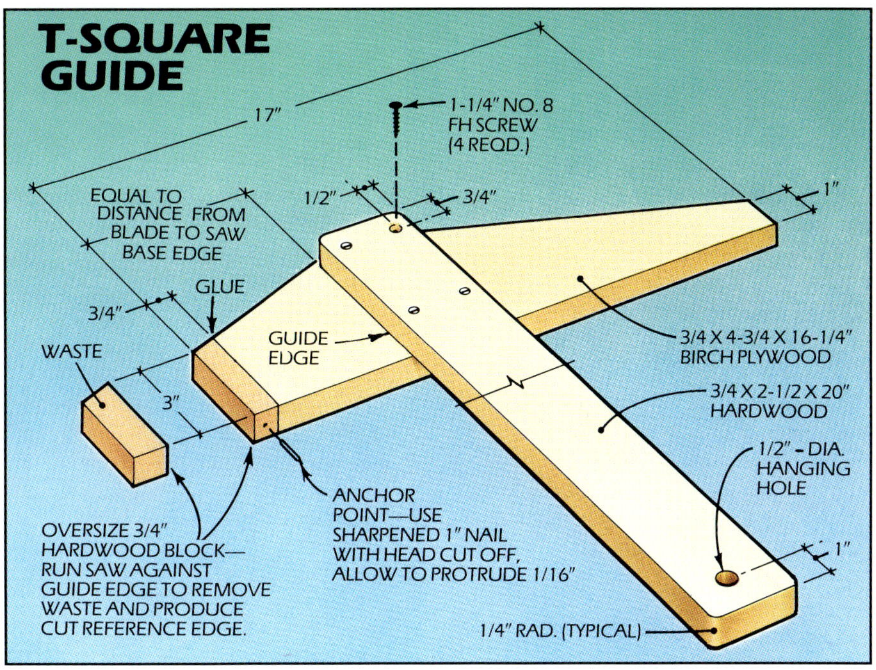

T-SQUARE GUIDE

The most common chore for a circular saw is a square crosscut. This jig does more than simply guide your saw square, however. Because the crossmember—the piece that rests on the stock edge—is initially longer than necessary, it's cut off the first time you use the jig. From then on, this trimmed end provides a precise kerf indicator for your saw and blade. The dimensions shown suit a Porter-Cable 368-1. You can, however, easily adapt the design to any model of circular saw.

First, cut $^{3}/_{4}$-in.-thick plywood to length and width for the crossmember. Then, glue a piece of $^{3}/_{4}$-in.-thick hardwood to the saw-blade end.

Measure the distance from the blade to the motor side of the saw base. Then, mark the position of the guide rail a distance from the hardwood end slightly greater than the blade-to-base edge distance. Cut the cross-member profile as shown. Then cut the hardwood guide rail to width and length. Bore pilot holes in the guide rail, but not yet into the crossmember. Then, tack-nail the pieces together. Use a square to accurately position the components, and then add another nail to hold the pieces in place while the screws are added (Fig. 10). Finish the job by boring a hanging hole as shown.

Make a cut to remove the excess on the hardwood block (Fig. 11). Check your first test cut for square and adjust the jig if necessary.

Of course, this type of jig isn't confined to 90° cuts. You can easily make versions that handle repetitive mitered cuts, as well.

Drill jigs

Drill Jigs was written by Rosario Capotosto. Photos by Rosario Capotosto. The three bushings for the *V-Block Drill Jig* are available as a set (No. 626-062) from Woodworker's Supply Inc., 1108 North Glenn Rd., Casper WY 82601.

HORIZONTAL BORING JIG

The portable power drill is probably the single most useful and popular power tool. Everyone owns one. The fact is, boring a hole is one of the most basic woodworking operations.

There are many times, however, when the eyeball method of hole alignment just isn't good enough for the job at hand. Of course, the pros turn to a drill press at these moments. Much of the work a drill press routinely handles, though, can be accomplished with a simple drill jig that holds the drill and bit at a consistent and controllable position in relation to the work.

The horizontal boring jig shown here is designed to handle a range of chores. In addition to simply boring aligned holes for screws and bolts, it's particularly well suited to doweling and preliminary waste removal in mortising—two woodworking jobs that standard drill presses aren't designed for. In this jig, a portable drill is mounted on a sliding carriage that pivots on a hinged platform. The pivoting action permits positioning the bit up to 3 in. from the bottom edge of the work. To keep the drill firmly and accurately mounted on the carriage, a custom-molded bed was used. This is an ideal solution because it easily suits the contours of typical drill housings and makes the jig suitable for any make and model of drill. The carriage dimensions shown will accommodate most drills. If your drill is large, you may have to modify the size of the drill carriage.

Drill Carriage

Start by building the drill carriage, because you'll use it later to bore accurate holes in other components. Cut the plywood carriage base to width and about 6 in. longer in length than shown (about 13 in.). Then, cut the 1/8-in.-thick edge banding to match the length of the long side edges and glue the edge banding to the plywood.

To make the custom drill-housing bed, first install a 3/8-in.-dia. bit in your drill. Then measure the distance between the top edge of the bit and the highest point on top of the housing. Add about 1/8 in. to this measurement and cut a 4-in.-sq. block to this thickness.

1 Align bit squarely on temporary bit-support block and tack cleats on each side. Bit is aligned with base centerline.

2 Install bit in drill and tape chuck so it won't turn. Then, clamp bit to support block to suspend drill housing over base.

3 With bit clamped and the drill handle vertical, nail enclosure strips around drill housing to contain filler.

HORIZONTAL BORING JIG

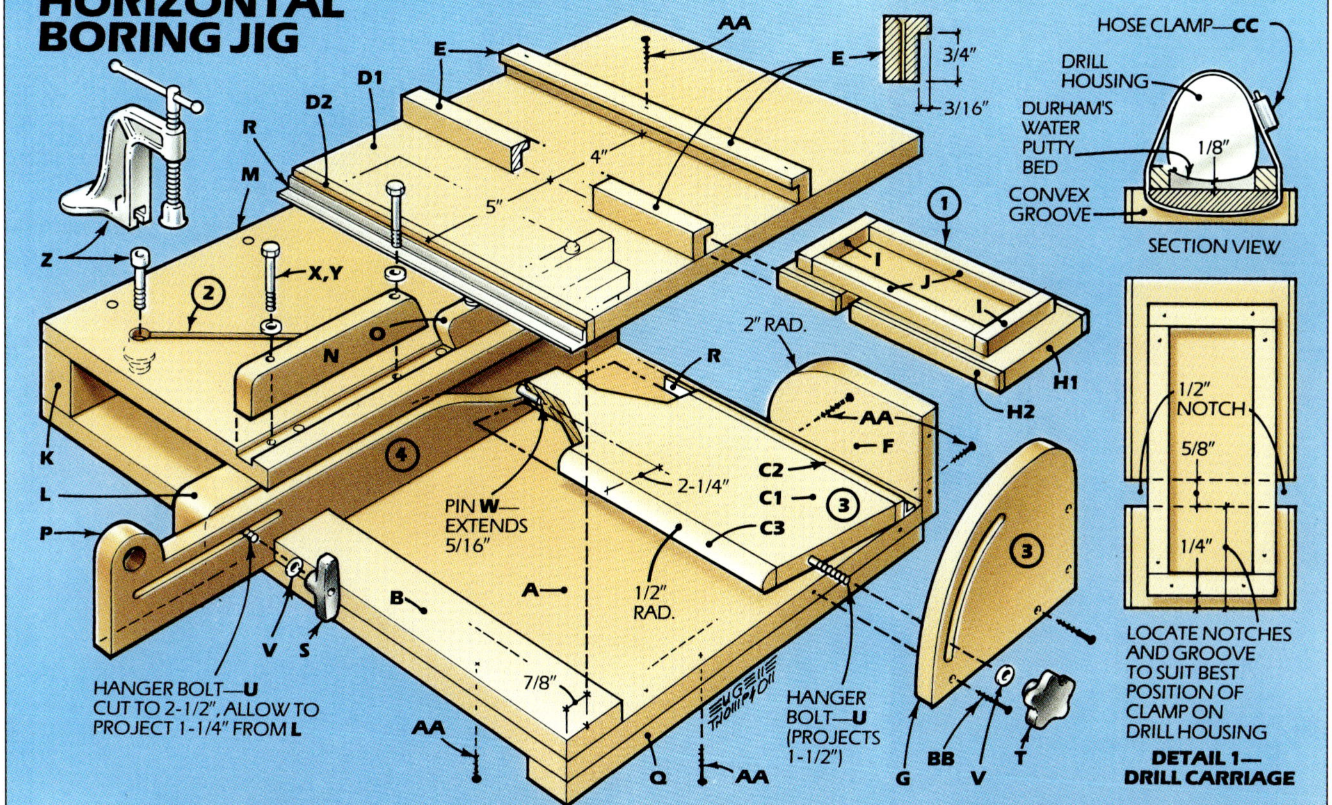

MATERIALS LIST—HORIZONTAL BORING JIG

Key	No.	Size and Description (use)
A	1	¾ x 16 x 24" plywood (base)
B	1	¾ x 2¼ x 12" plywood (platform support cleat)
C1	1	¾ x 6 x 12" plywood (platform support)
C2	1	⅜ x ¾ x 12" hardwood (trim)
C3	1	½ x ¾ x 12" hardwood (trim)
D1	1	¾ x 12 x 14¾" plywood (platform)
D2	1	⅜ x ¾ x 12" hardwood (trim)
E	2	¾ x 1 x 12" hardwood (carriage guide)
F	1	¾ x 4 x 6" plywood (side bracket)
G	1	¾ x 6 x 7" plywood (front bracket)
H1	1	¾ x 3¾ x 7⅝" plywood (carriage base)
H2	2	⅛ x ¾ x 7⅝" hardwood (edge band)
I	2	½ x ½ x 3" hardwood (end block)
J	2	½ x ½ x 5¾" hardwood (side block)
K	1	1½ x 2½ x 16" pine (table support)
L	1	1½ x 2½ x 18" pine (table support)
M	1	¾ x 11⅝ x 16" plywood (table)
N	1	¾ x 1½ x 7⅜" hardwood (fence)
O	1	¾ x 1½ x 7⅞" hardwood (fence)
P	1	¾ x 4¼ x 18" plywood (sliding support)
Q	1	¾ x 1½ x 16" hardwood (bench stop)
R	2	1¹⁄₁₆ x 12" hinges
S*	1	¼"-20 T-knob
T*	1	¼"-20 5-star knob
U	2	¼"-20 x 3" hanger bolts
V	2	¼" ID washer
W	1	¼"-dia. x 1" steel pin
X	4	¼"-20 Teenut
Y	4	¼"-20 x 2" hexhead bolt and washer
Z	1	3" hold-down clamp
AA**		1½" No. 10 fh screw
BB**		2" No. 10 fh screw
CC	1	hose clamp

Misc: 1¼" brads; glue; Durham's Water Putty; plastic wrap; sandpaper.

* 5-star knob (No. 71548) and T-knob (No. 71506) available from The Woodworkers' Store, 21801 Industrial Blvd., Rogers, MN 55374.

** As required.

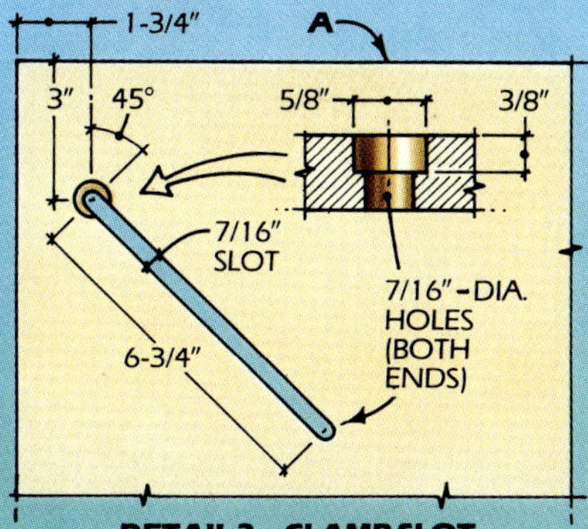

DETAIL 2—CLAMP SLOT

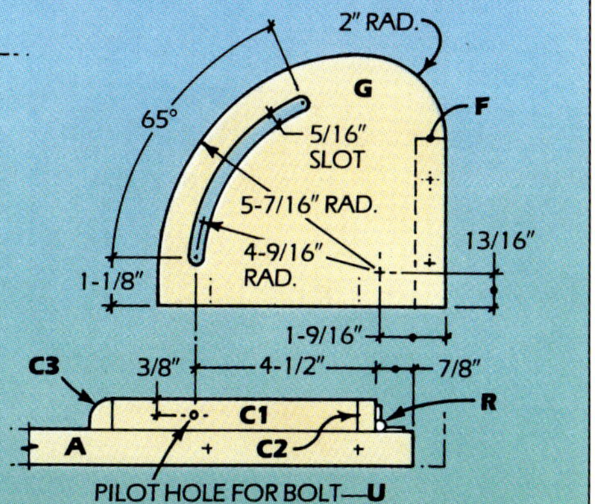

DETAIL 3—PLATFORM SUPPORT

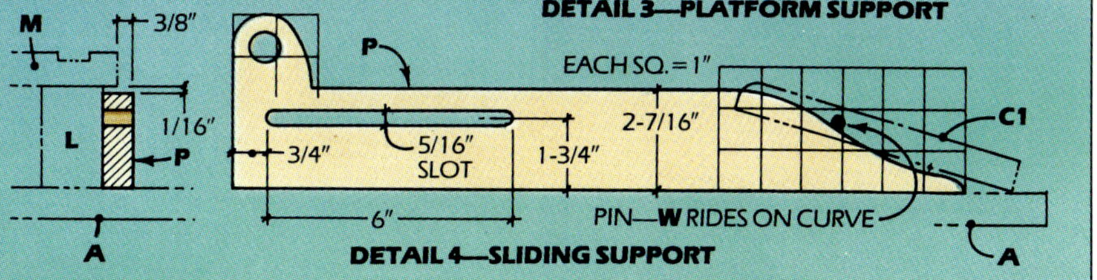

DETAIL 4—SLIDING SUPPORT

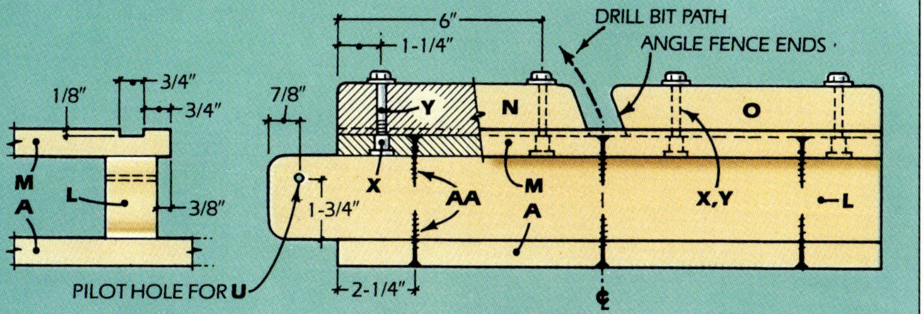

SECTION VIEW AT CENTER

PM TECHNICAL ART BY EUGENE THOMPSON

4 Remove drill and fill area with Durham's Water Putty or a similar compound that sets hard but can be sanded.

5 Cover drill housing with plastic wrap and set the drill in the soft putty. Clamp bit firmly between cleats on support block.

6 After putty has hardened, remove drill and sand surface flush with enclosure strips. Contoured recess holds drill securely.

7 Align hose clamp with the section of the housing that affords the best grip. Then, mark the base for clamp notches.

8 After sawing edges of hose clamp recess, use a chisel to remove the rest of the waste on bottom of the drill carriage.

9 Use the drill carriage to bore accurate holes in platform support piece. Guide carriage against strip clamped to bench.

Draw centerlines along the top, down both ends and around the bottom of the block. Temporarily nail the block near one end of the carriage base so it's aligned with the base centerline. Remove the bit from your drill and place it on the block centerline. Cut two small wooden cleats, $^3/_4$×3 in. long and just shy of $^3/_8$ in. thick. Butt each cleat securely alongside the centered bit. Then, nail the cleats to the block (Fig. 1).

Reinstall the bit in the drill and wrap tape around the chuck and housing to keep the chuck from turning. Place a scrap block over the bit and clamp the bit between the cleats (Fig. 2). In this position, the drill is cantilevered over the carriage base, with a $^1/_8$-in. space between the housing and the base. Then, add the $^1/_2$-in.-sq. enclosure pieces, as shown, to suit your drill (Fig. 3).

Remove the drill from the carriage base and cover the housing with clear plastic wrap. Stretch the wrap, press it to the housing so it covers smoothly and apply tape so it doesn't come off. Mix up a relatively soft batch of Durham's Water Putty (available at most hardware and paint stores), pour it into the enclosure and level the top (Fig. 4).

Carefully place the drill into position with the housing seated in the putty and the bit clamped firmly in the channel between the cleats (Fig. 5). Using a square as a reference, check that the drill handle is vertical. Allow the putty to set overnight. Remove the drill and sand flush the top of the molded enclosure (Fig. 6).

Return the drill to the molded bed and determine the best location for the hose clamp (Fig. 7). Then cut the hose clamp notches in the base sides and around the bottom as shown (Fig. 8). Finally, cut the base carriage to the finished length as shown in the drawing on page 131.

Platform and Table

Cut the plywood jig base to 16×24 in. Then, cut the $2^1/_4$×12-in. cleat (B) and secure it to the jig base with glue and nails as shown. Next, cut a 12 × $14^3/_4$-in. plywood board for the tilting platform (D1), and add the $^3/_8$×$^3/_4$-in. strip (D2) on one end to receive the hinge. Cut the assembly to $15^1/_8$ in. long by trimming the opposite end. Cut a 12-in. length of $1^1/_{16}$-in. continuous hinge. Attach the hinge first to the hardwood strip on the tilting platform and then to the cleat on the base, taking care to align the hinge properly with both components.

Next, make the smaller tilting platform support board that fits under the tilting platform. First, glue $^3/_8$- and $^1/_2$-in.-thick strips to each long edge of a 6×12-in. plywood board. After the glue is dry, use a router to round one corner of the $^1/_2$-in.-thick strip with a $^3/_8$-in. rounding-over bit.

You can use the drill carriage to bore perfectly aligned holes in each end of the support board for the hanger bolt and the $^1/_4$-in.-dia. steel pin. First, clamp a straight guide strip to your bench so it's aligned with the edge. Then, align the support board with the bench

10 Secure platform support hinge with one screw. Check alignment with base and tilting platform. Install remaining screws.

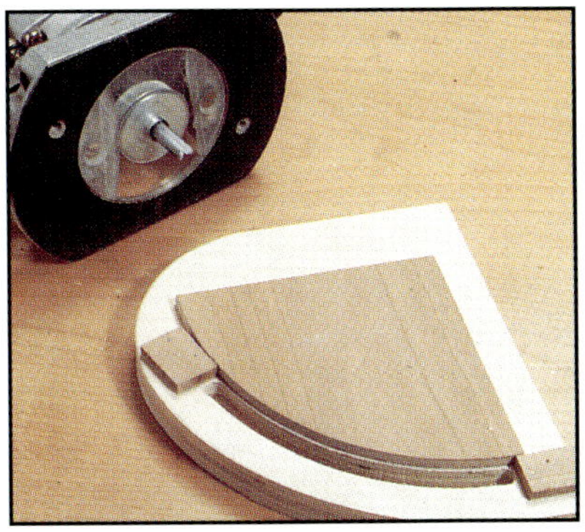

11 After using a sabre saw to rough cut the bracket slot, trim to finished shape with a router, guide bushing and template.

12 Use a wingnut to install hanger bolt in platform support hole. Bolt goes through bracket slot and locks platform.

13 Tack rabbeted carriage guides to tilting platform and check for alignment. Then, secure guides with screws.

14 Bore holes at ends of hold-down-clamp adjustment slot in base. Finish cutting slot with a scroll saw or sabre saw.

15 Temporarily secure fence, and use a drafting triangle to align table squarely with carriage guides on tilting platform.

edge, shimmed to the correct height for a centered hole. Install your drill in the carriage, then place the carriage against the guide strip and bore the holes (Fig. 9).

Attach the hinge to the support board, and then attach the assembly to the jig base with a single screw through the hinge at one end. Align the support board with a square, and use tape to secure the other end of the hinge to the jig base (Fig. 10). Rest the tilting platform on the support board, and test the assembly by tiling the support board upward to raise the tilting platform—the rounded edge should remain in contact throughout the swing. Adjust the free end of the hinge, if necessary, and install the remaining screws.

Cut the upright corner brackets to size and temporarily join them with screws. To scribe the precise position of the curved slot, first whittle the end of a short pencil so it fits into the hanger bolt hole in the support board end. Then, butt the side bracket (F) against the side of the base while advancing the end bracket (G) until it touches the pencil. Hold the bracket in position and tilt the support to scribe the line. Disassemble the corner pieces and use the drill carriage to bore $^5/_{16}$-in.-dia. holes at each end of the arc. Draw the slot outline and use a sabre saw to cut the slot. You can also use a router, guide bushing and template to trim the slot (Fig. 11). After the slot is cut, use a wingnut to install the hanger bolt into the hole in the support board (Fig. 12). Make and install rabbeted hardwood carriage guides as shown (Fig. 13). Make both guides in a single length of stock, using a router or table saw to cut the rabbet. Then, cut the finished piece to produce the two 12-in.-long guides.

Cut the fixed table (M) to size and use a router to make the $^1/_8$-in.-deep × $^3/_4$-in.-wide groove for the fence. Then, lay out the clamp slot as shown by marking the centers of the end holes. Bore $^1/_8$-in. pilot holes at these centers and counterbore the $^5/_8$-in.-dia. × $^3/_8$-in.-deep recess from the bottom side of the table as shown. Rebore the pilot holes from the top with a $^7/_{16}$-in. bit. Finish the slot with a sabre saw or scroll saw (Fig. 14). Next, make the 2-piece fence out of a single piece of hardwood. Cut this after the table has been accurately positioned and fastened. Then, cut the table support pieces from 2×4 softwood and bore the $^1/_4$-in.-dia. hole in the forward support for the hanger bolt as shown. Attach the supports to the jig base.

Use the sliding carriage and drill to bore four $^1/_8$-in. pilot holes through the fence stock at the bolt locations. Then, remove your drill from the carriage, position the fence and continue the holes through the tazle. On the bottom of the table, bore $^1/_{16}$-in.-deep × $^3/_4$-in.-dia. counterbores for the Teenuts. Then bore out the $^1/_8$-in. table pilot holes to $^5/_{16}$ in. and install the Teenuts. Switch to a $^1/_4$-in. bit and rebore the pilot holes in the fence.

Temporarily attach the fence and place the table in position on the supports. Use a square or drafting triangle to accurately align the table so the fence is square with the carriage guides (Fig. 15). You'll have to tilt and lock the platform to allow the triangle or square to contact both the fence and the carriage guide. When the table is aligned properly, tack-nail it to the rear support and bore screw pilot holes. Then, remove the fence and bore screw pilot holes in the fence groove for securing the table to the forward support. Permanently secure the table to the supports with screws. Cut the fence into two pieces to create an opening for the drill bit.

Lay out the sliding support on 3/4-in.-thick hardwood stock and use a sabre saw to cut the shape. Bore the finger-pull hole and lay out the slot so it's aligned with the hanger bolt hole in the forward table support. Cut the slot with a sabre saw or scroll saw after boring holes at the slot ends. Finally, install the sliding support and the T-knob and hanger bolt (Fig. 16).

16 After making sliding support, install and check action. Curved edge supports platform pin at shallow height settings.

HOLE SPACING GUIDE

This jig aids in boring screw pilot holes, shelf pinholes and any other series of holes that must be placed at a uniform distance from an edge.

To make the jig, first cut a piece of acrylic sheet to size. Then, tape a piece of paper to the sheet and mark the hole centers. Clamp a backup block to the work, and use a brad point bit to bore the holes (Fig. 17). Attach the sheet to a hardwood guide strip with two wood screws as shown in the drawing.

The hole spacing and diameter shown in the illustration produce a general-purpose jig that's useful for boring pilot holes. You can easily vary the dimensions to suit specific applications that require a larger hole size or different spacing.

17 Use the horizontal boring jig to make this spacing jig. Change the hole diameter and spacing to suit the application.

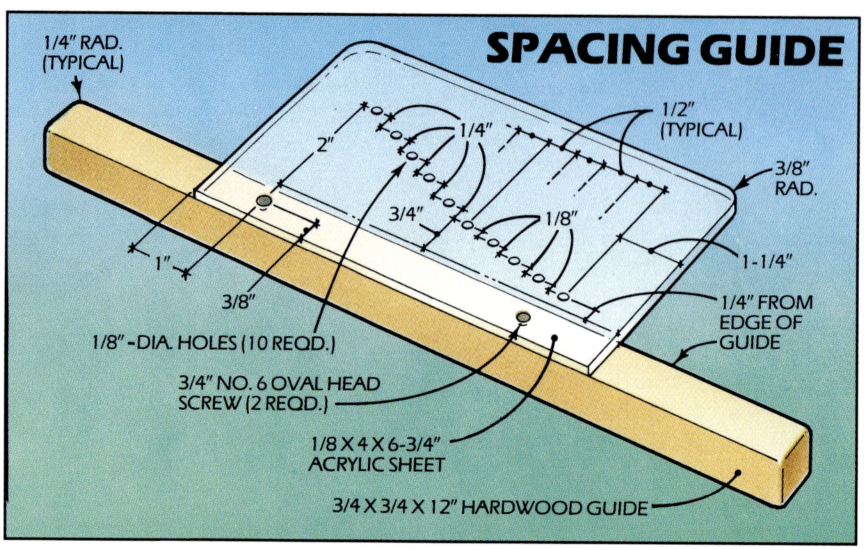

18 Use a black fine-point pen to mark the graduations. Make sure graduations on each side are aligned accurately.

19 To position jig with layout mark on workpiece, align similar graduation marks on opposite sides of jig.

20 To use jig, install steel bushing to suit bit. Place jig over work and bring the pins in contact with the workfaces.

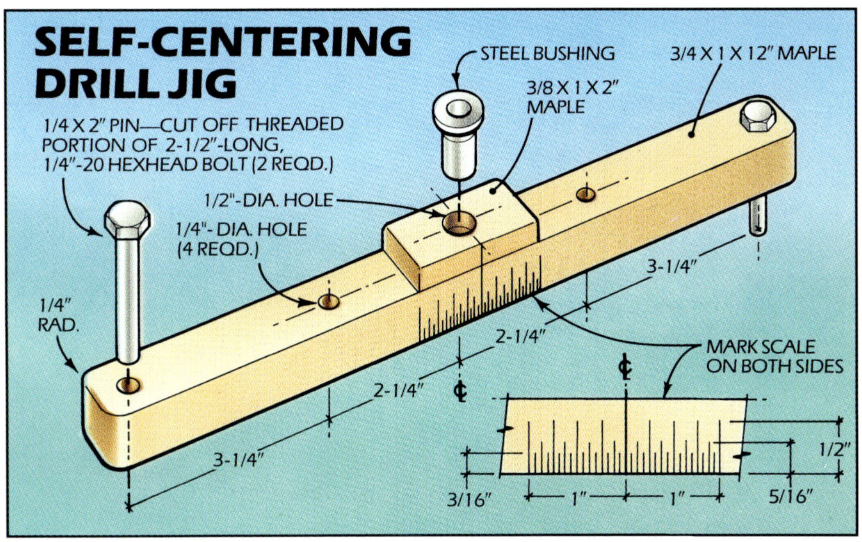

SELF-CENTERING JIG

If you've tried to position centered holes by measuring the thickness of the work and dividing in half, you know that the holes rarely fall exactly where you want them. This jig automatically centers holes regardless of stock size. To use it, you simply place it diagonally over the work and turn it to bring the pins on each end in contact with the workfaces. The design features two sets of pinholes to handle thick and thin stock. The graduations drawn on the jig aid in aligning the hole with a mark on the face or edge of the workpiece.

To make the jig, cut the hardwood parts to size and glue the small block to the center to hold the bit bushing. Then, accurately lay out the hole centers and bore the holes on the horizontal boring jig or a drill press.

Use a fine-point felt-tip pen to draw the graduations on both sides of the jig as shown (Fig. 18). To make the pins, cut off the threaded portion from $2^1/_2$-in.-long, $^1/_4$-in. bolts. Steel drill-bit bushings are available in $^1/_4$-, $^5/_{16}$- and $^3/_8$-in. sizes from mail-order suppliers.

To align the jig with a centerline marked on the workpiece, simply line up diagonally opposed graduations with the centerline (Fig. 19). Then, with a bushing that matches the bit installed in your drill, insert the bit in the bushing and bore a perfectly centered hole (Fig. 20).

21 Set table-saw blade at 45° and align fence and blade height to produce a centered V-notch. Use pushstick for safety.

22 Align the work with an offset mark that matches the distance from the bushing to the block end. Then bore your hole.

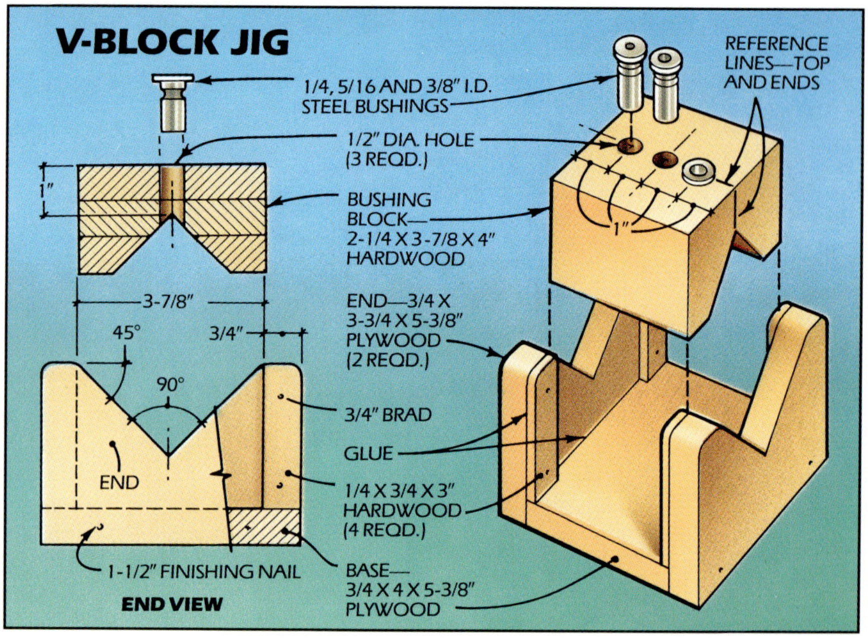

V-BLOCK DRILL JIG

With this handy jig, you can easily bore centered and perpendicular holes in round stock that ranges from $^3/_8$ to 2 in. in diameter. The hardwood V-block holds three hardened-steel bushings that guide the drill bit for boring $^1/_4$-, $^5/_{16}$- or $^3/_8$-in. dia. holes. A plywood cradle holds and stabilizes the workpiece.

To construct the jig, first glue together three pieces of $^3/_4$-in. hardwood to make up the $2^1/_4$-in.-thick V-block. After cutting the block to exact size, lay out the centerlines for the holes so they're spaced 1 in. apart and 1 in. from each end. Use a drill press or drill guide to bore the three $^1/_2$-in.-dia. holes for the bushings. Mark the lines for the V cut, then tilt your table saw blade to 45° and make two passes to form the V in the block (Fig. 21).

Lay out the V-shaped cutouts on the cradle endpieces, and cut exactly to the line with a sabre saw or band saw. Nail the four $^1/_4$-in.-thick guide strips to the cradle pieces, as shown. Use finishing nails and glue to join the cradle ends to the base. Mark a vertical centerline on the ends of the V-block, then apply sanding sealer to all surfaces.

To straighten work in the jig, make an offset index mark on the work that corresponds to the distance from the desired bushing center to an end of the V-block. Then, align the centerline of the hole position on the workpiece with the centerline of the V-block, and align the offset index marks with the appropriate end of the V-block. Insert the bit in the bushing and bore the hole (Fig. 22).

Router jigs

Text and photographs for *Router Jigs* by Rosario Capotosto. Technical art by Eugene Thompson.

SURFACING JIG

The jig is comprised of two L-shaped tracks that hold the work. An adjustable carriage that holds the router rides on top of the tracks. In operation, the router, equipped with a large-diameter straight bit, moves across the work on its carriage while the bit levels a strip across the surface. After each pass, the carriage is moved along the L-shaped tracks for the next pass.

This surfacing jig is dimensioned to handle work up to 18X30 in., but its capacity can be modified by changing the size of the carriage and the length of the tracks.

1 Make the carriage tracks and place them on the track joiners. Adjust spacing and then mark for joiner dadoes.

2 After the dadoes have been cut in the joiners, secure one joiner with glue and screws. Opposite joiner is adjustable.

3 Position router carriage over L-shaped tracks and lock sliding joiner. Then adjust bit depth for shallow cut.

Begin by cutting the stock for the carriage tracks and the track joiners to size. You can use your router to cut the track rabbets, but a table saw is faster. Make each rabbet in two passes—the shallow cut first, followed by the deep cut that removes the waste.

The dadoes in the joiner pieces are positioned to suit the size of your router base. To ensure accurate placement, set the tracks parallel to each other on the joiner pieces and space them so the router fits in between (Fig. 1). Attach one end of each track to one joiner piece with screws (Fig. 2)—the other joiner is adjustable. Cut the clamp blocks for the adjustable joiner to size, and use a sharp chisel to shape the recesses for the $^{1}/_{16}$-in.-thick iron clamping bars.

Then, attach the clamping blocks to the adjustable joiner with screws. Bore the holes through the clamping bars as shown, and attach the bars to the blocks with 1-in. No.10 pan head screws. Using the bolt hole in the clamping bar as a guide, bore a corresponding bolt hole through each end of the joiner. Install the bolts and T-knobs. Make and install stops on the joiners that limit router travel. Set these back $^{1}/_{4}$ in. farther than the router-base-to-cutter distance so the cutter travel extends past the work edge.

To make the tracks, rip the track members to width and assemble both L-shaped pieces with screws and glue. Then, bore and countersink the holes for the drywall screws that hold the stock.

Make four stepped leveling blocks as shown. Use these to support the work while the L-shaped tracks are screwed to the work edges. Adjust the carriage to fit over the tracks, tighten the clamps and set the bit depth for the first pass (Fig. 3).

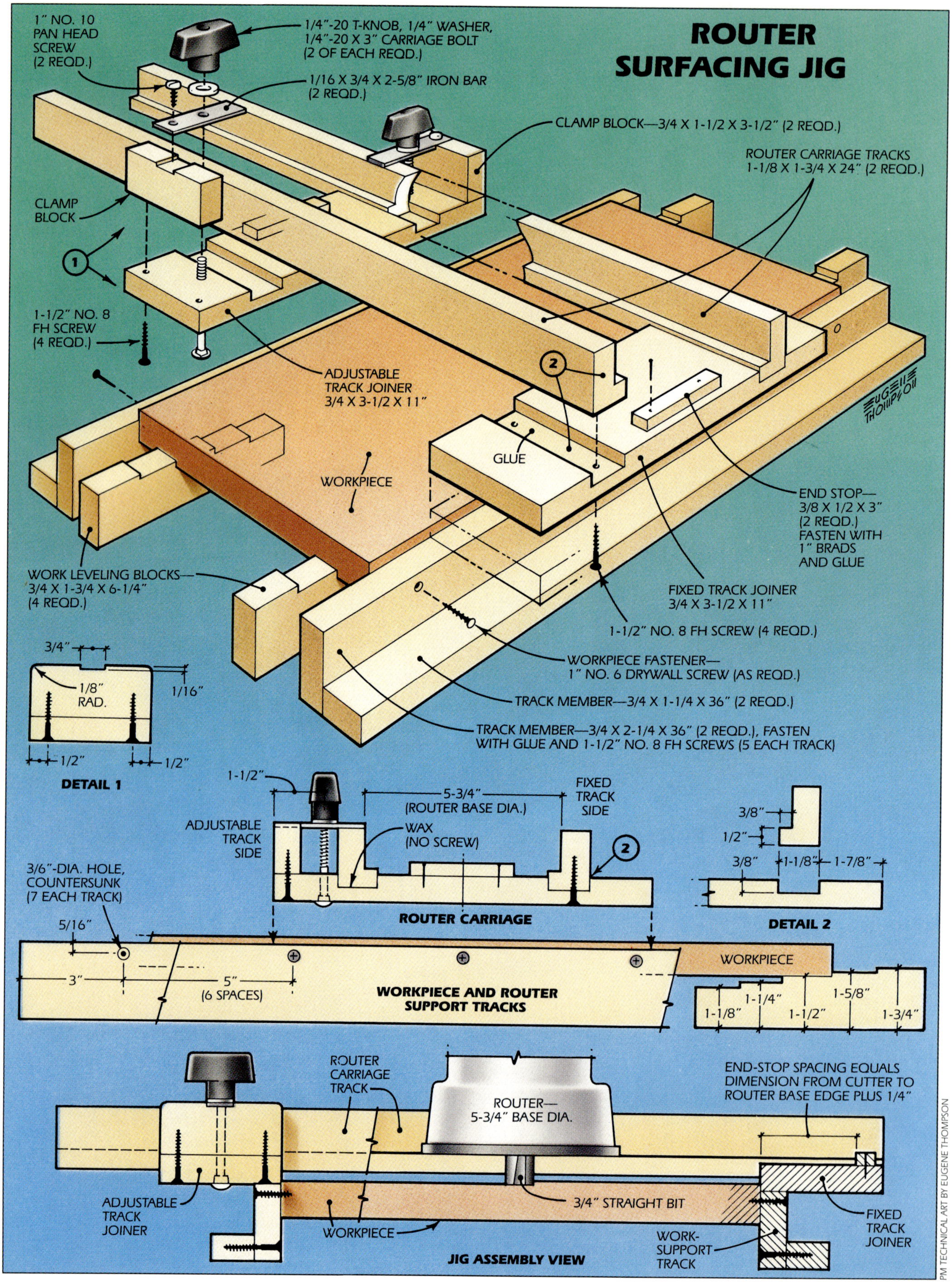

PM TECHNICAL ART BY EUGENE THOMPSON

EDGE GUIDE

Of all the jigs that you can buy or make to enhance your router, a basic edge guide, or fence, is the most essential. Considering its usefulness, however, it's surprising that many routers don't come with one—you have to buy it as a special accessory.

Actually, you don't have to buy one; you can make it yourself. This edge guide is based on an oversize clear-acrylic baseplate with a pivoting fence that's adjusted at one point.

Begin by cutting a sheet of $^1/_4$-in. acrylic plastic to 12 in. square. Leave on the protective paper. You'll use this for marking layout lines.

You can cut the curved edge freehand with a scroll saw, band saw or sabre saw, but it's best to use a stationary tool equipped with a simple pivoting jig to guide the cut. First, bore a small nail hole at the baseplate pivot point. Then, drive a nail through this hole into a board clamped to the scroll saw or band saw table. Align the hole with the front edge of the scroll or band saw blade.

Remove your router's baseplate, place it on the acrylic sheet and trace the screwholes and central router-bit hole (Fig. 4). Use a 2-in. hole saw to bore the center hole. Then, bore and countersink the screwholes.

Cut the fence to size and bore the pivot hole with a $^1/_4$-in.-dia. bit. To bore the $^1/_4$-in. half hole, first mark the hole location. Then, clamp a piece of scrap wood to the face of the fence and use the seam between the two pieces as a centerline for the hole.

Shape the clamp recess by first boring a $^1/_2$-in.-dia. hole into the end as shown. Then, remove the remaining waste by boring a $^5/_{16}$-in. hole and finishing the slot with a sharp chisel.

Attach the router and fence to the new baseplate and secure a $^1/_4$-in.-dia. alignment rod (cut from a bolt) in the router collet. Glue a piece of paper to the end of the alignment rod and mark centerlines on the end.

Tape a rule with fine graduations to a small block of wood to act as a square. Align a whole number on the rule with the inside edge of the block.

To make the zero mark on the baseplate, align the fence so the alignment rod is seated in the half hole (Fig. 5). Subsequent graduations are marked in $^1/_4$-in. increments. They are offset from the original zero mark, however, by $^1/_8$-in. to align with a similarly offset index mark on the fence.

Using the shopmade square, pivot the fence $^1/_8$ in. from the alignment rod center and mark a 2-in.-long line on the baseplate. From this position, mark lines on the baseplate that indicate fence positions as you move it in $^1/_4$-in. increments (Fig. 6).

4 Remove the base from the router and use it to mark the screwholes and the router-bit hole on the acrylic sheet.

5 Install a $^1/_4$-in.-rad. rod in router and attach router and fence to the new base. Seat rod in half hole to find zero mark.

6 Tape a block to a finely graduated rule. Pivot fence while aligning rule graduations with rod center to locate base graduations.

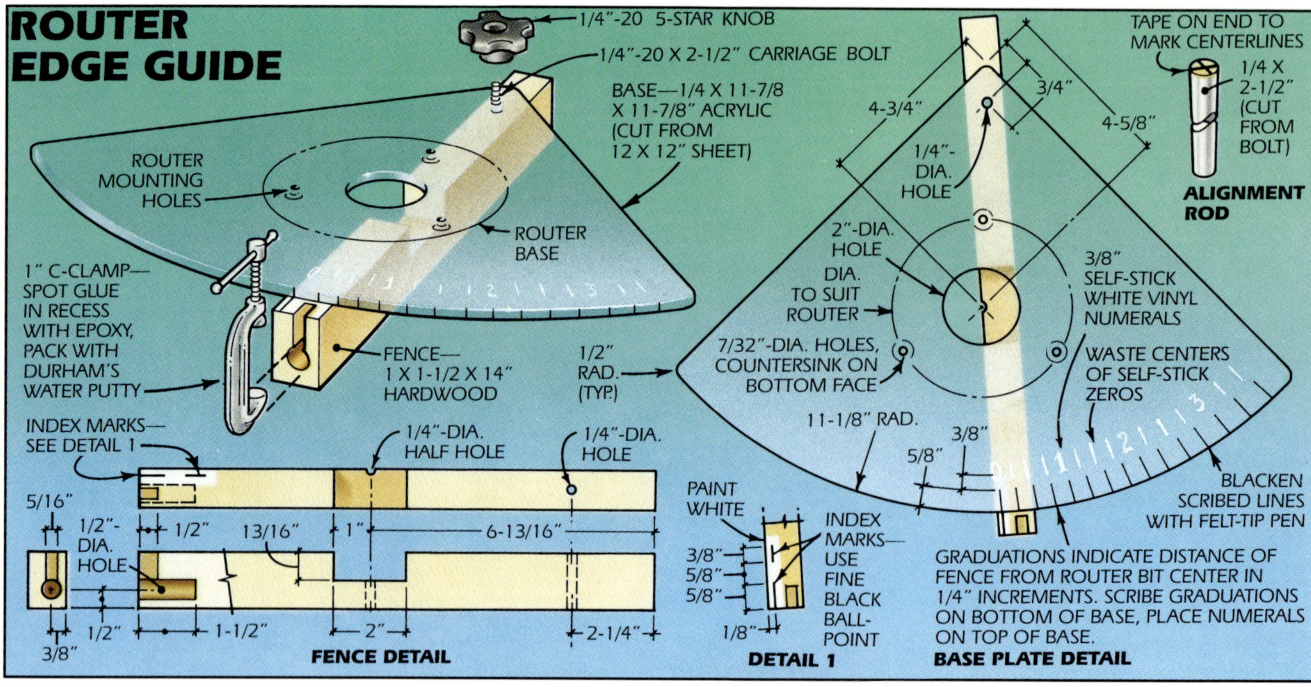

Peel away a 5/8-in.-wide strip of the protective paper from the arc edge. Use a rule and a plastic-laminate scoring tool (available where laminate is sold) to scribe a line at each graduation (Fig. 7). Then, ink the scribed lines with a black felt-tipped pen, and wipe away the surplus ink with an alcohol-dampened cloth.

Peel away the remaining protective paper. Use 3/8-in. self-stick vinyl numerals, available at stationery and art supply stores, to designate each graduation. To create bars between the numerals, use the waste centers from the zero self-stick numerals.

Fill the clamp recess with Durham's Water Putty, then firmly seat the clamp in the recess. Paint a white spot on the fence end, and mark the index line on the white spot 1/8 in. from the fence edge.

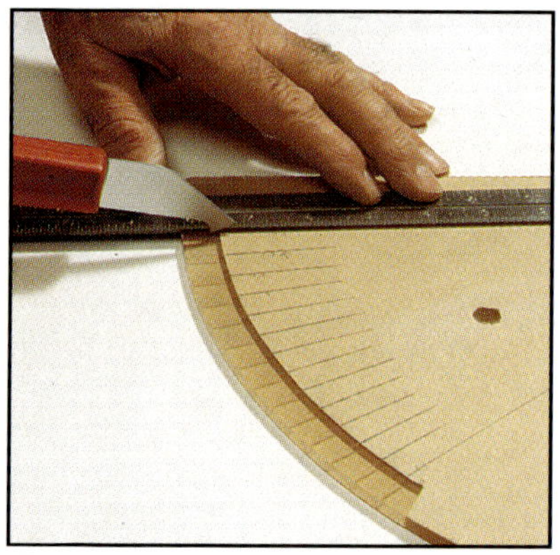

7 Peel away a 5/8-in.-wide strip of protective paper at the arc edge. Continue graduation lines by scribing an arc.

Raw materials

It used to be that if you wanted to assemble material for a furniture or cabinet project, you had to visit a minimum of three or four suppliers—your local lumberyard, the corner hardware and paint stores and maybe even the closest tool supply outlet. Today, however, with the coming of the home-center mega-stores, you can get everything you need for almost any project at just one location. While this may remove some of the romance from your woodworking pursuit, it can also remove much of the frustration of tracking down a long list of materials.

Raw Materials was written by Neal Barrett with photos by Rosario Capotosto.

Wood

The foundation of most woodworking projects is some type of solid lumber. While a typical home center won't carry the same selection of species and grades as a specialty lumberyard, you can expect to find a reasonable assortment of both softwood and hardwood stock.

For general millwork, pine lumber is still the most popular material. Pine is most often stocked in the No.2 Common grade, which allows quite large and plentiful knots, although they must be solid. Some stores will also carry Select grade pine with tiny pin knots that are hardly visible.

Select pine is the material of choice for pieces of elegant design that must have a smooth, unblemished surface. But the use of Select grade lumber comes at a considerable price, since its cost is about $2^1/_2$ times more than that of Common grade.

For pieces that have a rustic design, the knotty appearance of Common pine can be a real plus. By buying a little extra material, you can often cut around the worst knots and end up with a very suitable piece for much less money.

Fine lumber is available in sizes ranging from 1×2 to 1×12, with lengths from 4 to 16 ft. Sometimes, 5/4 stock ($1^1/_{16}$-in. actual thickness) is carried in the same grades, widths and lengths. It's easy to make the thicker pieces that are often needed in woodworking projects by simply gluing together thinner pieces.

Specialty pine stock is also carried at many home centers. These items might include 1×6 tongue-and-groove beaded boards and shiplap siding for exterior use.

The hardwood species most often found at home centers are poplar and red oak. One nice feature about buying hardwoods at a home center is that they are sold already surfaced on all four sides (unlike most lumberyards). Another is that hardwood stock can be available in an incredible variety of sizes, ranging from $^1/_4$-in. thick × 2 in. wide and 12 in. long to standard 1×12 dimensions in 10-ft. lengths. Note that lengths are often formed by gluing up narrower-width boards. Also available are 2×2-in. and 3×3 squares in 36- and 48-in. lengths. Compared with Select pine, expect to pay about one-third more for poplar and twice as much for red oak.

The selection of moldings found at a home center also can be quite impressive. A wide variety of architectural and cabinet profiles are usually stocked in pine and red oak, and occasionally poplar. These profiles might include casing, baseboard, chair-rail, cove, crown, half- and quarter-round and panel moldings—all in different sizes. One particularly useful item, with many project applications, is the $^1/_4$-in.-thick lattice stock, usually sold in $1^3/_4$-in. width. Costs for these millwork items can run from 20¢ per ft. to $5 per ft., depending on size, species and complexity of the profile.

Dowel stock is most often found in either birch or maple, with some centers stocking red oak as well. Available sizes range from $^3/_{16}$ to $1^1/_4$ diameters in 36- and 48-in. lengths.

If your woodworking project calls for construction lumber you can expect to find a complete range of sizes from 2×4×8s to 2×12×16s. Most often, a general construction grade will be carried, but sometimes an economy grade will be substituted. Check that the grade offered is suitable for your intended use. Economy-grade material is generally not appropriate for use in structural applications.

Panels

Most home centers carry a good selection of manufactured panel products. The standard size for panels is 4×8 ft. in $^1/_4$-, $^1/_2$- and $^3/_4$-in. thicknesses. At many centers, however, you can find panel stock in various precut sizes as well, from 1×2 ft. up to 4×4 ft. Panels are available in construction grades, made of fir or pine veneers and cabinet grades, with poplar or lauan veneer cores and lauan, birch, red oak or poplar face veneers. These more expensive hardwood panels are typically used for cabinet and furniture parts, although they find uses in architectural applications as well. These panels are ideal alternatives to laminating smaller boards when the surface appearance isn't critical.

In addition, flakeboard and medium-density fiberboard (MDF) panels are available in full sheets and cut sizes. These composite materials are extremely stable and flat, though quite heavy and make excellent substrates for plastic laminate. You might also find melamine-covered flakeboard panels. Melamine is a thin, hard plastic surface that is permanently bonded to the flakeboard. It is most often used as an interior surface for kitchen and bathroom cabinets, since it's washable and relatively inexpensive.

The more complete home centers also carry a limited selection of plastic laminates. Plastic laminates (Formica, Nevamar and WilsonArt are the most widely available brand names) are frequently installed in kitchen and bathroom cabinets and on countertops. They can, however, be effectively used as a surfacing material on furniture and as a durable shop worksurface. These materials are manufactured in literally hundreds of different patterns and colors, and it is beyond the scope of a home center to stock more than a representative sample. But you can often special order a particular color or pattern, giving you many options to explore. Standard sizes for plastic laminates range from 25×97 in. up to 60×144 in., but the sizes available will vary with the supplier.

Paints and Coatings

The paint department is where many home centers really shine. Your are likely to find a remarkably complete selection of paint and wood-finishing products, as well as the tools for their application. For opaque finishes, oil and latex-based paints are the standard materials. For stained work, you will find oil-based and polyurethane. There are also new water-based clear finishes available that claim less environmental damage and personal hazard potential in their use than many traditional finishes.

Although the variety of finishes might seem confusing, the truth is that many of these products won't be an appropriate choice for your project. Shellac, for example, can be tricky to apply, has a limited shelf life and offers only average surface protection for your project, especially against water or alcohol damage. Oil finishes, though quite attractive on some hardwoods, also offer reduced protection. These products do have their uses, but for most do-it-yourself projects, you'll find that a polyurethane varnish or water-based finish is the easiest to use and is the most resistant.

Fasteners

When it comes to fasteners, you will again find a wide selection of items. Nails come in many styles and sizes. For general construction use, common nails are the traditional choice, with flat heads and thick shanks. Coated nails are of the same configuration, but they have thinner bodies and are covered with a resin that makes them hold better than their common counterparts. This type of nail is also less likely to split the lumber when it's used near an edge.

For trim- and cabinetwork, use finish nails. These nails have a small, round head with a dimple in the top to facilitate setting them below the surface of the wood.

Exterior work requires nails that will not rust, so either aluminum or galvanized-steel nails should be used. These nails come in many configurations, from common and finish styles to specialty nails such as ring-shank siding nails, roofing nails, and spiral nails, designed specifically for use with pressure-treated lumber.

The size of the nail is designated by a "penny" number, varying from 2-penny (2d) at 1 in. long, up to 60-penny (60d) at 6 in. long.

Screws are the fasteners of choice for many projects. They, too, are available in a wide assortment of styles, sizes and materials. For some woodworking projects, traditional wood screws are a reasonable choice. These screws are classified by material, length, gauge of the body and type of head. Phillips and slot head styles are available as well as oval, round and flat head configurations.

If the fastener head will not be seen, a drywall screw is a better option in many cases. Drywall screws have thinner shanks, finer threads and sharper points than wood screws. They tend to drive easier and are less likely to split wood than the fatter wood screws.

For metal fastening, self-tapping screws are the best choice. These screws have sharp points and hardened shanks with threads all the way from the head to the tip. They come in both flat and pan head varieties, with the option of either a slot or Phillips head.

Hardware

In the big home centers, you can get lost in the hardware department for hours. If you make it past the fastener section, you still have lots of hinges, nuts, bolts, washers and knobs to browse through before you're done. The selection of nuts and bolts will include the basic machine bolts in all sizes and nearly every length, plus the washers, lockwashers, capnuts and locknuts to go with them. Usually, you'll also find a nice selection of carriage bolts and lagscrews in most lengths and diameters.

You're also bound to encounter a wealth of specialty items, from glass-mirror hangers to picture-frame mounting devices and much more. There should be dozens of sizes and varieties of screweyes and screwhooks as well.

The hinge selection should be similarly comprehensive, including standard butt hinges and overlay door hinges for cabinetwork. You can usually find small specialty hinges for fine furniture work. Finally, the deep variety of drawer and doorknobs and pulls can be enough to make anyone dizzy. If you start to feel overwhelmed, don't worry. Just step outside to get a breath of fresh air and then come back for more.

Woodworking tools

Woodworking Tools was written by Thomas Klenck. Photo by Rosario Capotosto.

While a few of us might lament the passing of the traditional hardware store—complete with oiled wooden floors, bins upon bins of every conceivable fastener and a clerk who not only knew your name, but also knew a capscrew from a carriage bolt—there's no denying that the superstore approach to woodworking has its benefits. With their vastly increased purchasing power, home centers and hardware stores now offer tool selections—and tool prices—too impressive to ignore.

It's not just the retail level that's changed. Thanks to consumer demand, manufacturers are working hard to produce professional-grade tools at weekend-woodworker prices. The entry-level tools are still there, but right alongside you'll find tools that your local contractor would be proud to own and use.

Portable Power Tools

For cutting wood, there are two basic power tools—the circular saw and the sabre saw. Circular saws are designated by the maximum blade diameter they can handle. Because of this tool's heritage as a construction saw, where most lumber tops out at $1^1/_2$ in. thick, you'll find $7^1/_4$-in. saws the most prevalent. There are smaller ones available for trimwork and larger ones to handle heavier stock. If you can afford to own only one, the $7^1/_4$-in. is the best all-around choice.

In terms of design, circular saws come in two flavors—worm drive and spur gear (sometimes called sidewinder). While the worm-drive design is a favorite in many areas of the country for construction, the spur-gear type is lighter, generally easier to handle and a better choice for fine work.

When it comes to notching, curve cutting and making irregular holes, it's time to switch to a sabre saw. Often called a jigsaw, this tool has a straight, reciprocating blade. While it's not as accurate as a circular saw for straight cutting, when equipped with a sharp blade, it's very effective for curved cuts.

Some sabre saws come with a pivoting blade that's controlled by a front knob on top of the housing. While this scrolling feature can help with a lot of tight, intricate curve cutting, it's otherwise unnecessary. On the other hand, one feature that's definitely worthwhile is orbital action. Orbital sabre saws have a mechanism that thrusts the blade back and forth in line with the cut as the blade moves up and down. The degree of orbiting action is controlled by a dial. At maximum orbit, the saw will cut almost as fast as a circular saw, although the accuracy of the cut will not be as good.

You may also come across a heavy-duty contractor's saw called simply a reciprocating saw. If your work includes serious home remodeling, this may be a tool to own. With it, you can cut through nearly everything—as long as you don't need to be too precise.

Drills are designated by the maximum bit diameter that will fit in the chuck. For most applications, a 3/8-in. drill is a good bet. Also, make sure your choice has variable speed and is reversible. With these features, your drill becomes a driver as well.

Larger 1/2 in. drills and hammer drills are also available. In addition to having more power, a 1/2-in. drill will accept up to a 1/2-in. shank bit. Hammer drills are designed for masonry. Because they also have a normal drilling mode, they're useful as dual-purpose tools.

For intricate joinery, molding and trimming, most power tool enthusiasts turn to routers. These pint-size portable milling machines come in two configurations—standard and plunge. A standard router will cut moldings, dadoes, rabbets, mortises and tenons, while a plunge router is far better for mortises and other cuts that are completely enclosed. Routers are designated by the router bit shank diameter that they accept, with 1/4 and 1/2 in. being standard. Routers are also rated by horsepower—and it pays to buy as much power as you can afford. A router is the easiest tool to convert to a stationary machine. Mounted in a router table, you have a small shaper that's capable of very accurate work.

When it comes to finishing, most home woodworkers start with a random-orbit sander. This tool removes stock almost as fast as a belt sander, with results that are comparable to better finish sanders. If you need to work into square corners, turn to a standard orbital sander or detail sander. Detail sanders, with their small triangular pads, are especially good at cleaning and smoothing tight, confined areas. Belt sanders are designed for removing material fast. They can be unruly and require care to avoid removing too much stock.

Power planes have straight blades mounted in a spinning cutterhead. They'll do a great job of taking that extra 1/8 in. off the edge of a door. Because they cut so fast, however, it's easy to plane off too much.

Until recently, your list for must-have portable power tools would now be complete. But today, you need one more—a plate joiner. This specialized tool does one thing—cut the slots for joining wood with small wooden plates, or biscuits. Fortunately for the home woodworkers, this once high-end professional tool is now offered at prices nearly everyone can afford.

Cordless Tools

While you probably don't need a cordless drill, once you get one, you'll never want to be without it. Today's offerings range in power up to 12 and even 14.4 volts, and they'll do just about anything your corded versions will. In addition, owning both corded and cordless drills cuts time dramatically when it comes to combination driving and hole-boring chores.

For light-duty screwdriving, cordless screwdrivers are great time-savers. Sanders and small circular saws also have recently appeared as battery-powered versions.

Benchtop Tools

Stationary benchtop tools provide precision and power without the space and budget requirements of full-size machinery. Benchtop circular saws come with all the features of floor models—tilting arbor, miter gauge and rip fence—plus you'll get a bigger blade.

A benchtop drill press is a handy tool for starting mortises and drum sanding. For curved cutting and resawing, benchtop band saws do a lot of work for a small price. For tight, intricate cutting, check out a scroll saw.

Radial-arm saws and power miter-boxes are both used for fast crosscutting. The radial-arm saw has the edge for large workpieces and can be set up for ripping. On the other hand, a power miterbox is far more portable making it the best choice for moldings, miters and other fine work.

A combination disc/belt sander goes a long way in speeding up small-part edge and face sanding, and it will even handle preliminary tool sharpening. Oscillating drum sanders are best at edge smoothing on curved work.

A bench grinder is indispensable for reshaping plane iron and chisel bevels as well as for touching up steel circular saw blades. You'll also find it useful for modifying any of the various metal components that go into your woodworking projects.

Hand Tools

Although there have been a few innovations, your home center's stock of woodworking hand tools isn't that different from what the hardware stores of 25 years ago offered. Handsaws for ripping have largely disappeared, replaced by fast-cutting saws with teeth, inspired by Japanese toolmakers.

Specialized saws such as coping saws and backsaws are both requirements for the well-equipped shop. Keyhole saws allow you to hand-cut enclosed holes when necessary.

Professional shops will have many sizes of hand planes, but you may find only one or two models at your home center. These—the smooth plane and jack plane—when kept sharp, will probably handle most jobs you encounter. A small block plane is handy for end-grain work and trimming tight areas.

One hand tool that hasn't been successfully replaced by a power tool is the wood chisel. Although these can be bought separately, a set of four—in widths from 1/4 to 1 in.—is a good investment. It even pays to have a few extra on hand just for rough work.

When it comes to hammers, small workshops rarely require a heavy one—a 16-ounce claw hammer will do just fine.

Although you'll find multibit screwdrivers economical, a set of single screwdrivers in the common tip designs is a good investment.

Important measuring and marking tools include tape measures, folding rules, try squares, framing squares, bevel gauges, marking gauges and straightedges. Don't forget some clamps—no shop ever has enough. Sliding bar clamps and handscrews are best for general work, while pipe clamps handle larger assemblies.

Power miter saw

You'll find one in nearly every professional woodworking shop, and even the well-equipped do-it-yourselfer has one for weekend projects. The tool is a power miter saw—a hybrid that combines the consistency and accuracy of a good miterbox with the power and speed of a circular saw.

These tools don't come cheap, though. If you consider that buying one duplicates the motor, housing and blade of a circular saw you already own, it's easy to think twice before getting out that checkbook.

You can build your own power miter saw out of plywood and some easy-to-find hardware. The design shown cuts 45° to the left and right, and has stops at the most common cutting angles. This power miter saw is based on the Porter-Cable model 368-1, $8^1/_4$-in. circular saw. This provides a cutting capacity of $1^1/_2 \times 6^1/_8$ in. at 90°. If you have a different saw, the cutting capacity may vary and you might have to modify some construction details.

Unlike commercial power miter saws that are spring loaded to keep the power head in the raised position, the circular saw in the version shown rests on the base. In operation, you simply lift the saw, insert the workpiece and then lower the saw to make the cut. The blade-guard lever is lashed to the rear of the base. In this way, the blade guard retracts for the cut in the low position and returns to cover the blade when the saw is raised.

The Pivoting Platform

Begin by cutting two pieces of plywood to 17×24 in. for the base and turntable support. Cut another piece to $18^1/_4$×24 in. for the turntable top. Lay out the pivot centers on all three pieces. Place pivot points $8^1/_8$ in. from the back edge on the base and turntable support, and position the turntable top pivot point 7 in. from the back edge. Center all pivot points from side to side.

Mark centerlines at 90° and 45° on the pieces (Fig. 1). These lines will help to orient the pieces later on. Use a beam compass to draw the circular outlines. Then lay out the turntable arm (Fig. 2).

1 Use a triangle to mark the 45° and 90° centerlines on the turntable pieces.

2 Lay out the circular pieces and mark the arm outline on the top turntable piece.

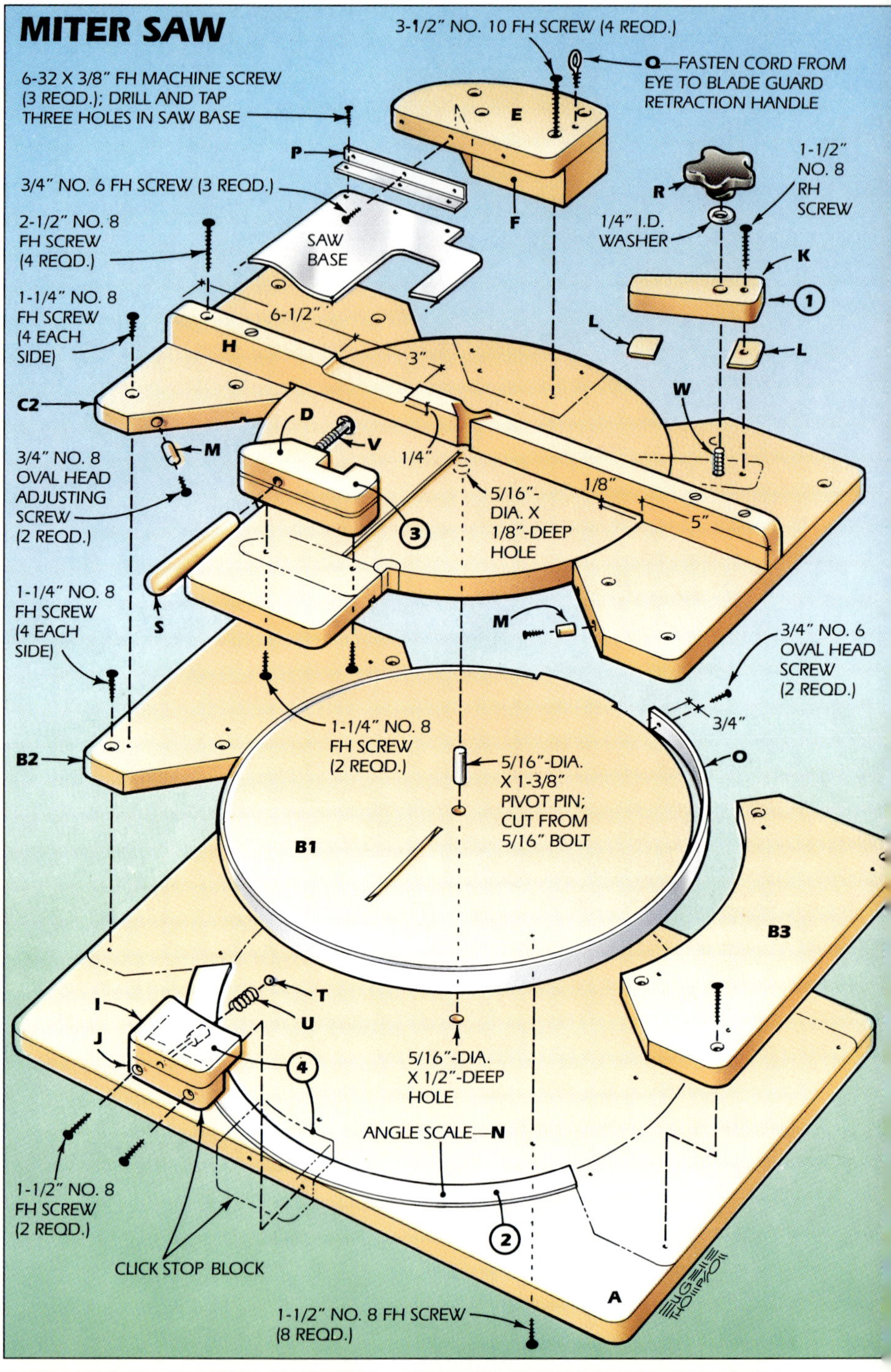

3 Cut circular pieces with a bandsaw or sabre saw and circle-cutting jig.

4 Drive a nail through the pivot holes of turntable pieces, align centerlines and tack.

5 Fasten turntable pieces with screws driven from bottom of turntable support.

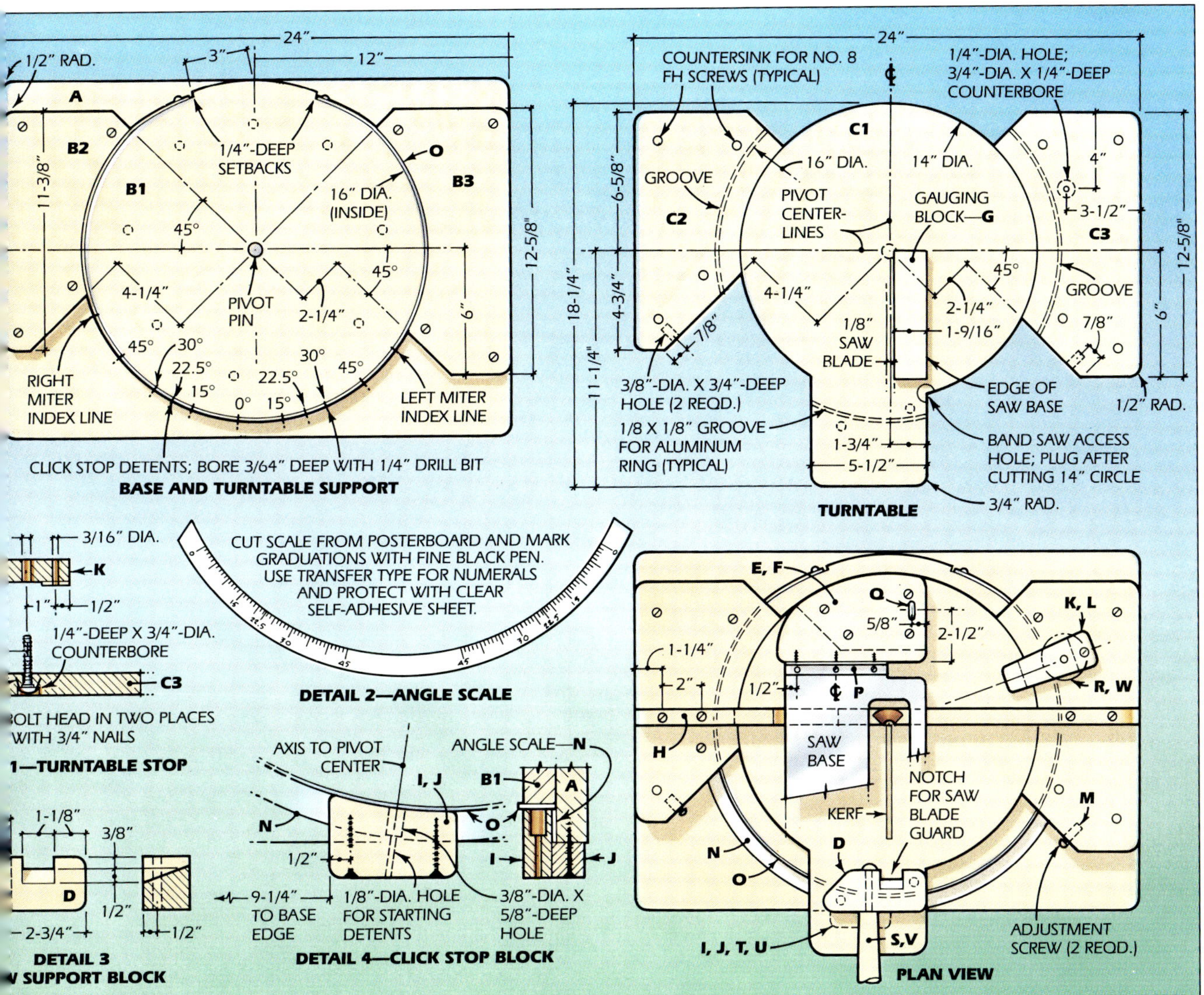

MATERIALS LIST—POWER MITER SAW

Key	No.	Size and description (use)
A	1	3/4 x 17 x 24" plywood (base)†
B1*	1	3/4 x 16"-dia. plywood (turntable support)
B2*	1	3/4 x 6 3/16 x 11 3/8" plywood (spacer)
B3*	1	3/4 x 6 3/16 x 12 5/8" plywood (spacer)
C1**	1	3/4 x 14 x 18 1/4" plywood (turntable)
C2**	1	3/4 x 7 x 11 3/8" plywood (retainer)
C3**	1	3/4 x 7 x 12 5/8" plywood (retainer)
D***	1	1 7/8 x 1 9/16 x 5" plywood (saw support block)
E	1	7/8 x 4 x 7" hardwood (saw mounting block)
F***	1	1 9/16 x 3 1/2 x 6" plywood (block support)
G***	1	1 9/16 x 1 11/16 x 6 1/8" plywood (gauging block)
H	1	3/4 x 1 1/2 x 24" hardwood (fence)
I	1	5/8 x 2 x 3" hardwood (click-stop block)
J	1	3/4 x 7/8 x 3" hardwood (click-stop block)
K	1	3/4 x 1 3/4 x 4 1/2" hardwood (turntable lock)
L	2	1/8 x 1 x 1 3/4" plywood (spacer)
M	2	3/8"-dia. x 3/4" dowel (plug)
N	1	8 x 16" white posterboard (scale)
O	1	1/16 x 3/4 x 44" aluminum bar
P	1	1 1/16 x 4 3/4" hinge
Q	1	3/4" screweye
R	1	1/4"-20 5-star knob (No. 71548)††
S	1	5/16"-18 post handle (No. 81505)††
T	1	1/4"-dia. steel ball
U	1	5/16" O.D. x 3/4" spring
V	1	1/4"-20 x 2" carriage bolt and washer
W	1	5/16"-18 x 2 1/2" carriage bolt

* Cut B1, B2 and B3 from one piece 3/4 x 17 x 24"
** Cut C1, C2 and C3 from one piece 3/4 x 18 1/4 x 24"
*** Laminate 1 9/16" from two pieces nominal 3/4" plywood and one piece 1/8" plywood
† Birch plywood (typical, 23/32" thick)
†† Available from The Woodworkers' Store, 21801 Industrial Blvd., Rogers, MN 55374

Misc: 5/16"-dia. x 2" bolt; 26 1 1/4" No. 8 fh screws; 2 1 1/2" No. 8 fh screws; 4 2 1/2" No. 8 fh screws; 4 3 1/2" No. 10 fh screws; 1 1 1/2" No. 8 rh screw; 3 3/4" No. 6 fh screws; 2 3/8" No. 8 oval head screws; 2 3/4" No. 6 oval head screws; 6-32 x 3/4-in. machine screws; self-adhesive clear plastic sheet; transfer-type numerals.

PM TECHNICAL ART BY EUGENE THOMPSON

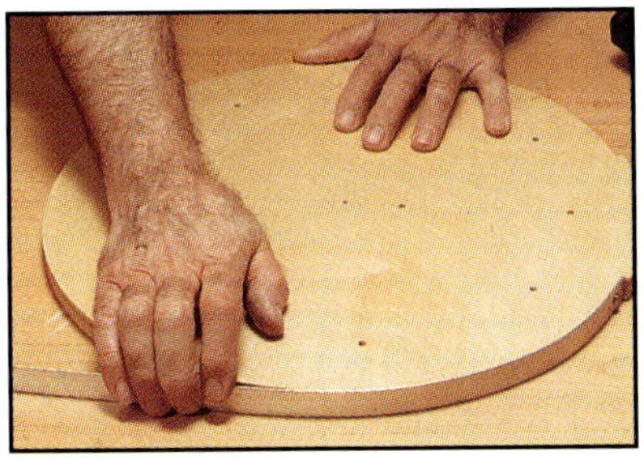

6 Screw end of aluminum strip in setback area. Apply contact cement and wrap strip around disc. Screw free end.

7 Width of aluminum strip is slightly greater than plywood thickness. Use a file to trim flush to surface in setback areas.

8 Use a router, guide bushing, template and veining bit to cut strip clearance grooves in retainer pieces and turntable.

It's best to cut the circular shapes on a bandsaw with a circle-cutting jig. Bore 3/32-in. holes at the pivot centers for the circle-jig pivot pin. Then, bore a 3/4-in. access hole centered at the intersection of the turntable circle and the arm layout lines as shown in the Turntable Detail in the drawing.

Make the two straight cuts up to the circle to define the arm. Position the panel on the bandsaw circle jig so the blade is in the 3/4-in. access hole. Then make the stopped circular cut from the access hole to the opposite straight cut of the arm. When the cut is finished, plug the access hole with a 3/4-in. dowel and trim flush.

Then, cut the full circle to produce the turntable support. Don't discard the cutoffs from the turntable support and turntable—you'll use these to make adjoining members (Fig. 3).

Insert a snug-fitting nail through the pivot holes in the turntable members, align their centerlines and drive in a few nails to keep the parts from shifting (Fig. 4). Then, bore screwholes from the bottom face of the turntable support for joining the pieces and temporarily install a few screws (Fig. 5). Bore the 5/16-in.-dia. blind hole for the pivot pin from the bottom of the turntable support. Also, bore the corresponding blind hole in the base.

Separate the two turntable pieces and make the setback cuts for the aluminum ring as indicated in the Base and Turntable Support Detail. Cut the aluminum bar to 44 in. and bore screwholes at each end for the 3/4-in. No.6 screws. Butt one end of the aluminum bar in one of the setback cuts and make sure the bottom of the aluminum is flush with the bottom of the turntable support. Then, bore a screw pilot hole into the plywood edge.

Apply contact cement to the wood and the aluminum. Screw the first end into the setback cut and gradually bend the aluminum around the turntable base (Fig. 6). When the bend is complete, bore a pilot hole for the second screw and secure the free end. Because nominal 3/4-in. plywood is slightly less than 3/4 in., file the bar flush with the wood surface in the setback-cut area (Fig. 7).

Use the cutoffs from the turntable base and turntable to make the retainers and spacers that fit up against each side of the two circular turntable components.

Next, cut curved clearance grooves in the bottom of the two retainers (C2, C3) and the turntable arm to match the projecting aluminum bar. Use a router with a template guide bushing and a 1/8-in. straight bit or veining bit to make the cut. Guide the router against a template made from 1/4-in.-thick plywood (Fig. 8).

To make the 1 9/16-in.-thick saw base support block (D), laminate two pieces of nominal 3/4-in. plywood (actually 23/32 in.) with a 1/8-in.-thick piece in between. Cut the saw support block as shown and bore the hole for the post-handle bolt. Secure the support to the turntable arm with 1 1/4-in. No.8 screws and install the handle. Reassemble the turntable members, insert the pivot pin and place the assembly on the base. Install a plug (M) in each retainer as shown. The plugs accept screws that act as adjustable stops for the 45° settings. Then secure the spacer and retainer blocks.

Cut the turntable lock slightly oversize, then glue the two 1/8-in.-thick spacers at each end as shown. Finish shaping the lock and bore the holes for the screw and the knob bolt.

Sand all the pieces with 220-grit sandpaper and apply two coats of a satin varnish or polyurethane finish.

9 With saw blade extended, align corner of 1 9/16-in.-thick gauge block with blade edge. Then, mark block position on base.

10 After placing saw and gauge block on turntable centerlines, tape free leaf of hinge to saw support. Remove hinge.

Attaching the Saw

The hinge that joins the saw to the saw mounting block must be free of play. To attach the hinge to the circular saw base, first remove the base from the saw. Then, mark the hinge hole positions and bore and tap holes in the base for the 6-32×3/4-in. screws. Resecure the saw's base and attach the hinge to the base. If your saw base is too thin for tapping, use nuts, washers and bolts.

Laminate the saw mounting block support (F) as you did when making the saw base support block to achieve the 1 9/16-in. thickness. Then, make the hardwood saw mounting block (E) and attach it to the support block with screws as shown. Bore and countersink holes for attaching the assembly to the turntable. Don't bore the pilot holes in the turntable yet.

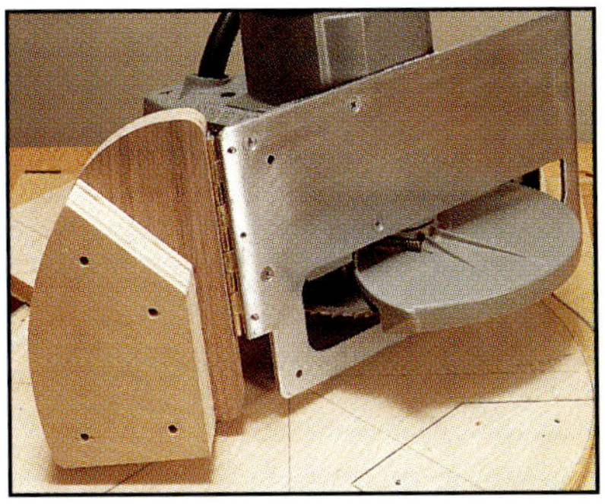

11 After securing hinge to saw mounting block, refasten it to saw base. Angled mounting block provides clearance.

12 Secure mounting block and check that blade is square to centerline. Butt fence against square and install.

For the miter saw to function properly, two conditions must be met. First, the center of the blade must be aligned with the centerline of the pivot. Second, when the blade is fully extended and the saw mounted, the intersection between the fence-side periphery of the blade and the turntable surface must be at the center of the pivot.

To align the saw, laminate a $1^9/_{16}$-in.-thick gauging block and cut it equal in width to the distance between the blade and the edge of the base. With the saw blade fully extended, hold the gauging block against the blade and position it so the bottom front corner aligns with the periphery of the blade. Then use a pencil to mark the block position on the top of the saw base (Fig. 9).

Draw a line on the turntable parallel to the pivot centerline (see Turntable Detail), spaced to the right a distance equal to the width of the gauging block plus one-half the blade thickness.

Completely retract the saw blade. Position the gauging block on the offset line drawn on the turntable, with its end aligned with the horizontal pivot centerline as shown in the Turntable Detail. Place the saw on the gauging block, and adjust the saw's position so the mark on the base is aligned with the pivot-center end of the block and the base edge is aligned with the edge of the block.

Without shifting the saw, position the saw mounting block to butt against the free leaf of the hinge. Once it's in place, tape the leaf to the block (Fig. 10).

Remove the hinge from the saw and mark the screw centers on the mounting block. Bore pilot holes and attach the hinge first to the block, then to the saw base (Fig. 11).

Position the saw and mounting block using the gauging block for alignment. Then mark the mounting-block screw centers on the turntable and attach the mounting block. Adjust the blade for maximum depth of cut. Tilt up the saw, turn it on, then lower it to cut the kerf in the turntable.

Next, cut the hardwood fence to size as shown and bore and countersink the screwholes. Temporarily tape a drafting square to the turntable so it's butted against the blade (Fig. 12). Then, align the fence against the square and secure it with screws. Turn on the saw and lower it to make the initial clearance cut in the fence. Then, make a series of cuts between the 45° left and 45° right miter positions to scoop away the blade clearance recess in the fence.

13 Use a shopmade beam compass to cut the posterboard scale. Press a razor knife into the beam and pivot to make cut.

14 Tape protractor to fence. Mark on paper shows turntable angle. Align marks on scale with index scribed on aluminum.

15 For a professional look, add transfer type at common miter settings. Then, apply clear, self-adhesive pastic to scale.

Finishing Touches

Make the angle scale out of white posterboard. Use a shopmade beam compass and fine felt pen to mark an $8^1/_2$-in.-radius accent line. Then, press a razor knife into the beam at an $8^5/_8$-in.-radius and cut the inner edge. Cut the scale to fit between the retainer blocks and secure it with contact cement.

To mark the graduations, first make an index guide block by cutting one edge of a small piece of wood to match the radius of the turntable base. Trim an adjacent edge so it extends geometrically to the pivot center. Place a protractor on the turntable and tape it to the fence so it's centered on the pivot centerline. Slide a piece of paper under the protractor and tape it to the turntable. With the turntable at the 0° position, make an index mark on the paper at the 90° mark on the protractor. Then, use a knife to scribe the right and left miter index lines on the aluminum ring as shown on the Base and Turntable Support Detail.

Rotate the turntable counterclockwise until the index mark on the paper aligns with the 45° mark on the protractor. Then, line up the edge of the index guide block with the index mark on the aluminum ring and mark a line on the posterboard scale with a felt pen. Finish the scale by rotating the turntable in 1° increments and transferring each position to the scale (Fig. 14). Then, repeat the process on the opposite side of the scale. Use transfer type to define the 0°, 15°, $22^1/_2$°, 30° and 45° positions on both sides of the scale (Fig. 15).

Cut the click-stop block to size and trim one edge to match the turntable-base radius with the block is positioned $9^1/_4$ in. from the base left edge (see Detail 4). With the block in position, mark the spring-hole axis so it extends to the pivot center as shown. Then, bore a $^1/_8$-in.-dia. hole through the block on this axis. If possible, use a drill press for accuracy.

Secure the block to the base. Use the $^1/_8$-in. hole to guide your drill in starting the detents in the aluminum at the standard miter positions (Fig. 16). Then, remove the block and use a $^1/_4$-in. bit in a handheld drill to enlarge the detents slightly. Bore the $^3/_8$-in.-dia. spring hole in the click-stop block as shown. Reinstall the block with the spring and $^1/_4$-in.-dia. ball in place (Fig. 17).

Finally, install a screweye in the top of the saw mounting block, in line with the saw's blade-guard lever. Then, secure the lever to the eye with a stout cord and check that the guard retracts properly as the saw is lowered (Fig. 18). Finally, install the turntable lock and knob.

Power Miter Saw was written by Rosario Capotosto. Photos by Rosario Capotosto. Technical art by Eugene Thompson.

16 Use $^1/_8$-in. hole in click-stop block to guide drill in starting detents. Place a detent at common miter settings.

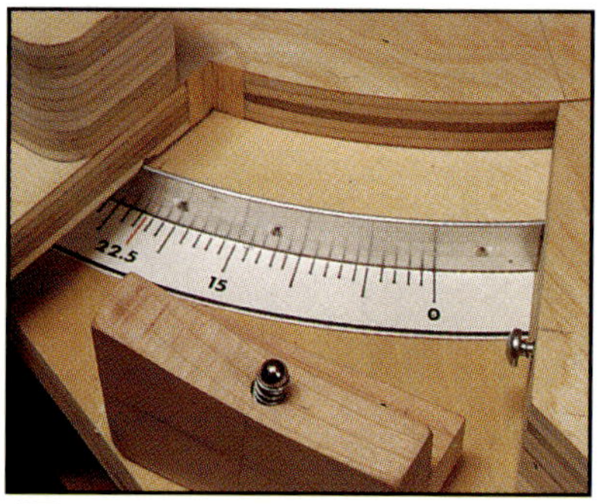

17 After enlarging detents with $^1/_4$-in. bit, enlarge click-stop block guide hole to accept spring and $^1/_4$-in.-dia. ball.

18 Tie string from screweye to guard lever. Adjust it so blade guard retracts properly as the saw is lowered.

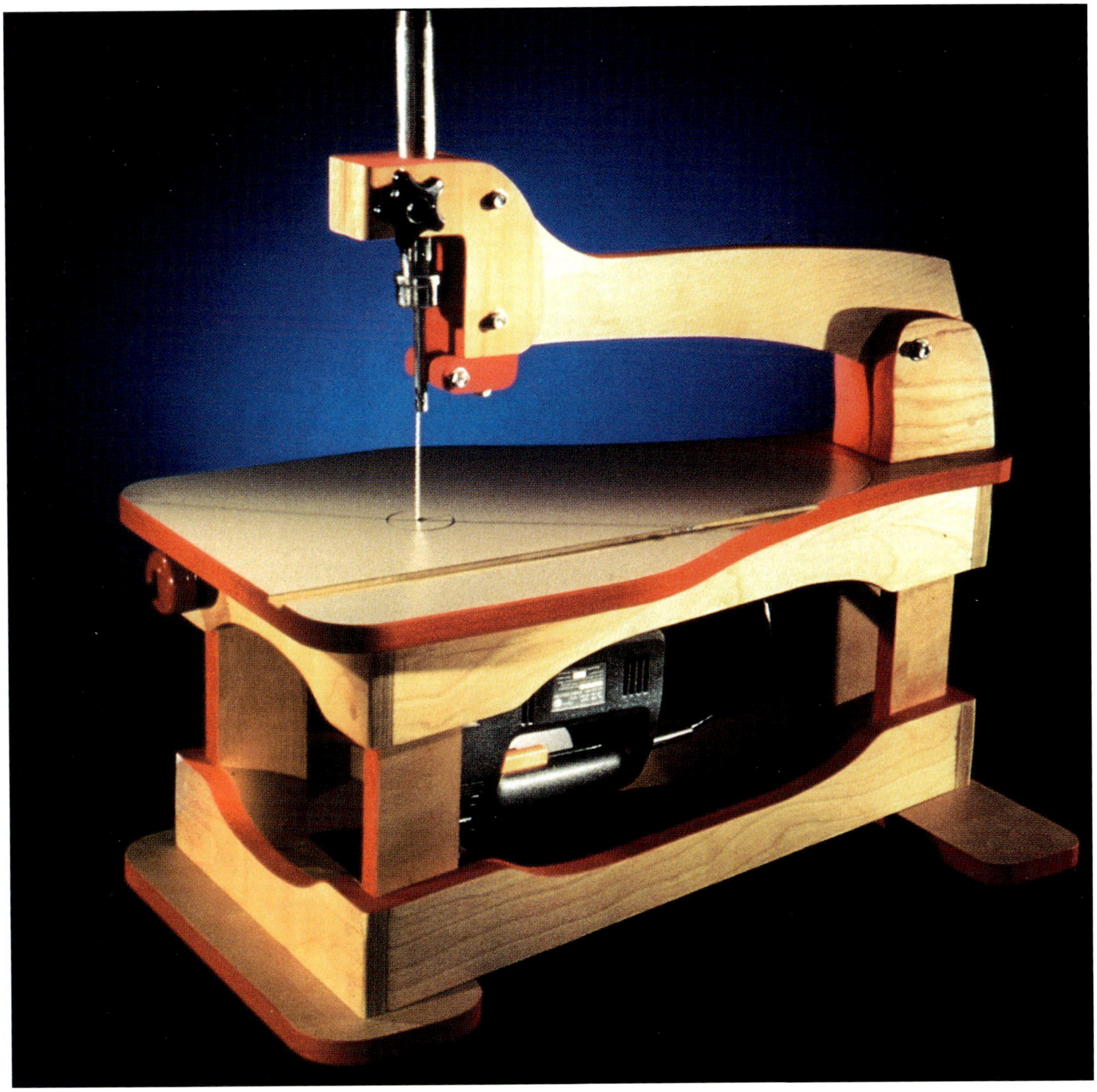

Sabre saw table

This sabre saw table is designed to convert your portable tool into a full-fledged scroll saw. It's able to do this without restricting utility—you can easily remove the sabre saw for portable use.

This sabre saw table provides a 16-in. cutting capacity and uses conventional 5-in. pin-end scroll saw blades. It works well with just about any sabre saw model that has electronically controlled preset variable speed.

Electronic circuitry is important because it helps the tool maintain speed under load, and the present feature is necessary for locking the tool at the required speed. This sabre saw table works best at low to moderate speeds. While making the sabre saw table requires a few special parts, you can find most of them at any well-equipped hardware store.

The table is surfaced with plastic laminate for friction-free operation and boasts a slot that accommodates a standard miter gauge. To provide stability, the two oversize footpads can be clamped to your worksurface. A convenient switch wired to the table's own outlet receptacle allows you to turn the machine on and off without touching the sabre saw controls.

Birch plywood and solid oak was used to build this table, but any other quality plywood and hardwood will work.

1 Mark the arm outline on 3/4-in. plywood. Then, cut to the line with a sabre saw and sand the sawn edges smooth.

2 Make templates for contoured pieces. Trace cheek template on oak stock. Hole at corner handles inside radius cut.

3 When gluing cheeks to spacer, use nails to maintain alignment. The spacer thickness should match arm thickness.

4 Use a 1 1/8-in-dia. spade bit ground down to 1 1/16-in. to make the hole for the 3/4-in. plunger-assembly pipe.

MATERIALS LIST—SABRE SAW TABLE

Key	No.	Size and description (use)
A	1	¾ × 10½ × 19⅝" plywood (arm)
B1	2	¾ × 5½ × 5½" oak (arm cheek)
B2	1	¾ × 2 × 3" oak (spacer)
C	2	1 × 4⅜ × 4⅝" oak (arm block)
D1	1	¾ × 14 × 27" plywood (table)
D2	1	1⅞"-dia. × ¼" plywood (insert)
E1	1	¾ × 6½ × 9" plywood (mounting plate)
E2	1	¾ × 6½ × 9" plywood (mounting plate)
F	4	¾ × 3 × 23⅝" plywood (frame side)
G	4	¾ × 3 × 10½" plywood (leg)
H	2	¾ × 3 × 12" plywood (front tie)
I	2	¾ × 3 × 4" plywood (rear tie)
J	1	¾ × 5½ × 14" plywood (front pad)
K	1	¾ × 4 × 14" plywood (rear pad)
L	1	⅜"-dia. × 10½" steel rod (plunger)
M	1	¾ × 8" pipe nipple (plunger housing)
N	2	¾" pipe cap (housing cap)
O	1	⅜" locknut
P	1	⅜" SAE washer
Q	1	6½"-long compression spring*
R	1	⅞"-dia. × 2" dowel (bushing)
S	1	1/16 × ½ × 2½" steel (blade holder)
T	1	1 × 2⅜ × 2¼" oak (bearing block)
U	1	¼ × ¾"-dia., ¼"-bore bearing**
V	As reqd.	plastic laminate (table surface)
W	As reqd.	1¼" finishing nail
X	3	2½" × ¼"-20 carriage bolt, washer, nut
Y	1	2½" × 5/16"-18 carriage bolt, washer
Z	1	5-star through-hole 5/16" knob***
AA	3	1¼" 10-32 rh screw
BB	4	¼"-20 Teenut, washer, 1½" × ¼"-20 thumbscrew
CC	4	1¼" No. 6 drywall screw
DD	22	1⅝" No. 6 drywall screw
EE	9	2" No. 6 drywall screw
FF	1	2½" × ¼"-20 hexhead bolt, 3 washers, nut
GG	2	1½" × ¼"-20 hexhead bolt, washers
HH	2	¼"-20 threaded insert

* Ajax No. 60, 9¾" × 11/16" OD, cut to 6½" long. Ajax Wire Specialty Co. Inc., 119 Bloomingdale Rd., Hicksville, NY 11801.

** Router bit pilot bearing.

*** Available from The Woodworkers' Store, 21801 Industrial Blvd., Rogers, MN 55374.

Misc: 16/3 wire; wire staples; plug; single receptacle; receptacle box; surface-mount switch.

Building the Arm

Begin by making cardboard templates of all the contoured arm parts. Cut the plywood arm with your sabre saw using a hollow-ground blade (Fig. 1). Then, smooth the sawn edges with drum and disc sanders, or hand sand them with a sanding block.

Next, trace the arm-check pieces onto 3/4-in.-thick oak stock (Fig. 2). Note that the grain direction of these two parts is vertical. Allow about 1 in. of extra stock at the forward end of the L-shaped pattern to help during assembly. Then, cut out the shapes with your sabre saw.

Cut the oak cheek spacer to size, leaving about 1 in. of extra material at one end to match the cheek pieces. Orient the grain direction of the spacer horizontally. Check the actual spacer thickness and compare it to the plywood arm thickness. If the plywood is slightly thinner, plane the cheek spacer to match.

Align the cheeks with the spacer in between and temporarily tape them together. Bore two 1/8-in.-dia. holes through the 1-in. waste area at the front of the assembly. Remove the tape, separate the pieces and apply glue to the mating surfaces. Reassemble the pieces, drive 3-in. finishing nails into the holes to ensure alignment and keep the parts from shifting, and then clamp them (Fig. 3). When the glue is dry, pull out the nails and cut off the waste area.

Next, use a drill press to bore the 1 1/16-in.-dia. hole for the pipe that serves as the plunger housing (Fig. 4). After marking the hole location, clamp the work squarely to the drill press table. If you don't have a 1 1/16-in. bit, grind 1/32 in. from each edge of a 1 1/8-in. spade bit. Bore a test hole to check for a good fit with the pipe before boring the workpiece. Then, bore the hole for the lock-knob bolt.

Use a table saw to cut the kerf in the center of the cheek assembly (see the top view in the Arm Pattern assembly in the drawing on page 155). To hold the piece during the cut, clamp it to a simple jig that straddles the table saw fence (Fig. 5). Place a scrap block between the cheeks before tightening the clamp.

With the slot cut, apply glue to the inner faces of the cheeks and the mating surfaces on the plywood arm. Join the components and clamp them until the glue is dry (Fig. 6).

To install the threaded inserts that allow the bearing block to be secured, bore two 1/2-in.-dia.×5/8-in.-deep holes into the bottom of the cheek assembly, as shown. You can do the job on a drill press, but you can also use a portable drill and doweling jig (Fig. 7). Apply epoxy to the insert threads, place them into the holes and let the adhesive cure (Fig. 8).

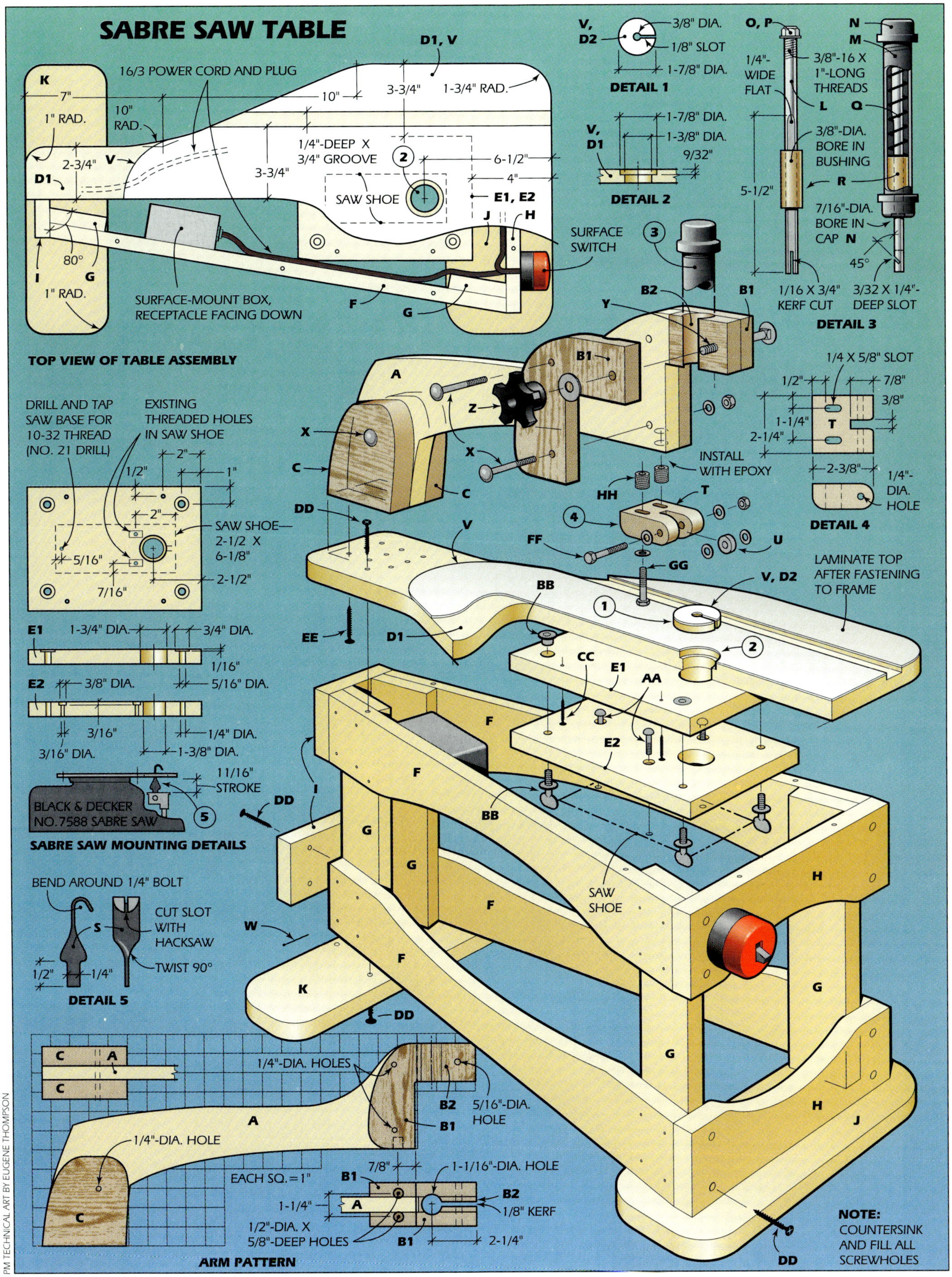
SABRE SAW TABLE
16/3 POWER CORD AND PLUG
D1, V
K
7"
10"
3-3/4"
1-3/4" RAD.
1" RAD.
10" RAD.
1/4"-DEEP X 3/4" GROOVE
2-3/4"
V
D1
3-3/4"
6-1/2"
4"
SAW SHOE
E1, E2
J
H
80°
I
G
1" RAD.
SURFACE-MOUNT BOX, RECEPTACLE FACING DOWN
F
G
TOP VIEW OF TABLE ASSEMBLY
V, D2
3/8" DIA.
1/8" SLOT
1-7/8" DIA.
DETAIL 1
V, D1
1-7/8" DIA.
1-3/8" DIA.
9/32"
DETAIL 2
SURFACE SWITCH
O, P
1/4"-WIDE FLAT
N
M
3/8"-16 X 1"-LONG THREADS
L
Q
3/8"-DIA. BORE IN BUSHING
R
5-1/2"
7/16"-DIA. BORE IN CAP N
45°
1/16 X 3/4" KERF CUT
3/32 X 1/4"-DEEP SLOT
DETAIL 3
B2
B1
Y
B1
A
Z
X
X
C
C
1/4 X 5/8" SLOT
1/2"
7/8"
3/8"
1-1/4"
2-1/4"
T
2-3/8"
1/4"-DIA. HOLE
DETAIL 4
DRILL AND TAP SAW BASE FOR 10-32 THREAD (NO. 21 DRILL)
EXISTING THREADED HOLES IN SAW SHOE
2"
1/2"
1"
2"
SAW SHOE—2-1/2 X 6-1/8"
5/16"
7/16"
2-1/2"
INSTALL WITH EPOXY
HH
T
FF
U
GG
DD
V
LAMINATE TOP AFTER FASTENING TO FRAME
V, D2
BB
EE
D1
CC
E1
AA
E1
1-3/4" DIA.
3/4" DIA.
1/16"
5/16" DIA.
E2
3/8" DIA.
3/16"
1/4" DIA.
3/16" DIA.
1-3/8" DIA.
11/16" STROKE
BLACK & DECKER NO. 7588 SABRE SAW
SABRE SAW MOUNTING DETAILS
F
F
E2
BB
DD
I
G
G
F
SAW SHOE
H
BEND AROUND 1/4" BOLT
S
CUT SLOT WITH HACKSAW
TWIST 90°
1/2"
1/4"
DETAIL 5
W
F
K
DD
G
G
H
J
C
A
C
1/4"-DIA. HOLES
B2
5/16"-DIA. HOLE
B1
A
1/4"-DIA. HOLE
EACH SQ. = 1"
C
7/8"
1-1/16"-DIA. HOLE
B1
1-1/4"
A
B2
1/8" KERF
1/2"-DIA. X 5/8"-DEEP HOLES
B1
2-1/4"
ARM PATTERN
DD
NOTE: COUNTERSINK AND FILL ALL SCREWHOLES
PM TECHNICAL ART BY EUGENE THOMPSON

5 Use a table saw to cut the kerf in the arm head assembly. A jig that straddles the fence makes the cut safe and secure.

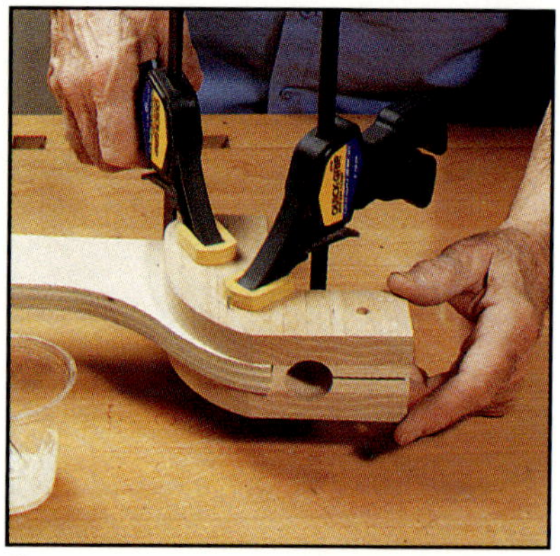

6 After boring the lock-knob bolt hole, glue and clamp the head assembly to the arm. Reinforcing bolts are added later.

7 Use an adjustable doweling jig to bore the holes for the threaded inserts. A drill press will also work for this job.

8 Dab epoxy on the inserts and install them in the holes. Inserts seat squarely in holes that match insert diameter.

Making the Table

Cut the parts for the table, and assemble the side frames with glue and finishing nails. When the glue is dry, tilt your table saw blade to 10° and make the bevel cuts on the front and rear edges of each frame (Fig. 9). Clamp the assembly together while boring screw pilot holes for joining the side frames to the end rails (Fig. 10). Assemble the table base with screws and glue. On the tabletop, locate the blade-hole center and bore the $1^7/_8$-in.-dia. inset recess $^9/_{32}$ in. deep. Finish the hole by boring through with a $1^3/_8$-in.-dia. bit.

9 After assembling the side-frame components with glue and nails, trim frame ends to a 10° bevel on a table saw.

10 Use pipe clamps to hold base together while the end rails are glued and screwed. Don't glue upper rear end rail.

Blade Holders and Plunger

The upper blade holder/plunger is comprised of a steel rod, a compression spring and a wood dowel bushing—all encased in a capped, 8-in.-long × $^3/_4$-in.-dia. pipe nipple.

When you shop for the pipe, hold it up to the light and check that the inside wall is free of irregularities. While you're at the hardware store, get the $^3/_8$-in.-dia. steel rod, $^3/_8$-in. SAE washer and the compression spring. An Ajax No.60 spring was used here. It has an outside diameter of $^{11}/_{16}$ in. and a length of $9^3/_4$ in.

Begin by boring a $^7/_{16}$-in.-dia. hole through the center of one of the pipe caps. To cut the spring to $6^1/_2$ in., first secure a bolt in your vise. Slip the spring over the bolt at the $6^1/_2$-in. mark on the spring. Stretch the waste end of the spring away from the bolt to allow room for a diagonal cutter to make the cut (Fig. 11).

Cut the $^3/_8$-in. rod to $10^1/_2$ in. long and thread 1 in. of one end with a $^3/_8$-in.-16 die. Follow by cutting the angled and straight slots with a handsaw. Double the hacksaw blade to cut the wider, angled slot.

Secure the rod in your vise and shape the flat area by draw filing, using a single-cut bastard file. Hold the file perpendicular to the work with both hands and move the file back and forth with even pressure (Fig. 12).

Make the lower blade holder from a piece of $^1/_{16}\times{}^1/_2\times2^1/_2$-in. steel stock. Form the hooked end by bending the metal around a $^1/_4$-in. bolt. Then, using an adjustable wrench as a lever, twist the bar 90° (Fig. 13).

When the bends have been completed, use a hacksaw to cut the shank end to fit your sabre saw's blade holder.

Because the inside diameter of the pipe nipple is $^{53}/_{64}$ in., the $^7/_8$-in.-dia. wood dowel bushing will need to be trimmed slightly to fit. First, bore the centered $^3/_8$-in. hole for the plunger rod on a drill press. Then, install a carriage bolt in the hole and secure it with a nut. Chuck the bolt in the drill press and use a coarse file to trim the dowel while it's spinning.

Cut the bearing block to size and shape as shown in Detail 4 on the drawing (page 155). Use a drill press to bore the hole for the bearing bolt. Begin the slotted holes by boring overlapping $^1/_4$-in.-dia. holes. Then, remove the waste area with a sharp chisel. The $^3/_4$-in. bearing is generally available where router bits are sold.

When all of the blade holder/plunger components are finished (Fig. 14), you're ready to begin final assembly.

11 To cut spring to length, place it over a bolt. Then, stretch waste side away from bolt and cut with diagonal cutter.

12 Use draw filing to produce flat on plunger rod. Hold file perpendicular to work. Push and pull with even pressure.

13 Bend the end of a steel strip around a bolt to form a hook on lower blade holder. Use a wrench to twist shank 90°.

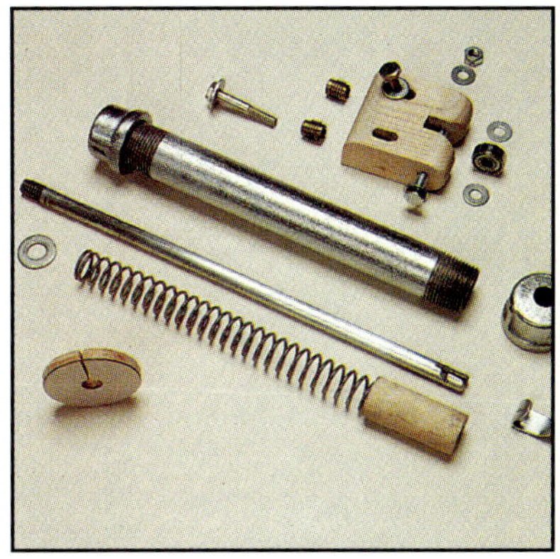

14 Compressed blade holder/plunger components. Bearing block at upper right reinforces plunger rod.

Final Stages

Start by cutting the two oak rear arm-mounting blocks to size and shape, and then bolt them to the arm with a single bolt.

Note that the mounting-block grain orientation is horizontal. Locate and bore the pilot holes in the tabletop for attaching the arm to the table and the table to the base.

To align the arm, first temporarily install the plunger assembly. Then, use clamps to hold the arm in position on the tabletop. Place a square on the tabletop so its edge is aligned with the center of the table hole (Fig. 15). Then, position the arm so the plunger rod is aligned with the blade of the square. Adjust the arm angle by pivoting the arm at the single rear mounting block. Then bore the pilot holes in the mounting blocks guided by the pilot holes in the table.

The sabre saw is secured to a double mounting plate that allows it to be easily removed. The saw base is attached to the lower mounting plate with three 10-32 screws—two of which are threaded into the existing holes in the tool's base that were originally intended for an accessory fence. The third screw requires a new threaded hole. After boring the hole with a No.21 bit, use a 10-32 tap to cut the threads (see Sabre Saw Mounting Details on the drawing).

After cutting both mounting plates to size, locate and bore holes in the top plate for the Teenuts and in the bottom plate for the thumbscrews that hold the pieces together. After driving the Teenuts into place, screw the plates together and mark the center of the blade access hole.

15 Clamp arm to table and use a square to align plunger rod with hole in table. Then bore pilot holes for mounting.

16 Remove shoe from sabre saw and place on underside of lower mounting plate. Then mark the screwholes.

17 Make sure Teenuts are installed in upper plate before gluing to table. Lower plate holds sabre saw.

18 After attaching the outlet box, single receptacle and switch to the base, connect switch and receptacle with 16/3 wire.

Bore a $^{3}/_{16}$-in. hole through both plates. Then, separate the assembly and, using the $^{3}/_{16}$-in. hole as a pilot hole, bore a $1^{3}/_{4}$-in. hole through the top plate and a $1^{3}/_{8}$-in. hole through the bottom plate.

Remove the base from the sabre saw and lay out the hole positions for the 10-32 rh screws on the underside of the lower mounting plate (Fig. 16). Then, bore $^{3}/_{16}$-in.-dia. holes for the screws. From the top, counterbore $^{3}/_{8}$-in.-dia. recesses for the screwheads. Reassemble the saw and mounting plates, and check for fit (Fig. 17).

Glue and screw the tabletop to the front and side top base rails. Cut the plastic laminate slightly oversize and glue it to the top with contact cement. Then, trim with a router and flush-trimming bit. Remove the rear top rail to provide screwdriver access, and glue and screw the arm to the tabletop.

Finally, cut and install the base pads, attach the switch and receptacle, and run the 16/3 cable (Fig. 18).

Sabre Saw Table was written and photographed by Rosario Capotosto.

Index

METRIC CONVERSION

Conversion factors can be carried so far they become impractical. In cases below where an entry is exact it is followed by an asterisk (*). Where considerable rounding off has taken place, the entry is followed by a + or a - sign.

CUSTOMARY TO METRIC

Linear Measure

inches	millimeters
1/16	1.5875*
1/8	3.2
3/16	4.8
1/4	6.35*
5/16	7.9
3/8	9.5
7/16	11.1
1/2	12.7*
9/16	14.3
5/8	15.9
11/16	17.5
3/4	19.05*
13/16	20.6
7/8	22.2
15/16	23.8
1	25.4*

inches	centimeters
1	2.54*
2	5.1
3	7.6
4	10.2
5	12.7*
6	15.2
7	17.8
8	20.3
9	22.9
10	25.4*
11	27.9
12	30.5

feet	centimeters	meters
1	30.48*	.3048*
2	61	.61
3	91	.91
4	122	1.22
5	152	1.52
6	183	1.83
7	213	2.13
8	244	2.44
9	274	2.74
10	305	3.05
50	1524*	15.24*
100	3048*	30.48*

1 yard =
.9144* meters
1 rod =
5.0292* meters
1 mile =
1.6 kilometers
1 nautical mile =
1.852* kilometers

Fluid Measure

(Milliliters [ml] and cubic centimeters [cc or cu cm] are equivalent, but it is customary to use milliliters for liquids.)

1 cu in = 16.39 ml
1 fl oz = 29.6 ml
1 cup = 237 ml
1 pint = 473 ml
1 quart = 946 ml
= .946 liters
1 gallon = 3785 ml
= 3.785 liters
Formula (exact):
fluid ounces × 29.573 529 562 5*
= milliliters

Weights

ounces	grams
1	28.3
2	56.7
3	85
4	113
5	142
6	170
7	198
8	227
9	255
10	283
11	312
12	340
13	369
14	397
15	425
16	454

Formula (exact):
ounces × 28.349 523 125* =
grams

pounds	kilograms
1	.45
2	.9
3	1.4
4	1.8
5	2.3
6	2.7
7	3.2
8	3.6
9	4.1
10	4.5

1 short ton (2000 lbs) =
907 kilograms (kg)
Formula (exact):
pounds × .453 592 37* =
kilograms

Volume

1 cu in = 16.39 cubic centimeters (cc)
1 cu ft = 28 316.7 cc
1 bushel = 35 239.1 cc
1 peck = 8 809.8 cc

Area

1 sq in = 6.45 sq cm
1 sq ft = 929 sq cm
= .093 sq meters
1 sq yd = .84 sq meters
1 acre = 4 046.9 sq meters
= .404 7 hectares
1 sq mile = 2 589 988 sq meters
= 259 hectares
= 2.589 9 sq kilometers

Kitchen Measure

1 teaspoon = 4.93 milliliters (ml)
1 Tablespoon = 14.79 milliliters (ml)

Miscellaneous

1 British thermal unit (Btu) (mean)
= 1 055.9 joules
1 calorie (mean) = 4.19 joules
1 horsepower = 745.7 watts
= .75 kilowatts
caliber (diameter of a firearm's bore in hundredths of an inch)
= .254 millimeters (mm)
1 atmosphere pressure = 101 325* pascals (newtons per sq meter)
1 pound per square inch (psi) = 6 895 pascals
1 pound per square foot = 47.9 pascals
1 knot = 1.85 kilometers per hour
25 miles per hour = 40.2 kilometers per hour
50 miles per hour = 80.5 kilometers per hour
75 miles per hour = 120.7 kilometers per hour